Preface Books

A series of scholarly and critical studies of major writers intended for those needing modern and authoritative guidance through the characteristic difficulties of their work to reach an intelligent understanding and enjoyment of it.

General Editor: JOHN PURKIS

A Preface to Wordsworth (*Revised edn*)	JOHN PURKIS
A Preface to Donne (*Revised edn*)	JAMES WINNY
A Preface to Jane Austen (*Revised edn*)	CHRISTOPHER GILLIE
A Preface to Lawrence	GAMINI SALGADO
A Preface to Forster	CHRISTOPHER GILLIE
A Preface to Dickens	ALLAN GRANT
A Preface to Shelley	PATRICIA HODGART
A Preface to Keats	CEDRIC WATTS
A Preface to Orwell	DAVID WYKES
A Preface to Milton (*Revised edn*)	LOIS POTTER
A Preface to the Brontës	FELICIA GORDON
A Preface to T S Eliot	RON TAMPLIN
A Preface to Shakespeare's Tragedies	MICHAEL MANGAN
A Preface to Hopkins (*Second edn*)	GRAHAM STOREY
A Preface to James Joyce (*Second edn*)	SYDNEY BOLT
A Preface to Hardy (*Second edn*)	MERRYN WILLIAMS
A Preface to Conrad (*Second edn*)	CEDRIC WATTS
A Preface to Samuel Johnson	THOMAS WOODMAN
A Preface to Pope (*Second edn*)	I.R.F. GORDON
A Preface to Yeats (*Second edn*)	EDWARD MALINS with JOHN PURKIS

Maurice Hussey died suddenly in June 1991. The publishers and author would like to pay tribute to his wisdom, inspiration and friendship as Editor of Preface Books. He will be sadly missed.

The new General Editor of Preface Books is JOHN PURKIS.

Yeats from about 1902–14

A Preface to Yeats

Second Edition

Edward Malins

*Revisions and additional material
by John Purkis*

Longman, London and New York.

Longman Group UK Limited,
Longman House, Burnt Mill,
Harlow, Essex CM20 2JE, England
and Associated Companies throughout the world.

*Published in the United States of America
by Longman Publishing, New York*

© Longman Group UK Limited 1994

First published 1994

ISBN 0 582 09093 8 PPR

British Library Cataloguing-in-Publication Data

A catalogue record for this book is
available from the British Library

Library of Congress Cataloging-in-Publication Data

A CIP record for this book is available from the Library of Congress
Malins, Edward Greenway.
    A preface to Yeats/Edward Malins. – 2nd ed./revisions and
additional material by John Purkis.
        p.   cm. – (Preface books)
    Includes bibliographical references and indexes.
    ISBN 0–582–09093–8 (pbk.)
    1. Yeats, W. B. (William Butler), 1865–1939 – Criticism and
interpretation.   2. Ireland – In literature.   I. Purkis, John
Arthur, 1933–   . II. Title.
PR5907.M26   1994   93–39017
821'.8 – dc20   CIP

Set by 15 in Monophoto 10/11 Baskerville

Produced by Longman Singapore Publishers (Pte) Ltd.
Printed in Singapore

Contents

LIST OF ILLUSTRATIONS AND MAPS   vii
FOREWORD TO THE SECOND EDITION   viii
INTRODUCTION TO THE FIRST EDITION   x
LIST OF ABBREVIATIONS   xiii
ACKNOWLEDGEMENTS   xiv

PART ONE: HISTORICAL AND LITERARY BACKGROUND

Chronological table   4

1   BIOGRAPHICAL SUMMARIES   14
   Education   14
   Appearance and characteristics   20

2   THE HISTORY OF IRELAND AS IT CONCERNED THE POET   25
   Tales of gods and heroes   25
   The coming of Christianity   28
   Gaelic Ireland in Norman, Tudor and Stuart times   30
   The Anglo-Irish of the eighteenth century   31
   The fight for freedom: 1800–1923   35
   The last years: 1923–39   42

3   THE POET'S READING   45
   Occult and magic   45
   Plato and the Neoplatonists   49
   Giambattista Vico, 1668–1744   53
   George Berkeley, 1685–1753   55
   Edmund Burke, 1729–97   57
   William Blake, 1757–1827   58
   Friedrich Nietzsche, 1844–1900   61

4   A VISION   65

PART TWO: CRITICAL SURVEY

INTRODUCTION   77

EARLY YEATS   79
The Stolen Child   79
Cuchulain's Fight with the Sea   83
The Players Ask for a Blessing on the Psalteries and on Themselves   86

Contents

POEMS 1910–20   89
The Magi   89
On a Political Prisoner   91
The Second Coming   94

POEMS OF THE 1920s   99
Meditations in Time of Civil War – Part VI   99
Sailing to Byzantium   102

LAST POEMS, THE 1930s   106
The O'Rahilly   106
The Circus Animals' Desertion   107

PART THREE: REFERENCE SECTION

Yeats's family, friends and acquaintances   112
Gazetteer   161
Places referred to either directly or by inference in the poems   192
Yeats's symbols: their origins, connections and attributes   197
Common Irish (Gaelic) place names   200
Further Reading   202

GENERAL INDEX   207
INDEX TO YEATS'S WORKS   215

List of illustrations and Maps

Yeats from about 1902–14   *frontispiece*

Family tree of the Yeats family   2

Genealogy of the Middleton and Pollexfen relatives of the poet   3

Yeats as a boy. Pencil sketch by his father   15

Yeats, Synge and Russell fishing on Coole Lake   23

Samuel Palmer: *The Lonely Tower*   51

Georgie Hyde-Lees, Mrs W. B. Yeats   66

A Vision, diagram by T. R. Henn   68

The Tower, cover design by T. Sturge Moore   100

Florence Farr with the psaltery   116

Maude Gonne   121

Map of Ireland   160

3 Blenheim Road, Bedford Park   178

Yeats country   193

Foreword to the second edition

Edward Malins's *Preface* has been praised for its persuasive manner in introducing Yeats to the general reader, and to those studying an apparently difficult poet for the first time. It also includes an enormous amount of information, especially about Yeats's dealings with his relations and friends, people who figure largely in his poetry. Yeats and his Irish background were subjects of long-term interest to Malins, who had spent years lecturing on Yeats and writing about the poet, and this book represented the culmination of a lifetime's work.

In revising the book – after such a long interval since first publication – I have tried to keep as much of Malins's original text as I could. The sections on 'historical context' have worn well; in this area the whole Preface Book series, which originated in the early 1970s, was ahead of its time. I have made only minor alterations here.

The Critical Survey, on the other hand, I have decide to rewrite entirely. It was not so much a matter of updating, as of adjusting the focus of the book to the expectations of the new reader of Yeats. I felt that the original selection of poems had been too limited in its approach, and Malins had avoided some of the more obvious texts. He had an aversion to certain kinds of 'close reading', and tended to stress the biographical links of the poems under discussion; but this has meant that I have been able to switch some of his original material to another position. The bibliography at the end of the book has also been further updated.

The general emphasis of the Preface Book series – under the direction of the first general editor, Maurice Hussey – was the provision of background materials for the study of poetry; the criticism of the poems was a secondary aim, and the series did not aim to reduplicate the many critical works available. In each case the critical survey acted as a kind of taster; and of course a book about the background to poems which did not include any examples would have seemed strange.

In the case of Yeats there is a problem peculiar to the study of that poet, and it is an open question whether the intensive study of the background material leads one towards or away from the 'poetry'. Yeats had a system of belief, a private revelation as it were, which he came to over many years of study. When he progressed from draft to final version of a poem he often revised the text so that the general 'meaning' of a poem emerged from the web of private and particular references – e.g. 'The Second Coming' (pp. 94–5) can be understood as a prophecy, or the utterance of an *oracle*, before the detail of Yeats's system has been encountered. This after all is the way in which most people become interested in Yeats in the first place – as I did myself at school under Malins's tuition – and the effect of such a poem is mysterious. The attraction lies in the mystery, and this leads us to wish to find out more; but the question is whether the further information enhances or diminishes the experience of reading the poem, or whether – in effect – it changes its meaning entirely. I feel that we must know something about Yeats's 'system', but that we must be sophisticated readers and understand that such knowledge does not necessarily increase our appreciation of the poetry, and may lead us into fascinating byways, leaving the poem behind. This may seem an odd note of caution to sound in the introduction to a Preface Book; in fact all readers of Yeats want to find out more about the poet and his ideas, and Malins tried to fulfil that need in a reasonable and civilized way.

In conclusion I should like to acknowledge the help of various friends and colleagues; in particular Michael Allen, who helped me in teaching Yeats to Extra-Mural and Open University students, and Carol Jones for information about Dublin and the Irish background to the poems. I should also like to thank my daughters, Lucy and Harriet, for helping me to obtain illustrations. Revising another person's work is not as easy, I have learned, as writing from the beginning on one's own, and I should like to thank my publishers for their patience.

JOHN PURKIS

For Felicia

Introduction to the first edition

Like others in this Preface Book series, this volume is primarily concerned with the background to the poet's life and poetry. In the case of Yeats, even though he is near to us in time, this background is as important to understand as it is difficult to acquire. Firstly, the average English-speaking man or woman knows little about Irish history, life and thought; and secondly, he is not equipped educationally to grasp the language of myth. Therefore the outline of Irish history and the study of magic and myth occupy two chapters of this book, for these may open the doors to the visionary land in which Yeats's poetry flowers. In comparison, the Critical Survey in Part Two is short, for there would be little point in adding here to the cairn of scholarly books and PhD theses lying at the top of the mountain of literary criticism. As can be seen, this section deals sometimes with lesser known poems, chosen to shed light on his consistent development as a poet during his long life, or to show the close connections between his poetry and his plays. But this section must be regarded as prolegomena, even though it is reinforced by critical examination of poems in the Reference section, under both 'Family, friends and acquaintances' and the Gazetteer.

One reason for the growing number of students of English literature in colleges and universities today must be the realization that the relationship of poetry to values in life is of first importance; and some may have sensed that those poets in touch with the wisdom of the ages through the archetypes of myth and its imagery may be able to give us, through the incantations of their verse, something which can no longer be said by priest and philosopher, if indeed it ever could be – and certainly not in a magically self-contained artefact like a poem. In a world which is dashing down the Gadarene slope of materialistic chaos at the expense of the spiritual, 'Things fall apart; the centre cannot hold.'

It was the realization of Yeats's awareness of this which prompted T.S. Eliot, the other major poet of this century, to say in his memorial tribute to Yeats:

> There are some poets whose poems can be considered more or less in isolation, for experience and delight. There are others whose poetry, though giving equally experience and delight, has a larger historical importance. Yeats was one of the latter. He was one of the few whose history was the history of our own time, who are

part of the consciousness of our age, which cannot be understood without them.

Yet, on the whole, Yeats held unpopular views: his mixture of Neoplatonism, magic and spiritualism, set out in *A Vision*, is beyond the scope of formal literary criticism, so by some he is called 'escapist' (whatever that may mean), and others see the poetry as stronger if divorced from his magical system. But as magic and myth are inherently expressed in images and symbols it is our fault and not the poet's if we do not reach the core of the matter to find reality as he saw it. This accounts for the somewhat forbidding list of names heading the subsections of chapter 3 'The Poet's Reading'; it is hoped that, brief though this section is, it may help the reader to trace some of the common links which the poet himself found, for example, in Neoplatonism, the Occult, the Hindu *Upanishads*, William Blake and Nietzsche. In two other ways also the poet's views are unpopular: in his scepticism of modern science, irrationally based on his own empirical judgements; and in his political views, in which he reveals an intense admiration for what the best of the Protestant aristocracy of eighteenth-century Ireland stood for – a long way from the chill climate of modern Irish democracy.

W.H. Auden has defined poetry as 'memorable speech', adding that 'No poetry . . . which when mastered is not better heard than read is good poetry.' This is especially so in the case of Yeats. Did he not compose his verse in this way, repeating aloud again and again variants on lines until they sounded right? No other modern poet is so packed with memorable verse, whether in the gentle lyrical strain of 'She bid me take life easy as the grass grows on the weirs', or the sure statement of 'A lonely impulse of delight/Drove to this tumult in the clouds', or the savagely prophetic 'And what rough beast its hour come round at last/Slouches towards Bethlehem to be born?' Eloquence like this has to be heard to receive the full incantations of 'articulated sweet sounds together', as he called them. And through such superb poetic statements as these and many others we begin to see Yeats as a poet in the great tradition of Milton, Blake, Coleridge and Shelley, all of whom find their imagery from the *Anima Mundi*, the source of life, according to Plato.

As a mature poet, Yeats, like those others, is concerned with the interpretation of the spiritual and the material, and the study of the migration of the soul. An examination of his reading, prose writing and thinking can often help more than analysis of a poem under a literary microscope, for the whole organism of the poem may thereby be unified rather than disorientated as is sometimes the case in analyses. The learning of the imagination (a tradition not usually taught in schools) will open up the visionary world to all who pass beyond the confines of material viewpoints, until 'soul clap its hands and sing'. Blake has shown us the way, which Yeats followed:

> I give you the end of a golden string,
> Only wind it into a ball,
> It will lead you in at Heaven's gate
> Built in Jerusalem's wall.

EDWARD MALINS
St Peter's College, Oxford

List of abbreviations

CP	*The Collected Poems of W.B. Yeats* ((2nd edn.), London: Macmillan, 1950).
CPl	*The Collected Plays* (London: Macmillan, 1952).
AU	*Autobiographies* ((2nd edn.) London: Macmillan, 1965).
E&I	*Essays and Introductions* (London: Macmillan, 1961).
EX	*Explorations* (London: Macmillan, 1962).
MY	*Mythologies* (London: Macmillan, 1962).
VIS	*A Vision* ((2nd edn.) London: Macmillan, 1937).

Acknowledgements

The author and publisher are grateful to the following for permission to reproduce photographs:

Yeats from about 1902-14 frontispiece, *Yeats as a boy. Pencil Sketch by his father* page 15, Florence Farr with the psaltery page 116, *Maud Gonne* page 121, *3 Blenhim Road, Bedford Park* page 178, The National Library of Ireland and Michael Yeats; Samuel Palmer: *The Lonely Tower*, page 51, courtesy of the Trustees of the Victoria and Albert Museum; *Yeats, Synge and Russell fishing on Coole Lake* page 23, Major R. G. Gregory and Colin Smythe Ltd.; *Georgie Hyde Lees, Mrs W. B. Yeats* page 66, reproduced from *W. B. Yeats and Japan*, Joseph Hone, 1942, Hokuseido Press; *A Vision* page 68, reproduced from *The Lonely Tower* by T. R. Henn, 2nd edition 1963, Methuen; *The Tower*, cover design by T. Sturge Moore, page 100, Henriette Sturge-Moore.

Part One
Historical and Literary Background

The Yeats family

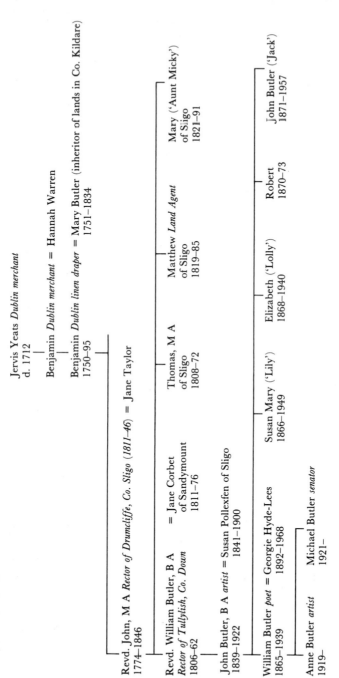

Jervis Yeats *Dublin merchant*
d. 1712

Benjamin *Dublin merchant* = Hannah Warren

Benjamin *Dublin linen draper* = Mary Butler (inheritor of lands in Co. Kildare)
1750–95   1751–1834

Revd. John, M A *Rector of Drumcliffe, Co. Sligo (1811–46)* = Jane Taylor
1774–1846

Revd. William Butler, B A   = Jane Corbet   Thomas, M A   Matthew *Land Agent*   Mary ('Aunt Micky')
Rector of Tullylish, Co. Down   of Sandymount   of Sligo   of Sligo   of Sligo
1806–62   1811–76   1808–72   1819–85   1821–91

John Butler, B A *artist* = Susan Pollexfen of Sligo
1839–1922   1841–1900

William Butler *poet* = Georgie Hyde-Lees   Susan Mary ('Lily')   Elizabeth ('Lolly')   Robert   John Butler ('Jack')
1865–1939   1892–1968   1866–1949   1868–1940   1870–73   1871–1957

Anne Butler *artist*   Michael Butler *senator*
1919–   1921–

Middleton and Pollexfen relatives of the poet

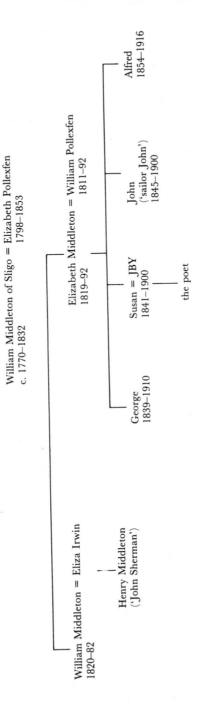

The genealogy is confusing because the poet's grandmother, Elizabeth Middleton Pollexfen, had a husband, brother and father, all of whom were named William.

There were many other children in each generation; for example, Henry Middleton and the poet's mother each had eleven brothers and sisters. Only the ones who concerned the poet are mentioned above.

For further details, see William M. Murphy, *The Yeats family and the Pollexfens of Sligo*, with drawings by John Butler Yeats (The Dolmen Press, Dublin, 1971).

Chronological table

YEATS'S LIFE	EVENTS IN IRISH AND ENGLISH HISTORY
1858	Foundation of Irish Republican Brotherhood (IRB).
1862 The Revd W.B. Yeats (grandfather) dies at Sandymount Castle, Dublin.	
1863 John B. Yeats (father) marries Susan Pollexfen at Sligo.	
1865 13 June: Yeats born in Dublin.	
1866 Susan Mary (Lily) born near Sligo.	
1867 The Yeatses move to London. Summer holidays in Sligo.	The Fenian Rising. Execution of the 'Manchester Martyrs'.
1868 Elizabeth (Lolly) born in London.	
1871 John Butler (Jack) born.	
1872–4 Yeats in Sligo.	
1873	Home Rule League founded.
1874 Yeats family move to West Kensington.	
1875	Publication of Standish O'Grady's *Bardic History*.

1877–81 Yeats at Godolphin School, Hammersmith.	Charles Stewart Parnell chairman of Home Rule League.
1879 The Yeatses move to Bedford Park, Chiswick.	Foundation of Irish Land League by Irish National Party of Parnell.
1881 The Yeatses return to Ireland to live.	
1881–3 Yeats attends the Erasmus Smith High School, Harcourt Street, Dublin.	
1882	Murder of Lord Frederick Cavendish and Mr Burke in Phoenix Park. Irish Land League suppressed.
1884–5 A pupil at Metropolitan School of Art, Dublin. Meets George Russell (AE).	
1885 Two lyric poems published in the *Dublin University Review*. First meets Katharine Tynan. Founding of the Dublin Lodge of the Hermetic Society. First meets John O'Leary.	
1886 Meets William Morris.	Alliance of Gladstone and Parnell for Home Rule. First Home Rule Bill defeated. Riots in Belfast.

1887	Yeatses move back to London. Yeats meets Pre-Raphaelites. (October) At his grandparents in Sligo.
1888	Yeatses move to Bedford Park.
1889	*The Wanderings of Oisin and Other Poems* published. First meets Maud Gonne.
1890	'The Lake Isle of Innisfree' published in Henley's *National Observer*.
1891	The Rhymers Club meets at the 'Cheshire Cheese' in Fleet Street. Yeats working on an edition of William Blake.
1892	Foundation of the National Literary Society (of Ireland). *The Countess Kathleen* is performed and appears in *The Countess Kathleen and Various Legends and Lyrics*. Pollexfen grandparents die.
1893	*The Celtic Twilight* published.	Gladstone's second Home Rule Bill passed in Commons, defeated in Lords. Foundation of Gaelic League by Douglas Hyde.

1894	(February) Visit to Paris; meets Verlaine with Arthur Symons. *The Land of Heart's Desire* produced in London. (Autumn) Sligo staying with George Pollexfen. Two visits to Lissadell House.	
1895	Yeats visits Wilde's house with letters of sympathy. *Poems* published. Moves to the Temple.	Arrest and trial of Oscar Wilde.
1896	Yeats contributes to *The Savoy* (successor to *The Yellow Book*). Moves to Woburn Buildings. Visits Aran Islands. First meets Lady Gregory. Visits Paris and meets J.M. Synge there.	
1897	Stays at Coole with Lady Gregory; plans Irish National Theatre. *The Secret Rose* (short stories) published.	The Queen's Diamond Jubilee.
1898	Meets James Connolly at Maud Gonne's house in Dublin.	Wolfe Tone Centenary.
1899	Visits Maud Gonne in Paris. *The Wind Among the Reeds* published.	The Boer War breaks out. Arthur Griffith founds the *United Irishman*.
1900	Yeats's mother dies.	
1901	Yeats first meets Hugh Lane, at Coole.	22 January: Death of Queen Victoria.

1902 Dun Emer Press (later Cuala Press) established by Lily Yeats. Maude Gonne in *Cathleen ni Houlihan*.	End of Boer War.

1903 *Ideas of Good and Evil* (essays) and *In the Seven Woods* published.
Maud Gonne marries John MacBride.
Irish National Theatre Society performs three Yeats plays in London.
(Winter 1903–04) Yeats lectures in United States.

1904 Abbey Theatre founded.

1905 Yeats becomes a co-director of the Irish National Theatre Society.

1907 Yeats's father goes to New York (never returns to Ireland).
J.M. Synge's *The Playboy of the Western World* causes riot at the Abbey Theatre.
Visit to Northern Italy with Lady Gregory and her son, Robert.

1908 *Collected Works* (eight vols) published.
(December) Visits Maud Gonne (now separated from her husband) in Paris.
Yeats's *Deirdre* performed in Dublin and London.

1909 (March) J.M. Synge dies.	(April) Swinburne dies.

1910   George Pollexfen dies.
(May) Yeats visits Maud
Gonne in Normandy.
*The Green Helmet and Other
Poems* published.

Edward VII dies (Abbey
Theatre remains open on day
of his death).

1911   Tour in United States with
Abbey Players.
First meets Georgie Hyde-
Lees (his future wife).

1912   Works with Rabindranath
Tagore on translations of
Gitanjali from Bengali.
(Winter) Controversy over
the Hugh Lane pictures.

1913   (August) Joins Ezra Pound
at Stone Cottage, Coleman's
Hatch, Sussex.
Given a Civil List pension
of £150 p.a.

1914   (January–March) Lecture
tour in United States and
Canada. *Responsibilities*
published.

Third Home Rule Bill
receives royal assent.
4 August: Outbreak of First
World War.

1915   Yeats refuses a knighthood.
Hugh Lane drowned in the
Lusitania.

1916   *At the Hawk's Well* produced
in London.
'Easter, 1916' written.

(April) Easter Rising of Irish
Republican Brotherhood.
3–9 May: Fifteen leaders
executed.

1917   Yeats buys Thoor Ballylee.
The Wild Swans at Coole
published.
20 October, Yeats and Miss
Georgie Hyde-Lees married
in London.

1918	(January and February) Oxford. (January) Robert Gregory killed on active service. Moves to Ireland with Mrs Yeats.	11 November: end of First World War. Armistice signed.
1918–21		The Troubles (Black and Tans)
1919	(February) Anne Yeats born. (Summer) Thoor Ballylee. (Autumn) Moves to Oxford	
1920	(January) Lecture tour of United States. 'All Souls' Night' written.	Lloyd George's Amending Act. (Six counties in Ulster vote themselves out.)
1921	*Michael Robartes and the Dancer* and *Four Plays for Dancers* published. (August) Michael Yeats born.	King George V opens the Northern Parliament at Stormont.
1922	(February) Yeats buys 82 Merrion Square, Dublin. J.B. Yeats dies in New York. (August) Bridge at Thoor Ballylee blown up by Republicans. Yeats made a Senator. D.Litt. from Trinity College, Dublin.	(January) Anglo-Irish Treaty signed. Civil War breaks out. Arthur Griffith, first president of Irish Free State dies. Michael Collins killed in an ambush.
1923	Yeats awarded the Nobel Prize for Literature.	de Valera orders Republicans to cease fire.
1924	(Winter) Visits Italy and Sicily.	

1926   (January) *A Vision*
published.
(June) Made Chairman of
the Senate Committee on
the design of the new Irish
coinage.

1927   (October) Ill with   (July) Assassination of Kevin
congestion of the lungs in   O'Higgins, Minister of
Spain and south of France.   Justice.
General breakdown of
health.

1928   (February) Rapallo, Italy.
The Tower published.
Resigns from the Senate.

1929   (Summer) Last time at
Thoor Ballylee.
(Winter) Rapallo.

1930   (Spring) Recuperating from
Malta fever at Portofino
Vecchio, Gulf of Genoa.
(November) *The Words upon
the Window-pane* produced at
the Abbey.

1931   Hon. Doctor of Letters,
Oxford.

1932   (May) Lady Gregory dies.   de Valera and Fianna Fail in
(July) Buys lease of   office.
'Riversdale', Rathfarnham,
Dublin.
(October) Lecture tour in
United States

1933   *The Winding Stair and Other   (July–August) Irish Blueshirt
Poems.*   movement attempt march on
Dublin.

1934   (April) Undergoes Steinach
       operation to relieve
       impotence.
       (June) Rapallo
       Wheels and Butterflies
       published.

1935   George Russell (AE) dies.
       (November) Majorca.
       Translates Hindu *Upanishads*
       with Shri Purohit Swami.
       A Full Moon in March
       published.

1936   Severe collapse with heart
       and kidney disease.
       Edits *Oxford Book of Modern
       Verse*, published in
       November.

1937   Yeats gives several BBC
       broadcasts.
       Publishes revised edition of
       A Vision.

1938   (January) Mentone.
       New Poems (last book seen
       through the Cuala Press by
       Yeats) published in May.
       (August) Dublin, for a
       performance of *Purgatory*
       (last public appearance).
       Olivia Shakespear dies.
       The Death of Cuchulain
       finished. Writes 'The Black
       Tower', his last poem.
       Finishes *On the Boiler*
       (published 1939).

1939   28 January: Yeats dies at   (September) Outbreak of
       Cap Martin. Buried at   Second World War.
       Roquebrune.
       (July) *Last Poems and Two
       Plays*.

1941   Coole Park razed to the
       ground.

1948   (September) Yeats's body
       reinterred in Drumcliffe
       churchyard, County Sligo.

1 Biographical summaries

Education

> Because I had found it hard to attend to anything less interesting
> than my own thoughts, I was difficult to teach.
>
> (*Autobiographies*)

Yeats was largely self-educated. In *Reveries over Childhood and Youth*
(*AU*), written in 1915, he reveals the chief influences on his childhood. Though the family was based in London, his memories are
mostly of Ireland. (Throughout his life he edited London out of his
reminiscences and his poetry.) His father was trying to make his way
as an artist, and the children were packed off to their grandparents'
house in the west of Ireland for long periods. At Sligo he received
hardly any formal education. His outstanding memories were of his
grandparents and many relations, both Yeatses and Pollexfens, and
they filled his mind; particularly his fear of his seafaring grandfather,
old William Pollexfen, with the great scar on his hand made by a
whaling hook, his brute strength, intolerable silences and violent
temper. Yeats as a small boy sailed model boats, listened to sailors'
tales, walked the country roads, visited cousins, or heard the family
history from his great-aunt Micky. His father was mostly an absentee
in London. His mother, a silent figure, was happiest listening to the
tales of cottagers or fishermen's wives; yet Yeats thought she was
'the right kind of mother for a poet or dreamer'. As was customary
at the time, the children seemed to have spent much time with
nurses.

In 1872 his father wrote from London to his wife in Sligo,
concerning Willie's development. The letter reveals as much about
his father as Willie:

> I think Willie [aged seven] was greatly disimproved by being at
> Merville [the large Pollexfen house outside Sligo]. He was coming
> on from being so much with his mother and away from his
> grandfather and dictatorial aunts. From his resemblance to Eliza-
> beth [one of his Pollexfen aunts] he derives his nervous sensitive-
> ness. I wish he could be made more robust – by riding or by other
> means – *not by going to school*. I was very sorry he could not have
> the pony more, but perhaps he might ride that donkey about
> which he used to tell me . . .
>   Tell Willie not to forget me.

W.B. Yeats as a boy. Pencil sketch by his father.

The Yeatses had little money, so were both envious of the Pollexfens' wealth acquired through trade, and conscious of the hard physical qualities which enabled them to keep it. They did not wish their children to appear to be lacking in either physical vigour or wealth, and on this occasion J.B. Yeats evidently wished Willie to become 'more robust' on a pony which was presumably lent them by the Pollexfens. J.B. Yeats also had eccentric ideas about schooling for children; he was not a very good father for a young child, tyrannizing over Willie, having little patience with his difficulties and not really understanding his dreamy turn of mind. However, he used to read much to him, often from Walter Scott's works, and to tell him the plots of Balzac novels – which do not sound very suitable for a child of Willie's age. Some of his aunts attempted to teach him to read, without much success; then his father also tried when he returned from London, but with even less success as he had less patience. There were few books in the Pollexfen household which he could have read. The so-called library at 'Merville' must have resembled the Petkoffs' library in Shaw's *Arms and the Man*, 'a single fixed shelf stocked with old paper covered novels, broken backed, coffee stained, torn and thumbed'.

On one occasion when his father had come back from London, he discovered that Willie had that morning been taught to sing at a dame's school:

> Little drops of water,
> Little grains of sand,
> Make the mighty ocean
> And the pleasant land.

From that moment Willie was forbidden to continue at the school, and except for visits to an old gentlewoman who laboured to teach him spelling (evidently with total failure) and some grammar, he received no formal education. Yet these years at Sligo were obviously happy ones, even if he could not read well at the end of them. Much worse was to come.

The family moved back to London in 1874, and on 26 January 1877, Willie, aged eleven and a half, entered the chilled Victorian portals of the Godolphin School in Iffley Road, Hammersmith, about a mile and a quarter from his home in Bedford Park, Chiswick. He describes the school as follows:

> It was a Gothic building of yellow brick; a large hall full of desks, some small classrooms, and a separate house for boarders, all built perhaps in 1860 or 1870. . . .
> For some days, as I walked homeward along the Hammersmith

Road, I told myself that whatever I most cared for had been taken away. I had found a small, green-covered book given to my father by a Dublin man of science; it gave an account of the strange sea creatures the man of science had discovered among the rocks at Howth or dredged out of Dublin Bay. It had long been my favourite book; and when I read it I believed I was growing very wise, but now I should have no time for it nor for my own thoughts. Every moment would be taken up learning or saying lessons, or in walking between school and home four times a day, for I came home in the middle of the day for dinner. But presently I forgot my trouble, absorbed in two things I had never known, companionship and enmity. After my first day's lesson, a circle of boys had got around me in a playing-field and asked me questions, 'Who's your father?' 'What does he do?' 'How much money has he?' Presently a boy said something insulting. I had never struck anybody or been struck, and now all in a minute, without any intention upon my side, but as if I had been a doll moved by a string, I was hitting at the boys within reach and being hit. After that I was called names for being Irish, and had many fights and never, for years, got the better in any of them; for I was delicate and had no muscles.

(*AU* p. 32)

The academic life at the Godolphin must have been as unpleasant for Willie as the social. He never won any prizes; he was weak in Mathematics, eighth out of a class of thirty-one in Latin at Christmas 1878; his French was 'faible, sans énergie'; and he was reported on by his form master with the usual pedagogic clichés which reveal a lack of insight: 'A very good boy. Tries to do as well as he can. He does best in Latin and History; with perseverance he will do better. Conduct very good.'

His hunger for Ireland and his hatred of London were mitigated by regular visits once or twice a year to his relations in Sligo. When he had embarked amid the bustle of Clarence Basin, Merseyside, on one of his grandfather's boats, the SS *Sligo* or the SS *Liverpool*, he would forget London; and when he awoke next morning to hear the Gaelic of the sailors, and then saw the cliffs of Donegal, he knew he was nearly home again. After thirty hours at sea the boat would dock alongside the quays of Sligo where his cousins awaited him. As he grew older, life at Sligo became more exacting, bringing with it more independence. He went fishing for trout in the loughs with Jim Healy, the stable boy, climbing Knocknarea and Ben Bulben, and riding his 'red' (chestnut?) pony past his great-grandfather's rectory at Drumcliffe, past the waterfall thrown back by the wind at Glencar, past the Holy Well of St Patrick and the monastery of St

17

Columba – through a countryside filled with Christian pilgrimage and Pagan myth, the very blood of his poetic inspiration.

After three years at the Godolphin school, J.B. Yeats decided to move the family back to Dublin, and Willie was enrolled in the Erasmus Smith High School in Harcourt Street at the beginning of the academic year of 1881. This turned out to be in striking contrast to the Godolphin:

> I was now fifteen; and as he did not want to leave his painting my father told me to go to Harcourt Street and put myself to school. I found a bleak eighteenth-century house, a small playing-field full of mud and pebbles, fenced by an iron railing, and opposite a long hoarding and a squalid, ornamental railway station. Here, as I soon found, nobody gave a thought to decorum. We worked in a din of voices. We began the morning with prayers, but when class began, the headmaster, if he was in the humour, would laugh at Church and Clergy. 'Let them say what they like', he would say, 'but the earth does go round the sun.' On the other hand there was no bullying and I had not thought it possible that boys could work so hard. Cricket and football, the collecting of moths and butterflies, though not forbidden, were discouraged. They were for idle boys. I did not know as I used to, the mass of my school-fellows; for we had little life in common outside the classrooms. I had begun to think of my school work as an interruption of my natural-history studies, but even had I never opened a book in the school course, I could not have learned a quarter of my night's work. I had always done Euclid easily, making the problems out while the other boys were blundering at the blackboard, and it had often carried me from the bottom to the top of my class; but these boys had the same natural gift and instead of being in the fourth or fifth book were in the modern books at the end of the primer; and in place of a dozen lines of Virgil with a dictionary, I was expected to learn with the help of a crib a hundred and fifty lines. The older boys were able to learn the translation off, and to remember what words of Latin and English corresponded with one another, but I, who, it may be, had tried to find out what happened in the parts we had not read, made ridiculous mistakes; and what could I, who never worked when I was not interested, do with a history lesson that was a column of seventy dates? I was worst of all at literature, for we read Shakespeare for his grammar exclusively.

(*AU*, p. 56)

Luckily, his father had read him Shakespeare with a different end in view, and had undoubtedly initiated in him a lifelong love of his plays. Blake's poetry read by his father also stayed with him. But his father's teaching methods were severe though well-intentioned, and he tried unsuccessfully to improve his Latin by regular coaching each evening. Perhaps it was as a result of this that the poet later decided that his son, Michael, should do Greek rather than Latin at school; although when he wrote *AU* he evidently saw the value of classical studies: 'He [his father] would have taught me nothing but Greek and Latin and I would have been a properly educated man, and would not have to look in useless longing at books that have been, through the poor mechanism of translation, the builders of my soul, nor face authority with the timidity born of excuse and evasion.'

Convincing his father that neither his Latin nor his mathematics was up to the standard of the Trinity College entrance examination, he enrolled in the Metropolitan School of Art in Kildare Street, where he attended classes from May 1884 to July 1885. He showed no special ability at drawing, though his water-colours and pastel drawings are pleasant, sensitive works in a sort of early Turner tradition. In fact, Turner's 'The Golden Bough' was then his favourite picture. Painted in 1834 (now in the Tate Gallery) it is Turner at his most Claudean – a landscape, with classical temples and dancing figures, with the Bay of Baiae near Naples in the distance. The Sibyl in the foreground is part of the legend, telling the story of her power to enable man to return from the underworld; art in alliance with poetry, as in the Pre-Raphaelite painters whom Yeats also much liked. On the other hand his tastes were not in the least affected by contemporary artists, such as the French Impressionists. As he pointed out:

> We had no scholarship, no critical knowledge of the history of painting, and no settled standards. . . . No influence touched us but that of France, where one or two of the older students had been already and all hoped to go. Of England I alone knew anything. Our ablest student had learnt Italian to read Dante, but had never heard of Tennyson or Browning, and it was I who carried into the school some knowledge of English poetry, especially of Browning, who had begun to move me by his air of wisdom. I do not believe that I worked well, for I wrote a great deal and that tired me, and the work I was set to bored me.
>
> (*AU*, p. 81)

A month or two at the Royal Hibernian Art School at the beginning of 1886 finished his formal education. During his last years at school he had written much verse, and in 1885 had had two lyrics published. To some extent he had formulated an aesthetic theory by reading Matthew Arnold, Herbert Spencer and others, but in general his education at all his schools had been anything but satisfactory. Academically he was true to form as a writer, and it might be said of him as Bernard Shaw said of himself: 'I cannot learn anything that does not interest me. My memory is not indiscriminate: it rejects and selects; and its selections are not academic.'

At the end of it all, Yeats could not spell, wrote in an untidy hand, was poor at languages and disconcerted by not having had to wrestle with any form of classical discipline at a university. But he was writing verse, and he knew himself to be a poet – nothing else mattered. Furthermore, he had lived much of his childhood at Sligo, which was to provide that verse with the marrow of Irish folklore, which he used again and again to the end of his life.

Appearance and characteristics

Throughout the poet's life women were undoubtedly attracted by his physical appearance. Men seemed to have been put off by his aloofness, his lack of small talk and his 'unclubbable' qualities. For instance, I cannot find any account of an occasion when he visited a pub, except once to drink lemonade in a theatre bar with Sir Herbert Grierson. If you were not prepared to listen but wished to talk, like the writer Monk Gibbon, you might not get on with him. If you let him talk and encouraged him, though not as a sycophant, you might receive a cornucopia of ideas, beautifully presented in his rich mellow voice with its subtle Irish accent. Were you one of those, like Francis Stuart (Iseult Gonne's husband, see below, p. 118) who was not always willing to follow the passionate and energetic presentation of his ideas, then he might have scared you.

Ezra Pound (see below, pp. 148–9) as a young man, dreaded having him to stay in a cottage in Sussex, and wrote to his mother in November 1913: 'My stay in Stone Cottage will not be the least profitable. I detest the country. Yeats will amuse me part of the time and bore me to death with psychical research the rest. I regard the visit as a duty to posterity.' But after a month he had changed his tune, for in a letter to William Carlos Williams, the poet, he wrote: 'Yeats is much finer *intime* than seen spasmodically in the midst of the whirl.' This change of opinion may have come about because Yeats had given him 200 dollars – in fact had transferred the money from a literary award he had just won himself.

There are many examples of Yeats helping poets with their work, and in other ways too, such as getting money for James Joyce when he was living in poverty in Switzerland. T.S. Eliot, twenty-three years younger than Yeats, spoke warmly of his relationship with him in 'The Poetry of W.B. Yeats', a talk delivered to the Friends of the Irish Academy, at the Abbey Theatre, June 1940:

People have sometimes spoken of him as arrogant and over-bearing. I never found him so, in his conversations with a younger writer I always felt that he offered terms of equality as to a fellow worker, a practitioner of the same mystery. It was, I think, that, unlike many writers, he cared more for poetry than for his own reputation as a poet or his picture of himself as a poet.

At the poet's birth, the doctor had remarked on his large *os frontis*, usually taken as a sign of intelligence. At the age of ten, when in school at Hammersmith, the poet was, on his own admission, 'delicate and had no muscles'. Katharine Tynan, his first girlfriend, remarked in 1885 on his 'dark face, its touch of vivid colouring, the night-black hair, the eager eyes'. He was then a frail and gentle aesthete, a dreamer of Celtic twilight, having a beard, but by 1893 had shaved it off. Out of doors he used to wear a weighty Inverness cape, once his father's, which gave him a more robust appearance. From 1895 Pádraic Colum remembered his velvet jacket, flowing tie, 'blue-black hair coming over his forehead, his frequent gestures and deliberate utterance'.

By 1904, aged thirty-nine, Yeats was no longer the aesthete of the Pre-Raphaelite type, but the fighter for the Abbey Theatre, Irish National Brotherhood member and a man of action. Augustus John's portrait, used as the frontispiece to *Collected Poems*, magnificently catches this change. These months, the poet said, were 'the worst in his life', as he was not able to find time or energy for writing verse. His utter absorption when reading his verse is described by Dr Oliver Gogarty in a letter to George Bell, afterwards Bishop of Chichester. The poet was at one of George Moore's salons, reciting *Deirdre*:

> He forgot himself and his face seemed tremulous as if an image of impalpable fire. His lips are dark cherry red, and his cheeks take colour, and his eyes actually glow black and then the voice sets all vibrating as he sways like a Druid with his whole soul chanting . . . I know no more beautiful face than Yeats's when lit with song.

On another occasion, in his *Memoir of W.B. Yeats*,[1] Dr Gogarty as a surgeon, is more anatomical: 'The jaw is clear-cut and firm. The mouth is beautifully modelled. The nose is aquiline with great breadth between the eyes, one of which, the right, is noticeably lower than the other.'

Many others who knew him mention his startling eyes. In point of fact he was very shortsighted. Dorothy Wellesley noticed this towards the end of his life, and deduced its effect on his poetry: 'His small dark eyes turned outwards, appear like those of a lizard and as

21

though at times they were hidden by a film. His perspective is therefore abnormal. Perhaps he cannot see very much out of doors. Certain it is he sees nothing, when we sit together in my walled garden, in the beauty of any flower.' From this she concludes that 'most of the Celtic poets are not concerned with nature at all. Yeats did not himself draw much inspiration from Nature, certainly from no details; only sometimes massed effects, such as a painter sees, influenced his verse.'

As he was also tone-deaf, it was a major disadvantage when he was choosing music for his plays; but he was far from deaf in his acute hearing of intonations in the reading of verse. There are many stories of his own method of composing verse by intoning the lines over and over again until he arrived at a solution that satisfied him. Staying with her grandmother, Lady Gregory, at Coole (see pp. 165–8), Anne Gregory used to hear him 'humming away for hours' while he was writing. Dorothy Wellesley's butler was once 'worried', as he said, by 'Mr Yeats a-moaning to hisself'. And I know an inhabitant of Steyning, Sussex, who heard Yeats practising variations of his epitaph, 'Cast a cold eye', when he was walking down the main street of the town in the 1930s.

A vivid description of the poet when he was in his late forties, is given by Mrs Alfred Lyttelton:

> His hair was rather long and it seemed very grand and black, and to have a life of its own which he could not always control: it swayed when he spoke, but often in a different rhythm from his speech, as if it were impatient of its owner's words. Then there were his eyes, burning with vehemence, smouldering with a deeper emotion than he was expressing, and finally a general sense that he did not belong . . . perhaps to the life of the Earth itself.

Austin Clarke, in *The Yeats We Knew*,[2] describes an incident in the woods of Coole: 'A tall sportsman, wearing an unusual rain-coat of sky-blue watered silk, and carrying the rods and fierce tackle of his craft . . . the angler was crossing a side lawn towards the portico of a Georgian mansion. To my complete astonishment, I saw that it was the poet himself.'

Fishing and swimming were the only sports in which Yeats indulged. He was 'useless at games' at school in Hammersmith. As a boy he had shot with a muzzle-loading pistol, but never did again after hearing a rabbit squealing in pain. Austin Clarke had noticed his height when he saw him striding across the Coole lawn: and George Moore,[3] remarked upon 'a tall black figure standing at the edge of the lake, wearing a cloak which fell in straight folds to his knees looking like a giant umbrella forgotten by some picnic party'.

George Russell, also known as AE (nearest), W.B. Yeats and J.M. Synge (in the bow), fishing on Coole Lake. Sketch by H. Oakley.

Equally irreverent was Anne Gregory's view of the poet in her *Me and Nu*.[4] When she was a child at Coole,

> He always seemed to be there, leaning back in his chair at table – huge with (in our eyes) an enormous tummy. He wore a signet ring with an enormous stone in it on his little finger and Nu [her sister] and I used to giggle like mad, and say he expected everyone to kiss it, like the Pope. She and I used to copy his habit of running his fingers through the great lock of hair that fell forward over his forehead, and then hold out our hand with the imaginary ring, saying: 'This ring is a holy ring: it has been in touch with my holy halo.'

At the age of sixty he was very much the smiling public man, with a black velvet coat, silver-buckled shoes, a wide black ribbon attached to tortoiseshell glasses, the large gold ring on his finger – the *grand seigneur* in his elegance, and putting on weight. Until the end of his life he continued to dress with distinction. Dorothy Wellesley was impressed, and describes him thus:

> His clothes perhaps belonged to the most elegant Bohemian sort that our generation has seen. He was always immaculately clean, always precisely shaved. . . . His suits were of soft corn or brown tweeds, with bright blue or dark green shirt, and always with handkerchief to match. The grand white-blue hair, which was raven blue in his youth, added much to his personality.[5]

William Force Stead, who has two poems in *The Oxford Book of Modern Verse*, after he had got to know the poet well when he lived in Oxford in the 1920s, told me he was the only man he had ever met of whose genius he was 'absolutely certain when talking to him'. More important, 'he was', in Augustus John's phrase which he used about Hugh Lane, 'one of those rare ones who, singlehanded, are able to enrich and dignify an entire nation'.

Notes

1. O. St John Gogarty, *Memoir of W.B. Yeats* (Dublin: Dolmen Press, 1963).
2. Francis MacManus (ed.), *The Yeats We Knew* (Cork: The Merrier Press, 1965).
3. George Moore, *Ave* (1911), p. 212.
4. Anne Gregory, *Me and Nu* (Gerrards Cross: Colin Smythe, 1970).
5. Kathleen Raine (ed.), *Letters on Poetry from W.B. Yeats to Dorothy Wellesley* (Oxford: OUP, 1940; reissued 1964).

2 The history of Ireland as it concerned the poet

This chapter is not a political or social history of Ireland, but a background to the Irish contribution to the civilization of Europe as it affected both Yeats's writing and his life: therefore invasions and battles, reigns and laws are important only so far as they become a part of the tradition he made for himself – his heroic mythical figures, his ancestors and his philosophy, all of which make up the core of his work. For Irish readers, it may not be sufficiently nationalist in concept; whereas English readers may find it patriotic and sentimental. But the answer lies in the significance of the event for Yeats, who as an Anglo-Irishman (although he did not use the term) was constantly tugged by his love-hate for Ireland, seeing Irish history and what was going on around him (now itself history) from two perspectives: inspired by its idealism but maddened by its politics.

> Out of Ireland have we come.
> Great hatred, little room,
> Maimed us at the start.
> I carry from my mother's womb
> A fanatic heart.
>
> (*Remorse for Intemperate Speech*, CP, p. 287)

It is as trite to repeat how little the English know of either the Gaelic epic legends or of the events of Irish history, as it is necessary to emphasize how vital both these are to an understanding of the nucleus of Yeats's thought.

Tales of gods and heroes

Gaelic Celts invaded Ireland, which they called Eriu (Erin) in about 350 BC. They found a Bronze Age culture, with hill forts such as Tara, hallowed burial grounds, sacred groves for gods, and one small, superior state, the Túatha de Danaan, among many others. Like the British Celts who conquered England, but came from further north in Europe, they were strong, tall and militant, and used tempered iron rather than bronze weapons. Most of the epic stories belong to the closing days of this prehistoric Iron Age, from the arrival of the Celts to the establishment of Christianity about AD 450. One of the features of these Celtic romances is their sense of the

Otherworld, of supernatural happenings and interventions by gods who have become reduced to the level of the *sidhe* (fairies) or hobgoblins. Yeats was lucky to be born into a culture so based, in which traditional memory still lived, and he took full advantage of it. 'The Unappeasable Host' from *The Wind Among the Reeds* (1899), *CP*, p. 65, shows this:

> The Danaan children laugh, in cradles of wrought gold,
> And clap their hands together, and half close their eyes,
> For they will ride the North when the ger-eagle flies,
> With heavy whitening wings, and a heart fallen cold:
> I kiss my wailing child and press it to my breast,
> And hear the narrow graves calling my child and me.
> Desolate winds that cry over the wandering sea;
> Desolate winds that hover in the flaming West;
> Desolate winds that beat the doors of Heaven, and beat
> The doors of Hell and blow there many a whimpering ghost;
> O heart the winds have shaken, the unappeasable host
> Is comelier than candles at Mother Mary's feet.

In this short poem he shows his knowledge of Danaan folklore, and his awareness of early Celtic culture. He knows all the details: the 'unappeasable host', the *sidhe*, who carry off children or substitute changelings; their disguises as birds or animals, here as a ger-eagle; and their beauty, 'comelier than candles'. Secondly, it is a possibility that the Danaan children indeed slept 'in cradles of wrought gold', for these Celtic people of the La Tène culture made ornaments, like the magnificent gold collar, the bronze dishes and horse trappings (as fine as any in Europe), which today can be seen in the National Museum, Dublin.

Yeats's poetry, with its roots in the great Irish folk-tales, cannot be fully appreciated unless these tales are known and loved: Oisín and Finn; Cuchulain and Emer; Deirdre and Naisi; Diarmuid and Grainne. Incomparably the best translations are those of Lady Gregory. Yeats wrote a Preface for her *Cuchulain of Muirthemne* (1902)[1] which we quote at some length, for it shows not only the beauty of Yeats's early prose and Lady Gregory's translation, but also how these stories pulled him like a lodestone.

> If we do not set Deirdre's lamentations among the greatest lyric poems of the world, I think we may be certain that the wine-press of the poets has been trodden in vain; and yet I think it may be proud Emer, Cuchulain's fitting wife, who will linger longest in the memory. What a pure flame burns in her always, whether she is the newly married wife fighting for precedence, fierce as some beautiful bird, or the confident housewife, who would awaken her

husband from his magic sleep with mocking words; or the great queen who would get him out of the tightening net of his doom, by sending him into the Valley of the Dead, with Niamh, his mistress, because he will be more obedient to her; or the woman whom sorrow has sent with Helen and Iseult and Brunnhilda, and Deirdre, to share their immortality in the rosary of the poets.

'And oh! my love!' she said, 'we were often in one another's company, and it was happy for us: for if the world had been searched from the rising of the sun to sunset, the like would never have been found in one place, of the Black Sainglain and the Grey of Macha, and Laeg the chariot-driver, and myself and Cuchulain.'

And after that Emer bade Conall to make a wide, very deep grave for Cuchulain; and she laid herself down beside her gentle comrade, and she put her mouth to his mouth, and she said: 'Love of my life, my friend, my sweetheart, my one choice of the men of the earth, many is the woman, wed or unwed, envied me until today; and now I will not stay living after you.'

The oldest national epic is the *Taín Bó Cualgne*, the *Driving away of the Bull of Cooley*, which tells the story of Maeve, Queen of Connacht and her war with Conchobar, King of Ulster, whose most famous Red Branch hero was Cuchulain. Contemporary with this were many anonymous lyric poets, some pagan and some Christian, whose poems are very beautifully translated by Frank O'Connor in his anthology, *Fountain of Magic*. These poets also tell the great stories: Oisín returning to earth from Tir-na-nÓg (the Land of the Young) to find St Patrick; Grainne singing as her lover Diarmuid sleeps when they are hunted by their enemies; Deirdre, after she has been separated by King Conchobar from Naisi, her lover, remembering her happiness with him. It is from these lyrics that one senses the life of these townless people who fought, hunted, loved, ate and drank, enjoyed the changing seasons and were mildly agricultural. As pagans they never worked out a detailed religion other than mere animism. The heroic stories show areas where there were groups under warrior kings or nobles: Ulaidh (Ulster) in the north; Mumha (Munster) in the south; in Laighin (Leinster) in the east and Connachta (Connacht) in the west. Until about AD 300 there was no idea of a High King and no Roman concept of unity, with roads and order; for although Roman influences did cross the sea, no legionary ever landed in Ireland. A semi-feudal set-up, in petty states still called *túatha*, organized on a family blood basis, was the usual form at this time. One of the first to unite many *túatha* and to make the sacred hill of Tara the capital of Ireland, was Cormac

MacArt, *c.* 300, and there he presided over the Feis, a law-making body, and led the Fianna, a warrior force. Heroic tales of the Fianna, led by Finn and his son, the poet Oisín, are the core of Gaelic legend known to Yeats.

By about 430 most of the island was Gaelic speaking and showing signs of a more advanced social and hierarchical set-up with specific Irish characteristics. One of these with particular interest for Yeats was the warrior aristocracy which supported poets who were the successors of the bards of the earlier La Tène culture. Between the nobles and the commoners was an influential group whom we might now call lawyers, Latin scholars, historians, clergy and poets. The druids were regarded as seers capable of prophecy and divination, the bards or poets were expected to write poetry and record heroic tales: and there was a Celtic writing called Ogam, based on Latin but used only on burial stones. For information on this mythology see M. Dillon and N. Chadwick, *The Celtic Realms.*[2]

The coming of Christianity

Christianity was brought to Ireland officially by Palladius, sent by the Pope from Rome in 431; but it had come earlier through emigrants, foremost of whom was Bishop Patrick, a romanized British Celt. Much of this period is shrouded in historical mist through which one peers to find tradition associating St Patrick with the Church at Armagh. Culturally the coming of Christianity meant a wonderful flowering of Celtic art, and the development of a direct link between this remote island and Mediterranean thought and writing. The early Irish saints founded hundreds of monasteries in Ireland during the sixth and seventh centuries; the best known, often mentioned in the writings of Lady Gregory, Yeats and James Joyce, are Enda of Killeany in Aran; Finnian of Clonard; Colum (Columcille) of Derry, Durrow and Iona, also known as St Columba; Ciaran of Clonmacnois; Kevin of Glendalough; Brendan of Clonfert; and Finnbar of Cork. The tales of these Irish saints and some of their hymns were translated from the Gaelic by Lady Gregory and were then read to Yeats. She tells the 'Breastplate of St Patrick' ('The Deer's Cry') or 'Blessed Cellach's Lament' in splendid poetic prose in her *Book of Saints and Wonders.*[3] St Brigit's hymn is typical of her style, based partly on Gaelic, partly on the Authorized Version of the Bible:

> Brigit, excellent woman; sudden flame, may the bright fiery sun bring us to the lasting kingdom.
> May Brigit save us beyond troops of demons; may she break before us the battles of every death.

May she do away with the rent sin has put upon us; the blossomed branch; the Mother of Jesus; the very dear young woman greatly looked up to. That I may be safe in every place with my dear saint of Leinster!

These tales of Irish saints are often joined to myths of animals, talking birds, giants or wizards, and human heroes with superhuman characteristics. We read of how St Patrick was told by the Angel to take down the stories of the Fianna from the fighting men, and how St Columcille pleaded for the poets who were driven out of Aedh's kingdom; so the interaction of Christian and pagan is the warp and woof of history. The last great pagan warrior, Oisín (Ossian), was in contact with St Patrick, a meeting between the two worlds movingly related by Yeats in *The Wanderings of Oisin* (1889). In *The Trembling of the Veil* (*AU*), he describes a mystical experience he had when crossing a stream in Coole Park. At that moment, he says, his 'whole imagination was preoccupied with the pagan mythology of ancient Ireland'. At Coole, the birthplace of St Colman, he must have heard the songs of beggars and travelling men, and, like St Columcille, been carried by their imagination 'over the plain in the company of the angels of God'.

At the time of the saints we have mentioned, Irish monasteries became internationally famous, being visited by students from all over Europe. The arts also benefited from their patronage: High Crosses were carved; metalwork flourished, for example, the eighth-century gold Ardagh chalice in the National Museum; and above all the monks were skilled at illuminated book illustration, as for example in the *Book of Kells*, one of the most beautiful books in the world, now in the library of Trinity College, Dublin.

A Viking raid on Lambay island off Howth, County Dublin, in 795 was the start of a continuing threat to much of the best of Irish monasticism and learning, being the first of many such raids for two centuries. The Norsemen were civilized neither by Christianity nor by Roman influences, though they have left some traces in Irish art, and founded the city of Dublin. Unfortunately the Irish seem to have adopted Norse methods by tribal fighting. Not until the tenth century does any one king again emerge as High King at Tara, and that was Brian Boru, who was titled 'Imperator Scottorum' (Emperor of the Irish). This was the zenith of Gaelic Ireland. Despite the Norsemen, unity in language, law, religion and culture had survived, and the Irish were the first nation north of the Alps to produce a national literature. Yeats could neither read nor speak Gaelic, so he had to be content with translations; yet it still fired his imagination and provided a mythological basis for his poetry such as no English poet could ever hope for.

Gaelic Ireland in Norman, Tudor and Stuart times

After Brian Boru's death in 1014, quarrels broke out with renewed vigour between the various rulers. Finally one of them, Dermot MacMurrough, King of Leinster, appealed to Henry II of England for help, so laying the way for the Norman conquest under Henry's lieutenant, the Earl of Pembroke, called Strongbow. His expedition was backed by the Pope's blessing, as he would carry religion to a barbarous people. However, Ireland for the next four centuries proved almost impossible to rule, even by the Normans; and weaker kings such as Richard II came to grief there.

In Tudor times a rigorous policy of Protestant Plantations, or colonization, established some form of order, though the burning of Edmund Spenser's castle at Kilcolman, during Desmond's Rebellion, was a far from isolated incident. The Plantation policy, giving land confiscated from the native Irish to such as Sir Walter Raleigh, who became the largest landowner in the south, aroused opposition which was put down with much severity.

This policy continued throughout the Stuart reigns. In Ulster the Earls of Tyrconnell and Tyrone were restored by James I in 1603, but soon quarrelled with the English and therefore, with more than a hundred chiefs, left Ireland for good. This 'Flight of the Earls' irreparably weakened Gaelic Ireland, leaving only the language, as Gaelic aristocracy did not long survive. The Plantations continued with renewed strength, 'undertakers' annexing 500,000 acres, including the lands of the earls which were the best. The town of Derry was presented to the City of London, and London Companies (absentees) received grants for business in the county. Many Scottish and English landowners were therefore established in the north: similarly, in Munster, an adventurer like the remarkable Richard Boyle (Earl of Cork, 1620) could arrive in the country penniless in 1588 and become a millionaire before he died.

In Charles I's reign Thomas Wentworth, later Earl of Strafford, was Lord Deputy, 1633–40, extracting subsidies and organizing the Irish equivalent of the Court of Star Chamber with efficiency, but in 1641 – the year he was executed in England for his illegal actions – there was a rising of Catholics in Ulster, many of the colonists being murdered or fleeing the country. Cromwell thought he was appointed by God to punish this rebellion and to root out the Catholics. He was nearly successful, as by famine, plague and war the population was reduced to about half a million. His memory lives on in the sack of Drogheda in which all the soldiers and civilians (about 3500) were massacred. He wrote: 'It has pleased God to bless our endeavours.' Wexford was similarly dealt with. His final objective – to drive all the native Irish into Connacht – failed through its impractability.

The Restoration of the monarchy in 1660 still meant a Protestant Anglican ascendancy in the country, with a Protestant state Church, only a few Catholics being restored to lands taken by Cromwellian followers. But the Catholics had about a third of the freehold land and during Charles II's reign they were protected by royal prerogative from religious persecution. The hopes, therefore, of Catholics stayed with the Stuart monarchy, and rose high on the accession in 1685 of James II, a Catholic. Three years later, after James had quarrelled with the Church and the Tory party in England, he was expelled; the Whigs invited William, Prince of Orange, to rule England, while the Irish still regarded James as their lawful king. Ireland now became a battleground. The Protestant apprentices of Derry closed the gates of the town on the Catholic armies of James and withstood a siege for 105 days. A Patriot Parliament was summoned by James to Dublin, which proved to be the last 'Old English' legislative assembly until 1922, and the last in which the Catholic faith was represented. William landed in Ireland and on 1 July the Battle of the Boyne decided the fate of the Jacobites. Yeats's Protestant ancestors were on the winning side:

> A Butler or an Armstrong that withstood
> Beside the brackish waters of the Boyne
> James and his Irish when the Dutchman crossed;
>
> *(CP,* p. 113)

Resistance continued in Limerick under Patrick Sarsfield, until he was forced to surrender after the Battle of Aughrim (1691). Subsequently, those Catholic soldiers who wished to were allowed to serve in France, where Sarsfield died fighting. The 'flight of the wild geese', as it was called, put an end to any Catholic hopes for a solution to their grievances.

The Anglo-Irish of the eighteenth century

At the start of the eighteenth century Protestants dominated the Irish Parliament. Penal laws tied and bound Catholics; they could not buy land or lease it for more than thirty-one years; estates had to be portioned among all sons rather than bequeathed to the eldest, unless he were to turn Protestant; higher posts in the government were given to Englishmen; rents were spent in England by countless absentee landlords; and no Catholic could vote or enter Trinity College, the only university.

Jonathan Swift, Protestant Dean of St Patrick's Cathedral, Dublin, from 1713 until his death in 1745, was one of the bitterest critics of English rule. *A Short Character of His Excellency t[he] E[arl] of W[harton], L[ord] L[ieutenant] of I[reland]* in 1711 denounces 'the

31

arbitrary power and oppression . . . whereby the people of Ireland have for some time been distinguished from all Her Majesty's subjects'. It was, in Swift's own words to Stella, 'a damned libellous pamphlet'. Again, in 1724, he took up his pen against a patent which had been granted to a certain William Wood of Wolverhampton to coin over £100,000 worth of halfpennies and farthings, which Swift pointed out in his four pseudonymous *Drapier's Letters* would devalue the coinage and enable Wood to make a possible profit of £40,000. In the fourth of these *Letters* he criticized the whole dependence of Ireland on England. The coinage scheme was dropped and medals were struck in Ireland in Swift's honour. His *Short View of the State of Ireland* (1727) and *Modest Proposal* (1729) further revealed the national tragedy.

Edmund Burke (see below pp. 57–8), as MP for Bristol, tried to get trading equality and religious emancipation for Ireland, but failed: 'Is Ireland united to the crown of Great Britain for no other purpose than that we should counteract the bounty of Providence in her favour?' he asked the citizens of Bristol. Similarly, Berkeley (see below, pp. 55–7) in *The Querist* (1737) asked questions about the unsatisfactory state of economic and social affairs in the country; but nothing was done because the legislative work of the Irish Parliament was limited by the Parliament at Westminster. Thus did three of Yeats's favourite figures from the eighteenth century protest at the inequalities suffered by the Irish in dealing with England.

Until 1760 Protestant rule was complete, and although there was peace in the country for a hundred years after the Battle of the Boyne, it was far from satisfactory for the majority of the population. Edmund Burke summarized the situation: 'The Protestant ascendancy is nothing more or less than the resolution of one set of people to consider themselves as the sole citizens of the Commonwealth and to keep a dominion over the rest by reducing them to slavery under a military power.'

The finest period in the Protestant ascendancy was during Henry Grattan's Parliament in the last fifteen years of the century. By 1770 Henry Grattan led a group called the Patriot Party which sought a 'free Constitution and freedom of trade' for Ireland. After the American War of Independence this party managed to obtain a relaxation of trade restrictions and some real independence for the Irish Parliament – the abolition of the severe penal code and the status of citizens for Catholics, as well as a period of economic prosperity. The reform of Parliament was one of Grattan's objectives, but he was always thwarted by the ruling class of landowners, from which he himself came. However, the French Revolution changed the political thinking of Europe, and soon the leaders for reform were to be found outside Parliament.

The chief of these was Wolfe Tone, a young Protestant lawyer who was an admirer of what the French Revolution had achieved in getting rid of a corrupt aristocracy. In 1791 he formed the Society of United Irishmen, which included Protestants and Catholics, its objective being to form a national Irish Parliament entirely free from the influences of Great Britain. He managed to obtain further concessions for Catholics, but they were still debarred from Parliament, from the higher positions in the state and from Trinity College. Small concessions were insufficient for the revolutionary Tone who, when in France in 1796, proclaimed himself to be a republican who hated England, and a defender of peasants against ruling tyranny. Conciliatory reforms were suggested at this point by Grattan in Ireland, but defeated in the English Parliament. Had these reforms taken place – full emancipation for Catholics, some increase in the number of voters, and certain rights for peasants with reference to tithes and land taxes by landlords – the 1798 rebellion would not have taken place. The last Parliament of the Kingdom of Ireland began in January 1798, and an armed insurrection broke out in May; before that Lord Edward FitzGerald, the much-loved commander-in-chief of the United Irishmen, had died of wounds received while resisting arrest. French troops, who intended to help Wolfe Tone, arrived too late in Killala Bay, County Galway, and were defeated in battle; Tone was captured. In his pride he asked to be shot as a soldier, but was sentenced by a court-martial to be hanged and disembowelled as a criminal. 'A fig for disembowelling if they hang me first', he replied, and eventually avoided that fate by a self-inflicted mortal wound from which he died in prolonged agony.

Yeats inherited

> The pride of people that were
> Bound neither to Cause nor to State,
> Neither to slaves that were spat on,
> Nor to the tyrants that spat,
> The people of Burke and of Grattan
> That gave, though free to refuse –
> Pride, like that of the morn,
> When the headlong light is loose . . .

> (*CP*, p. 222)

From then on, William Pitt, the British prime minister, was determined on an Act of Union between the two countries. Grattan opposed it, but his supporters were eliminated by bribes, or offered places and pensions by Pitt's government, and the Bill was carried. Ireland was to have a hundred MPs in the House of Commons at Westminster, the Churches of England and Ireland were to unite,

Catholics were to have equal rights, and there was to be free trade. But Grattan knew that all was not well for Ireland. His final speech was a poetic lament for his life's work: 'Yet I do not give up my country. I see her in a swoon but she is not dead; though in her tomb she lies helpless and motionless, still on her lips is the spirit of life, and on her cheeks the glow of beauty.' Pitt subsequently defaulted on Catholic emancipation, and the Union never in Irish eyes became 'a treaty between two nations'.

One of the outward signs of the prosperous period of Grattan's Parliament is the grace and magnificence of Irish eighteenth-century town architecture, expressed in countless squares, terraces and crescents in Dublin, Limerick and other towns. With fine public buildings, this was excellent town planning, and Yeats knew it when he lived in Merrion Square, and passed by the Rutland Memorial and through some of the most elegant eighteenth-century streets on his way to the Seanad Éireann (Irish Senate) in Leinster House. Throughout the country, landlords built elegant Palladian houses, known to their tenants as 'the Big House', surrounded by pleasant gardens and landscapes, often formed by them into a special Irish picturesque style, using the scenery of the many loughs and mountains. In 'Private Thoughts' (*EX*), Yeats remarks that the best landed gentry were 'great architects' and 'travelled everywhere, read the classic authorities and designed buildings that still stir our imagination'. This is an idealized view, for most of the gentry were more interested in country sports; but Yeats was influenced by the modest example of Coole Park (see below pp. 165–8) in providing a haven for writers, in the tradition of those friends whom Swift used to visit in the summer months.

The Irish eighteenth century, 'that one Irish century that escaped from darkness and confusion', as Yeats wrote in *Wheels and Butterflies* (1934), provided for him a union of opposites: 'all the delirium of the brave' in the rebel-martyrs who knew that death did not mean failure, and were able to laugh in its presence, combined with the order, grace and splendour of living in the country houses:

> Beloved books that famous hands have bound,
> Old marble heads, old pictures everywhere;
> Great rooms where travelled men and children found
> Content or joy; . . .
>
> ('Coole Park and Ballylee, 1931', *CP*, p. 276)

With his passionate love of the eighteenth century in Ireland, Yeats is not popular with Irish historians. This is a period for them when Gaelic resistance to the English was at its lowest; when Gaelic bards lamented the disappearance of Gaelic traditions, in ballads which either personified Ireland as Cathleen ni Houlihan or Dark

Rosaleen – the beautiful girl deprived of her birthright – or sang of their hopes for a restoration of the Gaelic aristocracy. Yeats's admiration is centred on a few figures, who he thought had the courage to fight against wrongs imposed by England. None of them, as Joseph Hone wrote, was from the landlord class: 'Neither Swift nor Berkeley was born in a great house; Goldsmith came from a country rectory; Burke was the son of a lawyer, Wolfe Tone of a coachmaker; Grattan's father was a Recorder . . . and these men were not only born in Ireland but educated there.'

The most important to Yeats was Jonathan Swift, whose plain and honest speaking seemed to him to be 'Passion ennobled by intensity, by endurance, by wisdom'. In *The Words upon the Window-pane* (1930), his play about Swift's spirit returning to a *séance*, one of the characters, a Cambridge undergraduate, expresses clearly what Yeats himself thought about the eighteenth century: 'when men of intellect reached the height of their power – the greatest position they ever attained in society and the State, that everything great in Ireland and in our character, in what remains of our architecture, comes from that day: that we have kept its seal longer than England'.

The fight for freedom, 1800–1923

Dublin, after the signing of the Act of Union, its Parliament gone, ceased to be a flourishing metropolis and became a provincial city. Soon the culture, independence and prosperity of the period of Grattan's Parliament became a memory. In 1803 there was one more brief and unsuccessful insurrection against English rule, similar to that of Tone and the United Irishmen, in which another hero, Robert Emmet, ended his life on the scaffold. Although his action had little effect upon subsequent history, we mention it as he also was a link in the chain of rebels, and was important for Yeats. In fact, Yeats idealized Tone and Emmet as much as he despised Daniel O'Connell, who was to dominate Irish politics in the first half of the nineteenth century. O'Connell was a Catholic landlord from County Kerry, speaking Gaelic yet spurning it, a man who thought nothing of the past, who expressed loyalty to the Crown (once presenting George IV with shamrocks and a laurel wreath), who did not believe in force as a method of achieving his ends; a demagogue, able to sway thousands by his oratory yet fundamentally unscrupulous and vulgar, in sharp contrast to Grattan, the dignified eighteenth-century aristocrat. Nevertheless, O'Connell, 'the Liberator', became a national hero from the moment he won the Clare election (in 1828) and, as a Catholic, demanded emancipation and the repeal of the Union. By this he meant national independence for

Ireland, but not national separation from Britain. During his leadership of the Irish party, the Catholic Emancipation Act was at last passed (in 1829), liberal reforms were made to the franchise, and Poor Relief and Tithe Acts helped the poor. In talking to Americans on his lecture tour in 1904, Yeats made clear his distinction between Emmet and O'Connell:

> I sometimes think that O'Connell was the contrary principle to Emmet. He taught the people to lay aside the pike and the musket, the song and the story, and to do their work now by wheedling and now by bullying. He won certain necessary laws for Ireland. He gave her a few laws, but he did not give her patriots. He was the successful politician, but it was the unsuccessful Emmet who has given her patriots. O'Connell was a great man, but there is too much of his spirit in the practical politics of Ireland.

Yeats was right. It is about the heroism of Tone, Lord Edward and Emmet that ballads are sung, whose portraits hang on cottage walls, and who have become symbols of freedom to the Irish poor for over a hundred years.

In 1842 another nationalist group called the Young Ireland Party survived for a few brief years, among them Thomas Davis and John Mitchel. At first they joined forces with O'Connell, but it was an uneasy partnership. Soon, however, the appalling crisis of the Great Famine (1845–48) descended on Ireland like the Angel of Death. The potato to the Irish peasant was as rice to the Indian – the staple crop. When epidemic blight killed the potato plant, thousands died of starvation. Despite charitable measures on a vast scale, the population fell from over eight million to six and a half, and thousands emigrated to the United States. It was the worst famine known in the history of Europe in peacetime, and it took Ireland years to recover, firstly because emigration increased, and secondly because most of those who died were Gaelic-speaking. By the 1850s the population was only five million. O'Connell did not live to see the full disaster, as he died an invalid on a journey to Rome, in 1847.

Of the three most important and positive movements in Irish nineteenth-century history – Catholic Emancipation, Land Reform and the Irish Literary Renaissance – only the first came before 1850. In that year a Land Act was passed that protected tenants from certain unjust forms of eviction and gave a fairer scale of rents, fixity of tenure and freedom to sell; but there were still many unfair evictions of tenants who were too poor to pay their rents, up to Maud Gonne's time (see below pp. 118–19). Also in 1850 the Irish Franchise Act increased the electorate to 160,000 voters, much to the advantage of the Irish Party in Parliament.

The Irish Republican Brotherhood (the Fenians, from Fianna the legendary followers of Finn McCool) was founded in 1858. As its name implies, it was based on Wolfe Tone's Jacobin ideas, and so was not content with the Home Rule movement (which hoped to achieve its ends through constitutional measures), but claimed complete national independence. One by one the long-established English injustices disappeared. Gladstone, a lifelong friend of Ireland, who came to power in 1869, saw an Act through Parliament by which the Protestant Church of Ireland was disestablished. A few years later, there followed an Act by which fellowships and higher degrees were open to all creeds at Trinity College. Then he decided to tackle the Home Rule question, and in this he had the cooperation of the most able Irish politician of the century, Charles Stewart Parnell. Parnell was a Protestant squire from County Wicklow – reserved, inscrutable, proud, with an inflexible attachment to the Irish cause. He may be said to have taken up the leadership of the Irish party where O'Connell left it; nevertheless, Yeats saw him as more in the tradition of Swift. In 1877, as MP for Cork City at the age of thirty-one, he was leader of about thirty MPs forming the Irish party in the House of Commons. He was determined first, that Irish farmers should own their land, and that the existing landlord–peasant relationship must become a thing of the past; and second, that Home Rule must be achieved as soon as possible.

Gladstone and his Liberal party returned to power in 1880, and a Land Act was passed which reduced Irish rents by about 20 per cent, giving both landlord and tenants a right in the land. When the first Home Rule Bill was introduced to the Commons in 1886 the Tories opposed it and some of Gladstone's party deserted him, forming the Liberal Unionists, so the Bill was thrown out. Only about a fifth of the population of Ireland, mostly landlords, supported the Union, except in the province of Ulster, which became the centre of the Unionist cause to resist Home Rule. At the height of the crisis, crowds of Orangemen burnt an effigy of O'Connell in Belfast during a riot. It soon became evident to politicians that the Plantation of Ulster, under James I, with Anglo-Scottish Protestants was a fact which could not be overlooked – indeed, it has affected the history of Ireland into our own times.

The partnership between Gladstone, aged eighty-six, and Parnell was now suddenly fractured. Parnell's attachment for the wife of a certain Captain O'Shea became the subject for a divorce in which he was found guilty; and, although Parnell afterwards married her, his supporters – the Pope and Catholic bishops, Gladstone himself, Nonconformists, and a majority of Parnell's own party – all deserted him on moral grounds. In a year's time he had died from the sheer strain and exhaustion of trying to fight his way back to the leadership. At his funeral in Glasnevin cemetery, Dublin, a shooting star was seen by many to fall across the clear sky at the moment that his body was lowered into the grave. Yeats was told about the incident by Maud Gonne, who was present.

More than thirty years later Yeats remembers this in 'Parnell's Funeral' (*CP*, p. 319), as he contrasts the 'animal' crowd beside the Great Comedian's tomb (O'Connell's) in Glasnevin cemetery, and the falling star, that symbol in its clarity for the pure intellect of Parnell, and his sacrificial death. Yeats goes on to contrast the fact that for the deaths of Emmet and Tone, England was responsible, but Parnell's own countrymen destroyed him.

> Through Jonathan Swift's dark grove he passed, and there
> Plucked bitter wisdom that enriched his blood.

It is Yeats's harshest political poem, as well it might be, for he passionately believed that this solitary proud man was sacrificed by the meanness of priests, politicians and people. His death was not rebirth but destruction. In 1913 he had first written in anger of Parnell's treatment (*CP*, p. 123). The lines here are addressed to Lady Gregory:

> A man
> Of your own passionate serving kind who had brought
> In his full hands what, had they only known,
> Had given their children's children loftier thought,
> Sweeter emotion, working in their veins
> Like gentle blood, has been driven from the place,
> And insult heaped upon him for his pains,
> And for his open-handedness, disgrace.

Yeats shows a similar reaction when he recounts an interview with a biographer of Parnell, who reveals the true story, in *The Trembling of the Veil*, Book II (*AU*). Gladstone retired from politics in 1894: the Home Rule Bill had failed to get through Parliament two years previously, having been thrown out by the House of Lords.

The second important movement of the century, which we mentioned, has a happier sequel. The Land Act (1903) offered a bonus to landlords who would sell, and enabled tenants to purchase on easy terms; tenant farmers therefore became yeomen farmers like their English counterparts. The Act affected Coole Park, where the Gregorys sold farms to tenants who became owners. Yeats did not like this dismemberment of the Coole estate and made his views quite clear in the twelve lines of 'Upon a House shaken by the Land Agitation' (*CP*, p. 106). He evidently did not appreciate the hard life that those who lived under 'mean roof-trees' had been forced to live as tenants, paying huge rentals. This was a mistakenly 'aristocratic' attitude on the part of someone who was a guest at Coole, since one of the leaders of the movement which managed to get landlords and nationalist leaders together, and helped to make recommendations for the Land Act, was Captain John Shawe-Taylor, a nephew of Lady Gregory's (see *E&I.* 'John Shawe-Taylor', and Donald Torchiana, *W.B. Yeats and Georgian Ireland*[4]).

The Irish Literary Renaissance (*c.* 1890–1920) was the work initially of Standish O'Grady, Douglas Hyde, Lady Gregory, George Russell (AE), and W.B. Yeats. The playwrights Synge and O'Casey followed, after the founding of the Abbey Theatre. The scholars who translated the folk-tales from Gaelic into English poetry and prose, and, indirectly, those who wrote their own work in Gaelic, contributed to the revival, during which the Gaelic language, with the oldest vernacular literature in Europe, became widely known.

In passing, it is worth noting that though the history and folk legends of Scotland are well known to English readers – Rob Roy, Robert the Bruce, Mary Queen of Scots and Bonnie Prince Charlie being household names – yet the deeds of Grainne O'Malley, Hugh O'Neill, Patrick Sarsfield and Robert Emmet, who are equally valiant Irish heroes, are unknown. Perhaps Ireland needs a Walter Scott to redress the English neglect of Irish myths and history.

In 1900 Gaelic was dormant, although about half a million people in the West still spoke it. In 1900 the Irish speakers in the West had a large vocabulary, estimated by Douglas Hyde at more than 5,000 words, and some could recite a saga of Cuchulain or of the Fianna, even though they could not read or write. (From 1922–73, the language was compulsory in Irish schools.) But English in Ireland is filled with Gaelic idiom to its advantage, and it is this tongue that Yeats heard about him as a boy. Pádraic Colum gives two examples which are relevant: in the first he deals with the English question, 'Are you selling a horse today?'

> The speaker of correct English has to move the emphasis from one word to another of the four last according to the information he seeks. For successive positions of the chief stress give four different meanings to the question. The Anglo-Irish idiom, which in this matter follows the locution of Gaelic, has no need of accentuating. Its user would say: (a) 'Is it you who are selling the horse?' or (b) 'Is it the horse you are selling?' or (c) 'Is it today you are selling the horse?'. Where the English purist depends upon stress to bring out his meaning, the Irish idiom employs construction for the same purpose, and much more effectively.

The second example is in reply to the query, 'Does it rain here?' The Irishman says:

'It bees raining' or 'It does be raining'. He is attempting to reach an exactitude that is possible in Gaelic; in that language there is a distinct form of the verb 'to be' to indicate habitual, the frequentative tense. The Irishman who has the tradition of Gaelic, even though he may never have heard it spoken, feels the want of a frequentative tense in English, and he attempts to supply it.

This may seem like a digression from Irish history with which this section is dealing: but the history of the Irish Literary movement, and its revival of Gaelic speaking and writing was an integral part of the nationalist spirit, which was about to come to fruition – apart from its influence on Yeats, as has been said, by revealing to him the glories of the Irish myths and sagas.

Despite Maud Gonne's fiery speeches, the Wolfe Tone Centenary celebrations in 1898 passed off without any major incident, and when in the next year the Boer War broke out, infinitely more Irishmen served in the British Army than in the Transvaal Brigade, which was commanded by Major John MacBride against the British. But in that year, Arthur Griffith, a journalist, founded a paper called the *United Irishman* (later Sinn Féin, meaning We Ourselves), and many of the younger men such as Pádraic Pearse (see below, pp. 143–7) eventually found that a solution within the Union was not satisfactory and broke away from those such as Griffith who supported the Union. In January 1913 the Third Home Rule Bill was at last passed in the Commons, and although it was again thrown out by the Lords, it was no longer possible, under the recent Parliament Act, for it to be held up by them for more than a year. Except for Ulster, under its leader Edward Carson, who vehemently opposed the Bill, the majority of Irishmen accepted it. To strengthen their position, Ulstermen openly drilled and armed themselves, and in October 1913 a National Volunteer Force to oppose them was organized in Dublin, in addition to a smaller Citizen Army under James Connolly (see below, pp. 112–13). It looked very like civil war as the two sides continued to arm. But the outbreak of the First World War (August 1914) radically changed the situation; the Home Rule Act could not be put into force until hostilities were over, whenever that would be. For the moment all seemed well as about 100,000 Irishmen voluntarily joined the British forces. However, the opponents of the Union saw their chance, and the Irish Republican Brotherhood prepared the ground for the Rising which broke out in Dublin in Easter Week 1916. (See the entry under Pearse, pp. 144 ff.) The subsequent sentences on the leaders united public opinion on Sinn Féin, and 1916, in Seán O'Casey's words, 'became the Year One in Irish history and Irish life'. That is so, but the first five years must be some of the worst suffered by any people trying to gain their independence, and having gained it to restore order and good government.

Home Rule was gradually pushed out of the picture as Sinn Féin, with de Valera as President, gained more and more MPs through by-elections; yet the successful candidates refused to take their seats at Westminster. By the time the war ended, there were more than 100,000 Sinn Féiners in clubs, and the rule of law and order started to break down as Sinn Féin terrorists started to commit atrocities as bad as any which have followed. At the general election in December 1918 Sinn Féin was triumphant and then formed an Assembly of delegates, Dáil Éireann, which declared itself the national government of Saorstát Éireann (the Irish Free State).

Lloyd George then proposed an Amending Act to the Home Rule Act, by which the Six Counties in the north with Protestant majorities should be self-governing, with a Parliament at Stormont. Although it may have pleased Carson, partition, when it became fact in 1920, did not satisfy Sinn Féin, nor was it a satisfactory solution in subsequent years. In southern Ireland, Lloyd George endeavoured to bolster up the Royal Irish Constabulary by recruiting a force of ex-soldiers, who came to be known as the 'Black and Tans' (on account of the dark green in their uniforms appearing to be black). Their atrocities, committed in answer to those of the IRA, make appalling reading, even to a generation which is seeing such things happen again. In the Gort district alone, Lady Gregory reports the Tans dragging young men behind lorries until their bodies were torn to pieces, and the shooting of an innocent widow on a bridge as she sat there. Details of some of these incidents were related by Yeats in his speech in the Oxford Union (see below p. 182). In May 1921 the IRA ambushed and killed four friends, who were with the widow of Major Robert Gregory, as they left a tennis party at Ballinamantane House on the Coole estate, where the Yeatses had lived in 1918 when Thoor Ballylee was being repaired.

> Now days are dragon-ridden, the nightmare
> Rides upon sleep; a drunken soldiery
> Can leave the mother, murdered at her door,
> To crawl in her own blood, and go scot-free;
> The night can sweat with terror as before
> We pieced our thoughts into philosophy,
> And planned to bring the world under a rule,
> We are but weasels fighting in a hole.
>
> (*CP*, p. 233)

In June of the same year, a truce was declared when the British Government decided to negotiate with Sinn Féin, and after a conference in London a Treaty was signed by which the Irish Free

State was recognized as a Dominion in the Commonwealth. When Dáil Éireann met in Dublin, it ratified the Treaty, despite opposition from de Valera, who resigned rather than accept anything but complete independence from the Crown. Griffith became President of the Executive Council, a post similar to prime minister. De Valera and his followers then formed the Republican Party in opposition to the government, and were supported by the IRA, who became known when in uniform as Irregulars. Gradually the situation drifted into civil war as ambushes, murders and reprisals followed one another with sickening regularity.

> An affable Irregular,
> A heavily-built Falstaffian man,
> Comes cracking jokes of civil war
> As though to die by gunshot were
> The finest play under the sun.
>
> (*CP*, p. 229)

In the next poem in the sequence (see pp. 99–101) Yeats calls on the honey-bees, those Platonic symbols of wisdom, patience and virtue, to build in the 'empty house of the stare'. In addition, sectarian hatred flared up in the Six Counties, and murders of Catholics by Protestants and vice versa became everyday examples of hatred. The material destruction was immense: twenty-three out of twenty-eight great houses in County Clare alone were burnt, and the Four Courts, which the Irregulars occupied, was bombarded. As they left the building, the Irregulars exploded a land mine which destroyed the Public Records Office with all the historical records of Ireland for centuries. Amidst this fighting, the Free State Cabinet, including Kevin O'Higgins (see below, pp. 141–2), continued the government of the country and in December 1922 the Dáil passed the Free State Constitution Bill, including the Oath of Allegiance to the Crown. Northern Ireland exercised her right to contract out. Gradually the Irregulars were captured and their supply of arms ran short, so that eventually on 23 May 1923 de Valera ordered them to cease fire. The drama which had opened with Pearse and Connolly in the Post Office had ended.

The last years, 1923–39

The Constitution of the first Irish Free State Parliament created two Houses: the Lower House of democratically elected members, and the Upper House or Seanad (Senate) of sixty members, half of whom were elected by the Dáil, and half appointed by the President of the Executive Council. Like the House of Lords, it could initiate legislation, except concerning finance, but could not reject legislation already passed by the Lower House. To qualify as a Senator, one had to have 'done honour to the nation by useful public service', or have special qualifications or attainments representing 'important aspects of the nation's life'. As the most distinguished Irish writer, especially with regard to his part in the Irish Literary Renaissance and his passionate support of Irish nationalism in his plays and verse, Yeats certainly qualified, and for six years he served as a Senator. He is chiefly remembered for his work as Chairman of the Committee which dealt with the design of the new coinage, which was outstandingly beautiful, and for his speeches on censorship and divorce, in both of which he expressed liberal views which were years ahead of the times in Ireland. In this public role he revealed an eloquence as a speaker which is reflected in the more oratorical structure and syntax of his later verse. His constant problem was how best to unite the best of what Anglo-Irish Protestant Ireland had stood for with the resurgence of Gaelic Ireland and its deep-rooted culture.

Though the Civil War was over, political assassinations did not cease, the most shocking being the murder of Kevin O'Higgins (see below, p. 142) to which 'Blood and the Moon' (*CP*, p. 267) and 'Death' (*CP*, p. 264), refer. (Even O'Higgins's father, a goodnatured country doctor, was murdered at his door by Republicans.) During the 1930s, Yeats kept clear of politics except for his brief flirtation with Eoin O'Duffy and his Blueshirt Fascists (see below, pp. 139–40). Basically Yeats hoped for a political system which would produce leaders who were honest, courageous, farsighted and statesmanlike, and he found it hard to find these in the Ireland of his later years. He sums up what he wanted in *On the Boiler*:

> I was six years in the Irish Senate; I am not ignorant of politics elsewhere, and on other grounds I have some right to speak. I say to those that shall rule here: If ever Ireland again seems molten wax, reverse the process of revolution. Do not try to pour Ireland into any political system. Think first how many able men with public minds the country has, how many it can hope to have in the near future, and mould your system upon those men. It does not matter how you get them, but get them. Republics, Kingdoms, Soviets, Corporate States, Parliaments, are trash, as Hugo said of something else 'not worth one blade of grass that God gives for the nest of the linnet'. These men, whether six or six thousand, are the core of Ireland, are Ireland itself. (p. 13).

Not until 1948, the year that Yeats's body was brought back to Ireland, did the 'Twenty-six Counties' secede from the British Commonwealth and become the sovereign republic of Ireland (Éire). But the end of partition still remains a dream. Yeats's ghost may well say:

One man, one man alone
In that outlandish gear,
One solitary man
Of all that rambled there
Had turned his stately head.
'That is a long way off,
And time runs on', he said,
'And the night grows rough.'

Notes

1. Lady Gregory, *Cuchulain of Muirthemne* (1902; Gerrards Cross: Colin Smythe, 1970).
2. Dillon and Chadwick, *The Celtic Realms* (London: Weidenfeld and Nicolson, 1967).
3. Lady Gregory, *Book of Saints and Wonders* (repr. Gerrards Cross: Colin Smythe, 1970).
4. Donald Torchiana, *W.B. Yeats and Georgian Ireland* (Evanston: North Western UP and Oxford: OUP, 1966), pp. 44–57.

3   The poet's reading

It is increasingly the habit of modern Yeatsian scholars to deduce, from an investigation of Yeats's reading, the source of his imagery. Thus many of his greatest poems become like a secret code which when cracked has a way of breaking open the poems into fragments also. Yeats makes it clear that *A Vision* (*VIS*), which is based on much of his philosophical reading, is not written to enable the ordinary reader to 'understand' his poetry better, but was 'intended . . . for my school-mates only'. He writes elsewhere: 'I have always come to this certainty: what moves natural men in the arts is what moves them in life, and that is, intensity of personal life, intonations that show them, in a book or a play, the strength, the essential moment of a man who would be exciting in the market or at the dispensary door.'

Although he may have found much in the philosophy of Vico, Berkeley or Nietzsche which became the source of the main stream of his ideas, it is the emotional effect of the poem on his readers which matters. His many philosophical readings, from which he takes ideas with which he feels in sympathy, lead to the ultimate truth of the poem. This is admirably summed up by A.G. Stock, in *W.B. Yeats: His Poetry and Thought:*[1]

> A poem is not great because of the beliefs it expounds, but when it convinces us of its greatness we know it cannot have been made from false or trivial thoughts. The images in his poems had to impress by their poetic rightness. What they symbolized was of no importance to the reader till their own power carried it home to him.

This chapter skims the surface of his literary and philosophic studies, which were extensive: theosophy and occult works; Plato and the Neoplatonists; St Thomas Aquinas; the Hindu Upanishads; the Kabbalah: Irish myth and legend; Dante, Shakespeare, Ben Jonson, Donne, Castiglione, Vico, Swift, Berkeley, Burke, Blake, Shelley, Kant and Nietzsche are but some of the fields in which he read widely. Yet I should emphasize that his poetry is illuminated by nothing so much as a reading, in conjunction with his life story, of his critical prose, autobiographical works and senate speeches.

Occult and magic

During his early life Yeats flirted with mystical and magical beliefs,

45

which were part of the underground culture of the late Victorian period. One of the unintentional results of British imperialism was the bringing to the West of the wisdom of India and Tibet. A Theosophical or Hermetic Society was founded in New York in 1875, and ten years afterwards a London headquarters also was opened by the founder, a Russian lady, Helen Petrovna Blavatsky (1831–91). Theosophy (from *theos*: god, and *sophia*: wisdom) originated in India, and was the study of the divine essence as expounded in mystical revelations from Mahatmas in India and gurus in Tibet. Madame Blavatsky, on her worldwide travels, had attached herself to one such Master, learning some of the secret doctrines which she then wished to make available to mankind. The aims of her society were: to found a universal brotherhood, irrespective of race, creed, colour and caste; to study comparative religion, philosophy and science from sacred books; and to investigate certain unexplained laws of nature (psychic phenomena) and latent powers in man, such as the spiritual body taking control of the physical body, which she had witnessed in India. The goal was Nirvana, in which the Lower Self is dead. These ideas are set out in her book *Isis Unveiled* (1877), which Yeats read. In acknowledging Man as a spiritual being, theosophy had much in common with the 'middle way' of Buddhism, and the Kabbalah, and with the mystic tradition of the Upanishads and Yoga systems of Hindu religion.

In 1885 Yeats helped to found a Dublin Hermetic Society to study oriental religions and theosophy, and he read books by A.P. Sinnett, a fellow-Irishman, entitled *The Occult World* and *Esoteric Buddhism*, as well as meeting Mohini Chatterjee, a Brahmin, to whom he was much attracted. Nearly forty years later, in 'Mohini Chatterjee' (*CP*, p. 279), he remembers meeting this Master and repeats the declaration of faith he then heard:

> I have been a king,
> I have been a slave,
> Nor is there anything,
> Fool, rascal, knave,
> That I have not been . . .

The Master established in Yeats's mind the belief in reincarnation, which he was later to find in the Neoplatonists and never to abandon. In the splendid second verse of the poem, he expresses his own belief, not found in either oriental philosophy or Neoplatonism, that God had contrived reincarnation so that all unsatisfied ones may live happily in another life. (F.A.C. Wilson deals with this poem in his book *Yeats's Iconography*.)[2] Yeats joined the Blavatsky Lodge of the Theosophical Society in 1887, and in 1890 was initiated into a Rosicrucian occult society: this was the Hermetic Order of the

Golden Dawn, whose leader, MacGregor Mathers (see below, p. 138), controlled the London temple. (Rosicrucian societies had been founded in Germany in the early seventeenth century: the name was derived from the alchemical and occult claims of Christian Rosenkreutz (1378–1484). There were ten initiation rites centred on the Sephirotic Tree of Life which one climbed by means of a series of spiritual deaths and rebirths, to reach, ultimately, union with God.

Mathers's interests were twofold: he sought to attain psychic phenomena or visions as a result of meditation on certain chosen symbols; and he practised ancient magical rituals which he had discovered. Yeats discusses this:

> I am confident from internal evidence that the rituals, as I knew them, were in substance ancient though never so in language unless some ancient text was incorporated. There was little that I thought obvious or melodramatic, and it was precisely in this little, I am told, that they resembled Masonic rituals, but much that I thought beautiful and profound. I do not know what I would think if I were to hear them now for the first time, for I cannot judge what moved me in my youth.
>
> (*AU*, p. 576)

Maud Gonne, who was also a member for a brief period, thought the ceremonies definitely smacked of freemasonry, and as she regarded this as a product of the hated British Empire, she resigned.

Of equal interest to Yeats were the visions of trancelike states which arose from the examination of symbols, and which so stimulated his imagination. In 'Ideas of Good and Evil. Magic' (*E&I*, p. 50) he explains this: 'The symbols are of all kinds, for everything in heaven or earth has its associations, momentous or trivial, in the Great Memory.' Here we have Yeats mentioning his belief in the *Anima Mundi* (see below, pp. 49–50). On other occasions he took part in group activities, and it seemed that visions which sometimes appeared might have been telepathically transmitted by the strongest member of the group.

Mathers's methods are described in *The Trembling of the Veil, Four Years, 1887–91* (*AU*):

> He gave me a cardboard symbol and I closed my eyes. Sight came slowly, there was not that sudden miracle as if darkness had been cut with a knife, for that miracle is mostly a woman's privilege, but there rose before me mental images that I could not control: a desert and a black Titan raising himself up by his two hands from the middle of a heap of ancient ruins. Mathers explained that I had seen a being of the order of Salamanders because he had shown me their symbol, but it was not necessary

47

even to show the symbol, it would have been sufficient that he imagined it.

The occult symbols would have included the Rose, the Cross, the Sun, the Moon, the Tree, the Water and the Bird. Poems in which these symbols and others occur are 'The Two Trees' (*CP*, p. 54) where one finds the Kabbalistic Tree of Life and the Tree of Knowledge; 'To Some I have Talked with by the Fire' (*CP*, p. 56) with its reference to the Ineffable Name of Jehovah, which in the four Hebrew letters can be anagrammatized countless times; and 'The Poet pleads with the Elemental Powers' (*CP*, p. 180) where the Seven Lights are the seven planets.

Although Yeats was admitted to the inner conclave, the Esoteric section of the Theosophical Society, his sense of fun did not desert him: 'A sad accident happened yesterday at Madame Blavatsky's lately. A big materialist sat on the astral double of a poor young Indian. It was sitting on the sofa and he was too material to be able to see it. Certainly a sad accident.' Soon, however, the internal quarrels of the Society were too much for him: 'The Society is like "the happy family" that used to be exhibited round Charing Cross Station – a cat in a cage full of canaries.' Even after he had shaved off his beard (a modest one), and Madame Blavatsky had predicted a severe illness through loss of mesmeric force which collects in a beard, he still continued to attend meetings for a few months. But an article in *The Weekly Review* brought matters to a head: he had criticized the Society and he refused to promise never to criticize it again. He was a member of the Blavatsky Lodge for only three years, but he progressed from the lowest to the highest grade of the Order of the Golden Dawn, becoming *Adeptus Exemptus* in 1916 after twenty-five years of involvement.

It is easy to laugh at or be shocked by Yeats's membership of these societies, as were his friends John O'Leary and George Russell, who thought he was wasting his time when he should have been writing. Yet one can now see how vital to Yeats was this searching for a non-materialist world, and the imagery, even though artificially inspired by conscious pictorial symbols, which was fuel to his poetic imagination. It is the start of Yeats's lifelong search for symbols and thought forms, after having been brought up by an agnostic father in a world whose poverty of spiritual symbols derived from its sacrifice of the spirit before the claims of the intellect. Yeats feared this separation of spirit and matter in the modern world, and used the Rose as a symbol of harmony which he came to call a 'unity of being', though this was not its only symbolism. His gratitude to these early theosophists and clairvoyants is shown in his subsequent dedication of *A Vision* in its first private edition (1925), to Mrs

MacGregor Mathers herself, one of the few survivors from these times.

Plato and the Neoplatonists

Lionel Johnson (see below, pp. 131–3) thought Yeats an 'unlettered lad' and told him he should read Plato; in the same way, Madame Blavatsky had recommended the Neoplatonist philosophers to him. The poet followed this advice, and by selective reading he gradually built up his own philosophic beliefs. Central to these was Plato's principle (from the *Meno* and the *Phaedo*) of the immortality of the soul, which confirmed what Yeats already thought concerning personal immortality. Put briefly, Plato thought the soul had many lives; when born into this world it had returned from another to inhabit the body, rather as a pilot does a boat. Or, to choose another image from Plato: 'the body is a garment with which the soul is invested'. But it is not always happy in its relationship with the body, which is at the lowest end of the scale of being. 'Supernatural Songs' v (*CP*, p. 330), reflects this:

> Thought is a garment and the soul's a bride
> That cannot in that trash and tinsel hide:

Death is but a separation of the soul from the body. In the various regions through which the soul has been passing it absorbs knowledge which, so to speak, is stored there. In the *Meno*, Plato writes: 'Since the soul is immortal and has been born many times and has seen the things of this world and of Hades and all things, there is nothing which she has not learned. So that it is no wonder that she should be able to recollect virtue and all other things, seeing that she has learned them previously.' This Anamnesis (Recollection) is therefore a calling to mind by the soul of its previous state (this is discussed in the opening of the *Phaedrus*) and shows the basis for a belief in reincarnation which Yeats had also found in his oriental occult studies. If knowledge is a recollection, the soul before our birth must have been acquainted with it in that state or region where it beheld 'ideas' or 'forms' as Plato calls them, or as Yeats would say, the symbols of *Anima Mundi*, the great storehouse of Knowledge.

The Greek Neoplatonist philosophers Plotinus (*c.* 200–270 AD) and Porphyry (*c.* 223–304 AD) combine much from Platonic philosophy with the mysticism of the East and even some of the beliefs of Judaism: a heady brew, examined by Berkeley in his discourse in *Siris* on 'The Aether or pure invisible Fire', and imbibed by such English poets as Milton, Blake, Coleridge, Shelley and Yeats, for whom a transition from philosophy to mysticism was not difficult. F.A.C. Wilson, in *W.B. Yeats and Tradition*[3] makes this very clear:

The symbolic system of Neoplatonism was fixed and one might even say rigid: the sea, for example, symbolized always 'the waters of emotion and passion', or more simply life; man was consistently thought of as the beggar, dressed in the rags of mortality; the tomb, the forest and the cave were all symbols of the material world; after death, the soul, often accompanied by a mystic escort of dolphins, crossed the sea to heaven, the Isles of the Blessed. Yeats knew this system of symbolism from several sources: from Madame Blavatsky, in his formative years; then from Taylor's translation of the commentators on Plato, and especially from Porphyry's essay on 'The Cave of the Nymphs'; also from Plato himself, Plotinus ... and the other Platonic philosophers he had read. He took it over into his verse in the confidence that it would prevent his own symbolism from being arbitrary or unintelligible; it was traditional, for it had persisted throughout the middle ages, where it influenced among others, Dante, and, later, Spenser; and, as the symbolism of a religious system which he himself was largely able to accept, it is clear that he thought of it as profound. In using it, again, he had precedent in the work of two English poets he particularly admired: Blake ... and ... Shelley.

The history of myth shows certain recurrent symbols, deep in human psychology and religion, which become a reservoir of thought, fed by the *Anima Mundi*, the Great Memory, which may be compared to the 'collective unconscious' of Jung. In this region all mythologies are one, expressed through symbols which speak to the unconscious and on which we can all draw. For a poet such as Yeats the Great Memory was reality: not the reality of science or materialistic philosophy which dominates the arts in our own age, but the reality which through myth restores the fullness of imaginative life and gives to poetry an absolute truth. This may be modified by individual genius, but it is never abandoned. Milton is expressing this view of tradition when he writes in 'Il Penseroso':

> Or let my Lamp at midnight hour,
> Be seen in som high lonely Towr,
> Where I may oft out-watch the *Bear*,
> With thrice great *Hermes*, or unsphear
> The spirit of *Plato* to unfold
> What Worlds, or what vast Regions hold
> The immortal mind that hath forsook
> Her mansion in this fleshly nook:

It is important therefore to know the traditional language of symbols used by Plato and by later Neoplatonists, for these symbols

Samuel Palmer: The Lonely Tower, illustrating the Milton passage on p. 50.

are, as Jung says in *Psychology and Alchemy*[4], all variants of certain central types and these occur universally. They are the primordial images from which the religions each draw their universal truth.'

In Plato and the Neoplatonists, soul is reality and form; body is a cloudy vapour with no entity or form. 'What's water but the generated soul?' The soul descends into the body because of some imperfection, and thereby loses its purity through contact with the body or external matter, which is evil. Therefore the soul's descent is a death, so from an earlier Greek philosopher, Heraclitus (513 BC), we have: 'We live their [the souls'] death, and we die their life', the body being the sepulchre of the soul.

'The Delphic Oracle upon Plotinus' (*CP*, p. 306) is a paraphrase of a passage from Plotinus which Yeats read in the translation of Thomas Taylor, the friend of Blake:

> Where streams ambrosial in immortal course
> Irriguous flow, from Deity their source.
> No dark'ning clouds those happy skies assail,
> And the calm aether knows no stormy gale.
> Supremely blest thy lofty soul abides
> Where Minos and his brother judge presides;
> Just Aeacus, and Plato the divine,
> And fair Pythag'ras there exalted shine
> With other souls who form the general choir,
> Of love immortal, and of pure desire.

How much better is Yeats's short, witty, yet serious poem! The Oracle, 'the last great oracle of Delphi', speaks, showing us Plotinus struggling to swim in the sea of life, having discarded his mortal rags. But as he has lived as a saint, and on more than one occasion has attained to a mystical state of ecstasy by the elevation of his soul to God, he needs no expiation as impure souls do on arrival at the Isles of the Blessed. 'Bland Rhadamanthus' (a typical sonority of Yeats), the son of Zeus and Europa, and, as one of the judges of immortal souls, the prototype of wisdom and virtue, beckons him, so all is well.

According to Plotinus, the three types of men who have visionary experience and who provide the welcome on landing at the Isles of the Blessed, are philosophers, lovers and musicians. Plato is here the philosopher, and Pythagoras the conductor of the heavenly choir of love. He had been in life the perfector of the Doric scale and thereby the establishment of certain musical intervals according to the number of their vibrations, scientifically worked out. But, more important, 'number' and 'measure' had for him an ideal significance in which the laws of harmony were the laws of nature, the seven notes of the scale being related to the seven planets in the music of the spheres.

'News for the Delphic Oracle' (*CP*, p. 378) is admirably dealt with by F.A.C. Wilson, *W.B. Yeats and Tradition*,[5] and this should be read in conjunction with Kathleen Raine, *Blake and Tradition*,[6] 'The Sea of Time and Space' in which she discusses Blake's drawing illustrating the theme of Porphyry's essay, 'The Cave of the Nymphs', which was well known to Yeats. Some critics would have us believe that these poems of Yeats are frivolous, but Dr Wilson rightly asserts that although there is levity in 'News for the Delphic Oracle', it is fundamentally a poem showing belief in the whole Platonic heaven. The choir of love and Pythagoras appear in both poems, but in the second the mythology is a mixture of Ancient Greek and Celtic – the Isles of the Blessed and Tir-na-nÓg. This mixture is equally evident in 'The Statues' (*CP*, p. 375), in which Pythagoras and Cuchulain 'stalk' through Athens and Dublin respectively.

Plotinus's six 'Enneads', as edited by Porphyry, revealed Man as an imaginative and remembering soul, in touch with the *Anima Mundi* and with the Divine Mind; not through discursive, logical reasoning but through intuitive thought. The approach of these Neoplatonists is therefore more mystical than that of Plato himself, rating as they do, matter at the lowest level, and spirit (*nous*) as the divine and highest. This is where Yeats found common ground with the religions of the East.

A knowledge of Platonic symbols such as the spindle or the honey bees, as well as such a story as that of the Cave in the Myth of Er, helps to elucidate such passages as the 'honey of generation' in verse five of 'Among School Children' (*CP*, p. 244), and the honey bees of 'The Stare's Nest by my Window' (*CP*, p. 230). But it should also be noted how many times Yeats declares his ultimate faith in man himself. See 'The Tower', III (*CP*, p. 222–5).

Giambattista Vico, 1668–1744

Before 1924 Yeats had read little philosophy, but in that year he attended lectures in London on Benedetto Croce's *Aesthetic*, also reading and annotating Croce's *The Philosophy of Giambattista Vico*, translated by R.G. Collingwood. When Yeats was in Italy the next year, Mrs Yeats summarized some of the passages from other Italian philosophers, as he could not read Italian. One discovery was Vico, a Neapolitan jurist and philosopher-cum-historiographer. Until the age of forty, Vico had cherished a contempt for history, having been under the influence of Descartes (1596–1650) who was famous for his mathematically inclined deductions, and in particular for his central statement, the only proposition in which he thought the truth could not be doubted, and therefore that he existed: *Cogito, ergo sum.* But gradually Vico found much of Descartes' thinking to be alien, in particular that the body was a machine united to the soul; and that mind or spirit is pure consciousness and matter its extension. Vico thus freed himself from the shackles of Descartes' intellectualism and mathematical thinking, by starting to work out from a study of the classical writers his philosophy of history, which culminated in his *Scienza Nuova* (New Science), 1725. Of particular interest to Yeats was Vico's premise, a revolutionary one at the time, that myths and traditions are historical, even though they need not refer to real men; that they are a form of Truth for primitive men, from whom, after the senses and feelings, comes that primary working of the mind, the imagination, which, allied to Art, he calls poetry. It is easy to understand how Yeats would have joined this to William Blake's belief in the imagination being born of the passions and being the language of the spiritual kingdom, to which primitive men and children both belong. Previous philosophers had considered the primitive state of nature as savage and brutal, so Vico strikes out a new route with regard to primitive man which Rousseau was to follow later, though he did not go as far as Vico in thinking primitive man was 'a poet speaking in poetic characters'. William Blake certainly saw children in these terms.

However, more emphasis should be placed on Vico's cyclical view of movements in both religious and political history. Religions, thought Vico, begin with unity, go on to heresy, then die with atheism before the cycle recurs (he was always a Catholic). States begin with monarchy, go on to enfeebled monarchy or democracy, then after chaos, return to monarchy; the cycle being interdependent and concentric with the religious cycle. Civilizations start with Gods, go on to Heroes, poetic creatures, during which state there is aristocratic government, then descend to men, during which time religion becomes mere morality and politics undesirable equality, which he calls the 'alphabetical age'. After which barbarism, then a return to unified monarchy. Above all, it is Man who fashions his own destiny, or makes his history in these cycles.

> Whatever flames upon the night,
> Man's own resinous heart has fed.

> (*CP*, p. 240)

This removes from Vico's cyclical theory the depressing determinist philosophy from which Yeats was always trying to escape.

In Vico Yeats found a number of important views which he already held or had partly thought out, as well as a statement of a cyclical view of history, to be used later by historians contemporary with himself, such as Toynbee and Spengler. In the opposition of the imagination to the intellect, Yeats, as we shall see, sided with William Blake in his belief in the former. In the importance of Myth and tradition, Yeats not only found echoes of *Anima Mundi* of Plato, but also in the work of the translators from the Gaelic which provides the heart of so much of his own work. Finally, he felt sympathetic to the virtues of a benevolent aristocracy as opposed to the chaos of democracy, because of what he had seen and experienced during the Civil War in Ireland. 'The Seven Sages' (*CP*, p. 271) shows Whiggery, in Yeats's sense, to mean liberal, intellectual and possibly scientific thinking, an error which, in somewhat flat verse, he absolves his beloved eighteenth-century figures from holding. Elsewhere he compares certain works of Swift's with Vico's thought:

> Whether they knew it or not,
> Goldsmith and Burke, Swift and the Bishop of Cloyne
> All hated Whiggery; but what is Whiggery?
> A levelling, rancorous, rational sort of mind
> That never looked out of the eye of a saint
> Or out of drunkard's eye.
>
> (*Wheels and Butterflies, EX*, pp. 353–4)

Above all, Vico's influence shows in the cyclical view of history as worked out in *A Vision*, with particular reference to certain human types, and which covers all life:

> The Primum Mobile that fashioned us
> Has made the very owls in circles move.
>
> (*CP*, p. 229)

In *On the Boiler* (1938) Yeats sums up what Vico meant to him by placing him as 'the first modern philosopher to discover in his own mind, and in the European past, all human destiny'. Vico's views, which are briefly summarized above, constantly recur in Yeats's late verse, and are an integral part of a consistent pattern in the poet's thought with relation to Man and Eternity.

George Berkeley, 1685–1753

> I declare this tower is my symbol; I declare
> This winding, gyring, spiring treadmill of a stair is my
>   ancestral stair;
> That Goldsmith and the Dean, Berkeley and Burke have
>   travelled there.
>   . . .

> And God-appointed Berkeley that proved all things a dream,
> That this pragmatical, preposterous pig of a world, its farrow
>   that so solid seem,
> Must vanish on the instant if the mind but change its theme;
>   ('Blood and the Moon', *CP*, p. 268)

Thus does Yeats place Berkeley on his 'ancestral stair' with Gold-smith, Swift and Burke. The second of the two stanzas above refers to the basic theme of Berkeley's philosophy as Yeats saw it – that spirit or mind is the sole reality of physical things: in Berkeley's words *esse est percipi*, the existence of objects consists in their being perceived in the mind. This was in direct opposition to the utilitarian philosophy of Locke, who thought there was 'nothing in mind that has not come from sense'. Berkeley therefore considered himself an 'immaterialist' in his denying that 'matter' and the external reality of space existed.

Berkeley's philosophy appealed to Yeats on many grounds. He was born and educated in Ireland, and Yeats noticed in his *Commonplace Book* these words – with reference to a refutation of Locke's ideas which reflected the English philosophical thought of the time – 'We Irishmen think otherwise', namely not in abstractions. In Berkeley's *A Theory of Vision* (1733), he states there is an 'omnipresent eternal mind, which knows and comprehends all things', and which communicates in mental perceptions to human minds. Nothing therefore exists outside the mind of God. This may be thought to be a difficult philosophical hurdle for Yeats to surmount, yet he leapt over it happily, by saying, in his essay on Berkeley in *E&I*, that this was 'Not the God of Protestant theology, but a God that leaves room for human pride'. Yet could Yeats really agree with Berkeley's bringing in God to help when all else in the worldly system had failed? Did he not believe that man fashioned his own destiny in so far as the gyres would let him? Fundamentally, Yeats connects Berkeley with the Neoplatonists in their view of reality, and de-scribes, in the same essay, Berkeley's *Three Dialogues between Hylas and Philonous in opposition to Sceptics and Atheists* (1713) as 'the only philosophical arguments since Plotinus that are works of art, being so well-bred, so sensible'.

Whether Berkeley was writing as the 'fierce young man' or as 'the good bishop' of Cloyne, there is a tightness and lucidity about his prose, which, in the best eighteenth-century manner, avoids abstrac-tions. Berkeley had a versatility in the Renaissance tradition of *uomo universale* (universal man), writing on such diverse subjects as Irish social evils (*The Querist*), mathematics, the American-Indian cure by tarwater, and what would now be called the psychology of vision. Yeats responded to this Protestant graduate of Trinity College in his opposition to the physical science of Locke and Descartes who 'took away the world (dreams) and gave us excrement instead'.

The *Irish Times* of 18 February 1933 reports Yeats as saying in a lecture to the Royal Dublin Society: 'Ireland has produced three world figures . . . George Berkeley, a philosopher – according to Bergson, the creator of modern philosophy . . . Jonathan Swift, the first great modern mind to deny the value of life . . . Edmund Burke, who rolled back the anarchy of the French Revolution, and perhaps saved Europe.'

Edmund Burke, 1729–97

Among his eighteenth-century literary and philosophic ancestors Yeats placed Burke. As we have said (see above, p. 32), Burke's mother and his Irish friends were Catholics, and it is very probable that the reason for his father turning Protestant was to enable him to take his law exams, which he was not able to do as a Catholic. However, his family were certainly not descended from English settlers, but from an older stock of 'native' Irish; therefore Yeats was mistaken in thinking of him as like Swift, Berkeley or Goldsmith – in the Protestant Anglo-Irish tradition.

Burke's influence on Yeats comes late, 'The Tower' III (1927), 'Blood and the Moon' II (1928), and 'The Seven Sages' (1932) being the only references to him by name. Basically Yeats sympathized with Burke's view that man's political duties result from tradition and inheritance rather than from rational thought, and particularly not from abstract thought concerned with liberty. 'The only liberty I mean is connected with order', he wrote in *An Appeal from the New Whigs to the Old Whigs* (1791), a book, so Mrs Yeats told Professor Torchiana,[7] which might be called Yeats's political bible. 'Men come (as young people) into a community with the social state of the parents, endowed with all the benefits, loaded with all the duties of their situation. . . . Our country is not a thing of mere physical locality. It consists in great measure, in the ancient order into which we are born . . .'

Burke opposed the French Jacobin revolutionaries' ideals and practices as they destroyed the social order he valued so highly; and he even thought they should be counteracted by war if necessary, (see his *Reflections on the Revolution in France*, 1790). This idea is mirrored in much of Yeats's thought in *Last Poems*, filled as it is with admiration for fighting and violence. Having suffered the turmoil of Ireland in the 1920s, Yeats longed for politicians of the statesmanlike calibre of Kevin O'Higgins (see below, pp. 141–2), but instead he saw lesser men, with qualities similar to those Burke attributes to Pitt's ministry, which tried to negotiate with the Jacobins (*Letters on the Proposals for Peace with the Regicide Directory of France*, 1796): 'In truth, the tribe of vulgar politicians are the lowest of our species. There is no trade so vile and mechanical as government in their hands. Virtue is not their habit.' Moreover, Burke wrote elsewhere, men of wisdom were needed (as Yeats constantly stressed when a Senator):

> None, except those who are profoundly studied can comprehend an elaborate contrivance of a fabric fitted to unite private and public liberty, with public force, with order, with peace, with justice, and, above all, with the institutions formed for bestowing permanence and stability, through ages, upon the invaluable whole.

Burke's rhetoric, much like Grattan's, was regarded by Yeats as having Irish rather than English qualities – eloquent, passionate yet noble. His speeches on the question of the American colonies, published in 1769 and 1770, and the speech which opened the trial at the impeachment of Warren Hastings, are classics of English oratory, having a perfect fusion of feeling and thought into a poetic whole on which they may be judged as literature.

'And haughtier-headed Burke that proved the State a tree' (*CP*, p. 268) refers to Burke's oft-repeated statement that the state was an oak tree, which, as Yeats said to the Irish Literary Society in November 1925, was 'no mechanism to be pulled in pieces and put up again, but an oak tree that had grown through centuries'. The adjective 'haughtier-headed' is used by Yeats as he remembers the set of Burke's head in his statue outside Trinity College, where he stands, hand on hip, looking boldly forward, very different in stance to the adjacent statue of Goldsmith, which portrays him 'sipping' a book, head bowed.

Yeats picked from Burke the philosophic ideas with which he found himself in sympathy, and it is easy to understand Burke's appeal for the poet when he discusses his union of discipline and self-assertion, which might well be Yeats's unity of being. Also, Burke's acute awareness of man's intuitions, added to his allowing human nature a right to irrationality and complexity – the very opposite of a Lockeian rationality – enables Yeats to base many of his aspirations and political ideas on his beloved Burke's 'great melody'.

William Blake, 1757–1827

> Grant me an old men's frenzy,
> Myself must I remake
> Till I am Timon or Lear
> Or that William Blake
> Who beat upon the wall
> Till Truth obeyed his call;

> A mind Michael Angelo knew
> That can pierce the clouds,
> Or inspired by frenzy
> Shake the dead in their shrouds;
> Forgotten else by mankind,
> An old man's eagle mind.

Thus, in these last two stanzas of 'An Acre of Grass' (*CP*, p. 346), does Yeats as an old man return to William Blake. When he was sixteen years old, his father lent him a copy of Blake, then he had edited his works with Edwin Ellis (see below, pp. 114–15) and now, forty years on, Blake's influence was still pre-eminent. The operative word in the stanzas above is 'frenzy', that passion which is stronger than reason, that can 'pierce the clouds' and was supremely possessed by King Lear, Timon of Athens and William Blake in their old age. Professor Torchiana[8] points out an explicatory prose passage from a talk (11 October 1936) given by Yeats on the BBC, referring to the growth of naturalism or realism in literature since the seventeenth century, and how we have been overwhelmed by a mechanistic philosophy (Locke and Newton), as well as by an art which merely mirrors nature rather than transforms man's aspirations. This state of affairs, said Yeats, 'lasted to our own day with the exception of a brief period between Smart's *Song of David* (1763) and the death of Byron (1824), wherein imprisoned man beat upon the door'. For Blake, who had lived through that period, poetry and the other arts were not just a mirror of life, but the chief lens of spiritual consciousness.

Blake believed that the imagination was the 'first emanation of divinity', and that the arts, which were the language of imaginative knowledge, were the greatest of divine revelations; in this he showed the traditional nature of his spiritual knowledge, tradition being by that 'golden chain' with the past by which imaginative experience was handed down in the language of myth and symbol. With amazing eclecticism he was able to include in his idea Neoplatonists, alchemists and Christian philosophers. In 'All Religions are One' he writes:

> Principle 5th. The Religions of all Nations are derived from each Nation's different reception of the Poetic Genius, which is every where call'd the Spirit of Prophecy.

> Principle 7th. As all men are alike (tho' infinitely various), So all Religions and, as all similars, have one source.

The true Man is the source, he being the Poetic Genius. Yeats would have had no difficulty in believing this and in finding similarities between the philosophical ideas of Berkeley and Blake, for the basis of their worlds was the same, namely, we may doubt the reality of a material object, but we cannot doubt we hear, feel and see. Compare Blake in *A Vision of the Last Judgement* (1810): 'Mental Things are alone Real; what is call'd Corporeal, Nobody Knows of its Dwelling Place: it is in Fallacy, & its Existence an Imposture. Where is the Existence Out of Mind or Thought?' with Berkeley in the *Principles of Human Knowledge* (1710) 'It is an opinion strangely prevailing amongst men, that houses, mountains, rivers, and in a word all sensible objects have an existence natural and real, distinct from their being perceived by the understanding.'

Yeats developed these ideas in 'William Blake and the Imagination' (*E&I*, p. 111): 'In his [Blake's] time educated people believed that they amused themselves with books of the imagination, but that they "made their souls" by listening to sermons and by doing or not doing certain things. . . . In our time we "make our souls" out of some one of the great poets of ancient times.' Thus for Blake and Yeats, 'the marriage of art with symbol' (referring to vision and not allegory) is first a revelation, and second an amusement.

Yeats also found in Blake's writing his idea of paired opposites – soul and self, body and soul, love and death, chance and choice, 'subjective' and 'objective', conflicting yet establishing a unity in a man's life and in history. A passage from 'The Marriage of Heaven and Hell' states: 'Without Contraries is no progression. Attraction and Repulsion, Reason and Energy, Love and Hate, are necessary to Human existence' (*The Complete Writings of William Blake*, ed. Keynes.)[9]

Concerning such opposites, Yeats writes epigrammatically in 'Those Images' (*CP*, p. 367):

> Seek those images
> That constitute the wild,
> The lion and the virgin,
> The harlot and the child.

As T.R. Henn points out in *The Lonely Tower*,[10] this is both Blakean in rhythm and influenced by an illustration in Blake's 'Marriage of Heaven and Hell'. Yeats knew all Blake's visionary drawings well: 'The Ancient of Days' hung in his rooms for many years, and he places him, before 'confusion fell upon our thought', with other visionary artists, including Samuel Palmer and Edward Calvert, who were Blake's disciples:

> Calvert and Wilson, Blake and Claude
> Prepared a rest for the people of God.

In the late 1920s, between writing 'Sailing to Byzantium' and 'Byzantium', Yeats was very ill, and after he recovered he turned again to Blake, quoting particularly a letter of Blake's written in the year of his death to his friend George Cumberland, junior: 'I have been very near the Gates of Death, & have returned very weak, & an Old Man feeble & tottering, but not in Spirit & Life, not in The Real Man The Imagination which Liveth for Ever. In that I am stronger & stronger as this Foolish Body decays.' Yeats was immensely moved by this letter, describing it as 'the most beautiful of all letters'. Obviously he found a physical parallel between his own life and Blake's, as also he had always found a likeness in Blake's thought. He saw him as the champion of the soul, fighting the mechanistic, abstract thought of Locke and Newton,

> Beating upon the wall
> Till Truth obeyed his call.

Friedrich Nietzsche, 1844–1900

In 1902 John Quinn (see below, pp. 149–50) lent Yeats a book of selections from the works of the German philosopher Nietzsche. After reading the book, Yeats wrote to his father of his admiration for Nietzsche's philosophy, concerning which John B. Yeats, some years later, remarked with his customary humanity: 'The sort of men whom Nietzsche's theory fits are only great men of a sort, a sort of Yahoo great men. The struggle is how to get rid of them, they belong to the clumsy and brutal side of things.' He could not have expressed himself in stronger terms, for the Yahoos of Gulliver's final voyage are the epitome of Swift's ultimate disgust with and contempt for humanity – physically repulsive, and 'the most unteachable of all Brutes'. Again, in 1909, Yeats's father, writing from New York, sums up the heart of the matter by saying that W.B.'s talent was 'benign' whereas Nietzsche's was 'malign'. He was right: Nietzsche had a violent 'objective' irreligious mind; Yeats was tolerant, 'subjective' and religious in the broadest sense.

What were the views which appealed to son but disgusted father? In *The Birth of Tragedy*, Nietzsche sees the essence of Greek art as not in calm, but in tension between Dionysiac forces of cruelty and frenzy, and the beauty, light and rational energy of Apollo. In this violent conflict we have the two opposed movements of the soul, like so much in Yeats's own thought. Nietzsche also admired Greek art for its aristocratic qualities, which fitted some of Yeats's political leanings. Nietzsche's admiration for the Greeks was accompanied by a contempt for Christianity (although he respected Jesus Christ), for its weakness and gentleness, and he believed that its morals were fundamentally wrong. For example, loving one's neighbour was merely a Jewish trick to get the strong to submit to the weak. Christianity was born of weakness – 'sided with all that is weak and base, with all failure' – therefore he saw it as the enemy of reason, honesty, sex, power, joy and freedom.

These qualities were to be developed by humanity whom Nietzsche called on, in *Thus Spake Zarathustra* (1883–5), to create *der Übermensch*, the Superman, full of daring, initiative, masterfulness, and freed from guilt, repression and introversion. This 'exuberant, vigorous and world-affirming man' was never far from Yeats, whose imagination repeatedly dwelt on Cuchulain. Fierce heroic action is thus glorified by 'that strong enchanter', as Yeats called Nietzsche, and he is put in *VIS* in Phase Twelve, the phase of the hero; in 'The Phases of the Moon' we find the only reference to him in Yeats's verse:

> Eleven pass, and then
> Athene takes Achilles by the hair,
> Hector is in the dust, Nietzsche is born,
> Because the hero's crescent is the twelfth.
> And yet, twice born, twice buried, grow he must,
> Before the full moon, helpless as a worm.
>
> *(CP*, p. 183)

The 'phases of the moon' are the twenty-eight types of human personality, phase one is infancy and phase fifteen maturity; likewise there are twenty-eight phases of the soul in incarnations, phase fifteen being the full moon of complete beauty, subjectivity at its height.

The reference to Athene leading Achilles to heroic action, mentioned by Homer in the *Iliad*, is repeated in words spoken by 'the Greek', a character in the play, *The Resurrection* (1931): 'When the goddess came to Achilles in the battle she did not interfere with his soul, she took him by his yellow hair.' In this way the Greek in this play exemplified the opposite of the 'self-surrender and self-abasement' of the followers of Dionysus, and then he went on to enlarge on his theory: 'The man who lives heroically gives them (the gods) the only earthly body they covet. He, as it were, copies their gestures and their acts.' Here we have the deification of the Hero as if it were the very moment described by Vico, when Gods hand over to Heroes in the cycle of history.

In fact, Nietzsche's ancestors were Empedocles and Heraclitus, with a view of history as an endless recurring flux, and an image of eternity as a circle. It is a depressing philosophy in its view of the world as ungoverned by a purpose, being but an eternal, senseless play, and we find ourselves in the orbit of Samuel Beckett, rather than of Yeats, who saw joy in man's will to perfect himself.

The horror with which J.B. Yeats reacted to Nietzsche's philosophic ideas – 'aristocratic' illusions, sacerdotalism, and the ferocious absurdity of the Superman – has been carried on with renewed intensity since some of Nietzsche's doctrines were unscrupulously twisted by Hitler to bolster the Nazi regime. Nevertheless, much of the revulsion for Nietzsche as represented by Yeats's father stems from ignorance of his works (which in Yeats's time had not been translated into English), rather like the reaction of Renaissance Englishmen to Machiavelli's *Il Principe*. Hitler indeed glorified the superman, the 'blond German beast' ('yellow hair'?); but Nietzsche was not antisemitic, though he disliked Jewish interpretations of Christianity; nor did he think the Germans a superior race – far from it, for he wholly despised his contemporary fellow-countrymen, and their culture.

Yeats's father once told W.B. that he was a poet and not a philosopher, and here again he was right; yet one must not ignore the philosophic ideas which Yeats tried to make systematic and which are the scaffolding of his poems. He would pick from each philosopher what suited him, and sometimes he would find, even in such disparate writers as Burke and Nietzsche, a common idea: for example, 'send war in our time' in certain circumstances would have been approved of by both. Over all, Yeats was consistent (as this chapter tries to show), but like Nietzsche he was maddeningly unsystematic in working out his ideas, despite the apparent categorization in *VIS*. Contradictions and paradoxes of a superficial nature worried neither Yeats nor Nietzsche, and sometimes, it must be admitted, Yeats made deductions which really will not bear examination, such as when he wrote to Lady Gregory: 'Nietzsche completes Blake and has the same roots.' On no occasion does Nietzsche think of Christ as Blake does, and their attitudes to Christ are basic to their philosophy.

Notes

1. A.G. Stock, *W.B. Yeats: His Poetry and Thought* (Cambridge: CUP, 1961).
2. F.A.C. Wilson, *Yeats's Iconography* (London: Gollancz, 1960), pp. 283–90.
3. F.A.C. Wilson, *W.B. Yeats and Tradition* (London: Methuen, 1958), p. 199.
4. C.G. Jung, *Psychology and Alchemy* (2nd edn, 1968).
5. Wilson, *W.B. Yeats and Tradition*, pp. 216–23.

6. Kathleen Raine, *Blake and Tradition*, 2 vols (London: Routledge & Kegan Paul, 1969) vol. 1, part II. 3.
7. See Donald Torchiana, *W.B. Yeats and Georgian Ireland* (Evanston: North Western UP and Oxford: OUP, 1966), p. 196.
8. Ibid., p. 244.
9. Keynes (ed.), *The Complete Writings of William Blake* (London: The Nonesuch Press, 1925), p. 181.
10. T.R. Henn, *The Lonely Tower: Studies in the Poetry of W.B. Yeats* (London: Methuen, 1950; 2nd edn 1965), p. 39.

4 *A Vision*

A discussion of *A Vision* is essential in order to understand Yeat's philosophic reading and thought, but the account given here is limited to those ideas which elucidate his poetry; otherwise it would be considerably longer and more complicated. In his introduction to *The Resurrection* (*EX*, p. 392) Yeats wrote: 'For years I have been occupied with a certain myth that was itself a reply to a myth. I do not mean a fiction, but one of those statements our nature is compelled to make and employ as a truth though there cannot be sufficient evidence.' He refers in this passage to his work on *VIS*, published first in 1926, then in a new and revised version in 1929 – after he had read many of the philosophic works already mentioned in Chapter 3 above; then in a final version in 1937.

Mrs Yeats was a spiritualist medium and very soon after her marriage she started to communicate to her husband, in automatic writing, much of the matter and imagery which he used in the first version of *VIS*. In Yeats's statement quoted above, it is essential to note that it is as a *myth* that he wishes *VIS* to be considered; not as an historical fact, whether true or false, nor as a piece of metaphysics to be reasoned out. It is a document speaking the language of myth and imagery through which he gives us a message which he can endorse. This was and is a stumbling block for many people in the understanding of the work. Much of the matter for *VIS* was initially provided by Mrs Yeats's trances, but later, as he worked out his system, he gained a store of mythological symbols which he drew from many traditional cultures: for example, swan, sword, spear, arrow, lion, serpent and eagle. These symbols are never extrinsic trimming for Yeats, but the inwrought core of his experience through his own imagination. It is through the spirals and cyclic patterns of history, in which he believed, that he is able to connect, for example, Helen and the burning of Troy with Deirdre, the burning of Emain and the death of Usna's children; or to identify the swan of Leda with the nine-and-fifty swans at Coole.

It seems strange, therefore, that *VIS* has been so much misunderstood. In 1926 I.A. Richards despaired of Yeats in *Science and Poetry*:

> Now, he turns to a world of symbolic phantasmagoria about which he is desperately uncertain. He is uncertain because he has adopted as a technique of inspiration, the use of trance, of dissociated phases of consciousness and the revelations given in those dissociated states are insufficiently connected with normal

Georgie Hyde-Lees (Mrs W.B. Yeats) 1892–1968. 'Red-brown hair and a high colour which she sets off by wearing dark green in her clothes and earrings' (Yeats to his father, 1917).

experience ... Mr Yeats takes certain feelings of conviction attached to certain visions as evidences for the thoughts which he
supposes his visions to symbolize.[1]

According to this, Mrs Yeats's clairvoyance, Yeats's occultism, spiritualism and his theory of gyres and lunar phases in *VIS* are just a
convenient machinery for systematizing his whole philosophy, and
therefore external to the central core. This is not so: it is the vital
nucleus because it embodies his basic beliefs, and without beliefs no
poet like Yeats can feed his own 'resinous heart', his imagination. It
never stems from an external consciousness; and as the presumptions
of the material world meant nothing to Yeats's imagination, so he
found (as we have said previously) the sources of his imagery in the
Anima Mundi, the collective unconscious of myth, on which, of
course, he was by no means the first poet to draw.

VIS is clearly divided into three parts: the first outlining a cyclical
view of history, the second, a view of human psychology, and the
third, a description of the soul's migrations after death.

The first, the theory of history, is the easiest to understand, for the
idea of the history of civilization in 2,000-year cycles comes from
certain Eastern religions, from Plato, the Neoplatonists and Vico,
among others whom Yeats had read. He divides the growth, maturity and decline of a civilization into twenty-eight phases – the
twenty-eight phases of the lunar month. In this cycle, maturity, or
the zenith, is therefore at the full moon of phase fifteen, the decline
lasting from phases sixteen to twenty-eight, which is the dark of the
moon. History therefore turns on the Great Wheel in helical movements which Yeats thinks of as three-dimensional, and refers to as
gyres (the 'g' is hard). The gyres are, as it were, conical spirals of
history to which and through which events and man move. The
idea is as old as Heraclitus and Plato. The illustration on p. 68
shows the gyres as two cones expanding and contracting as they
whirl. They are, therefore, space-time symbols, gyrating as if any
one point moved from one place in an axis, tracing widening gyres
as it does so, until it reaches the circumference of the sphere.
Simultaneously another point is gyring its way from the opposite
end of the sphere as if unwinding the thread. Then occurs a
complication: in the double triangle, formed and interlaced by these
points going in opposite directions, moves a perne or spool, also
unwinding the thread spirally. (The word 'perne' may indeed be
unfamiliar as it is an Irish word not to be found in the *Shorter Oxford
Dictionary*.) This internal whirling, like a tornado funnel, eventually
reaches a catastrophic climax at which it breaks up.

> Turning and turning in the widening gyre
> The falcon cannot hear the falconer;

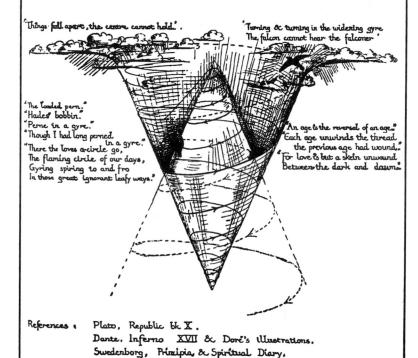

THE GYRE & ITS IMAGES

The cones are traced by the revolving spindle which carries the thread. As the gyre disintegrates a new cone starts in a reverse direction. The spiral is associated with the winding stair

'Things fall apart, the centre cannot hold.'

'Turning & turning in the widening gyre
The falcon cannot hear the falconer'

'The loaded pern.'
'Hades' bobbin.'
'Perne in a gyre.'
'Though I had long perned in a gyre.'
'There the loves a-circle go,
The flaming circle of our days,
Gyring spiring to and fro
In those great ignorant leafy ways.'

'An age is the reversal of an age.'
'Each age unwinds the thread
the previous age had wound.
For love is but a skein unwound
Between the dark and dawn.'

References : Plato, Republic bk X .
Dante, Inferno XVII & Doré's Illustrations.
Swedenborg, Principia & Spiritual Diary.

A Vision, *diagram by T.R. Henn.*

> Things fall apart; the centre cannot hold;
> Mere anarchy is loosed upon the world . . .
>
> ('The Second Coming', *CP*, p. 210)

In several important poems by Yeats, the so-called Great Year (*Magnus Annus*) is referred to. This time scheme derived from the belief in Plato that the planets would eventually return to their starting points in the heavens. Yeats took 24,000 years as the time needed to achieve this, and this 'year' is broken up by twelve cycles, corresponding to twelve lunar months of 2,000 years each in the gyres. One of these cycles or eras is from 2,000 BC to AD 1, Greek civilization having driven out an earlier one. 'Leda and the Swan' is an annunciation heralding this period. The second era, beginning with the Annunciation to the Virgin Mary, ushered in the 'Galilean turbulence' of Christianity, with the gyre widening until modern times when 'things have fallen apart'.

Thus the Great Wheel or the gyres are based on the Heraclitean principle of conflict, as the cones whirl and interpenetrate, 'living the other's death, dying the other's life' (as Heraclitus said), the one expanding as the other contracts; a conflict of opposites throughout: subjective and objective; natural and supernatural; love and hate; war and peace.

The phases of the moon can also be applied to the various reincarnations of the human soul, and therefore to human psychology: see Michael Robartes's reply to Owen Aherne in 'The Phases of the Moon':

> Twenty-and-eight the phases of the moon,
> The full and the moon's dark and all the crescents,
> Twenty-and-eight, and yet but six-and-twenty
> The cradles that a man must needs be rocked in:
> For there's no human life at the full or the dark.
> From the first crescent to the half, the dream
> But summons to adventure and the man
> Is always happy like a bird or a beast;
> But while the moon is rounding towards the full
> He follows whatever whim's most difficult
> Among whims not impossible, and though scarred,
> As with the cat-o'-nine-tails of the mind,
> His body moulded from within his body
> Grows comelier. Eleven pass, and then
> Athene takes Achilles by the hair,
> Hector is in the dust, Nietzsche is born,
> Because the hero's crescent is the twelfth.
> And yet, twice born, twice buried, grow he must,
> Before the full moon, helpless as a worm.

> The thirteenth moon but sets the soul at war
> In its own being, and when that war's begun
> There is no muscle in the arm; and after,
> Under the frenzy of the fourteenth moon,
> The soul begins to tremble into stillness,
> To die into the labyrinth of itself!

(CP, pp. 184–5)

Phase 15 is symbolized by what Yeats calls pure 'subjectivity'; objectivity at its height is therefore at phase twenty-eight. It is salient to understand what Yeats means by these terms – 'subjective' and 'objective': 'objective' deals with the treating of outward things and events rather than inward thought; the converse, 'subjective' is therefore the consciousness of self. From this it is not difficult to follow how Yeats categorized orthodox Christianity as an objective religion, for it largely relies on salvation imposed externally from a salvation-god, whereas the religions of the East, and in particular India, have a subjective faith in which the self, always aware that God is within, is exalted. The former tends to worship God by self-denial, self-abasement and mortification; the latter, by a joyful unification with God within oneself. This is briefly expressed by the second verse of the short poem in 'Supernatural Songs', vi, 'He and She' (*CP*, p. 331), and can be further understood by examining the rest of that poem:

> She sings as the moon sings:
> 'I am I, am I;
> The greater grows my light
> The further that I fly'.
> All creation shivers
> With that sweet cry.

The two views are clearly exemplified by the different philosophical positions which T.S. Eliot and Yeats arrived at in the 1920s, the former seeking Truth through the *objective*, accepting his human inadequacy as a Christian and the necessity for self-denial; Yeats himself claiming a 'subjective' ('antithetical') personality, trying, as he said 'to embody truth' through self-sufficiency.

Much is clarified on this point if one considers the passage in part 2 of *Little Gidding*, Eliot's fourth *Quartet*, in which the poet describes his meeting, in the deserted street after the air-raid, with the 'familiar compound ghost', in whose voice he recognizes his own, 'assuming a double part'. The opinions expressed are more those of Yeats than of any other poet, and the understanding shown by Eliot of Yeats's philosophic concepts is very remarkable. It has been pointed out that 'speech impelled us to purify the dialect of the tribe' is from Mallarmé's sonnet – 'Donner un sens plus pur aux mots de la tribu'. This sonnet, entitled 'Le Tombeau d'Edgar Poe' is a tribute to all poets (as well as specifically to Edgar Allan Poe) who have, like the angel of long ago in this poem, given a purer meaning to the words of the tribe. Mallarmé, of all poets in France at that time, gave dignity to the language, and as a Symbolist was a vital influence on Yeats and Eliot. In fact, both these poets, with symbols taken from tradition, such as the Rose, speak to the mind through the senses rather than the reasoning faculties in a language

> Too strange to each other for misunderstanding,
> In concord at this intersection time
> Of meeting nowhere, no before and after . . .
>
> (T.S. Eliot, *Little Gidding*)

In concord, with no misunderstanding, because both Yeats and Eliot had read Heraclitus, whose thoughts are reflected in this conversation. Images from Heraclitus appear throughout *Four Quartets* and in Yeats's verse. The dance, for example, as the image of life; to be sensed and apprehended rather than known: a momentary incarnation. Compare

> O body swayed to music, O brightening glance,
> How can we know the dancer from the dance?

ending 'Among School Children', with 'at the still point, there the dance is' from *Burnt Norton*, v. However, these two passages outline the essential difference in the two poets' interpretation of Heraclitus. In Yeats there is no still point in the whirling gyres, but only conflict. The condition of Fire, the chief element of Heraclitus, dominates both *Little Gidding* and the 'Byzantium' poems; the 'refining fire' of the Eliot poem, and the fire in which the sages stand in 'Sailing to Byzantium', and the constant image of joy when used with the dance in 'Byzantium'.

> Where blood-begotten spirits come
> And all complexities of fury leave,
> Dying into a dance,
> An agony of trance,
> An agony of flame that cannot singe a sleeve.

Yet fundamentally Eliot's objective Christianity is looking outwards for spiritual guidance: a form of mysticism which must be approached through deprivation and leading to an ultimate avoidance of sin; whereas Yeats accepts every part of existence, by looking inwards to form a unity of being by a faith in self.

To have introduced Yeats (whom I believe the 'compound ghost' to be) into the *Four Quartets* is very remarkable and represents a change of attitude in Eliot. Only in 1933, in a lecture, published in *After Strange Gods*,[2] Eliot had written:

> Mr Yeats's 'supernatural world' was the wrong supernatural world. It was not a world of spiritual significance, not a world of real Good and Evil, of holiness or sin, but a highly sophisticated lower mythology summoned, like a physician, to supply the fading pulse of poetry with some transient stimulant so that the dying patient may utter his last words.

After this censorial, orthodox Christian judgement of Yeats's supernatural world a complete volte-face occurs. In his memorial address Eliot describes Yeats as 'the greatest poet of our time – certainly the greatest in this language, and so far as I can judge, in any language'. Two circumstances are of much significance. Firstly, Eliot and Yeats met and talked on a number of occasions when Yeats was in England between 1934 and his death in 1939; and secondly, Eliot saw a performance of Yeats's last play, *Purgatory*, in August 1938. Apart from an immense admiration for the brevity and tautness of Yeats's verse line in this short play, he was much moved by the theme (a supernatural one). An Old Man sees his mother's ghost as she returns annually from Purgatory to re-enact what she regards as a transgression – the begetting of a child by a drunken and worthless groom. The Old Man tries to save her by breaking the links of consequence which fall on succeeding generations. To ensure this he stabs to death his own son. But there is no hint that his violent action does help his mother's spirit; and in the final lines of the play we see that it is to God he turns:

> O God,
> Release my mother's soul from its dream!
> Mankind can do no more. Appease
> The misery of the living and the remorse of the dead.
>
> (*CPl*, p. 689)

The dead of *VIS* are each in the appropriate circle of their particular purgatory, but in this last play Yeats has gone a step further, which leaves him overlooking a deeper abyss than any he had tackled in *VIS*.

In the second section of *VIS*, men are classified by the amount of subjective and objective qualities they possess; but, as 'The Phases of the Moon' quoted above makes clear, with regard to Man there are only twenty-six phases, rather than twenty-eight, as phase one and phase fifteen, complete objectivity and complete subjectivity, are never possible. A further detail in this section is Yeats's division of the soul into what he terms Four Faculties, two pairs of contraries: termed Will and Mask; Creative mind and the Body of Fate. These Four Faculties are gyres superimposed on the existing gyres, so making Yeats's ultimate philosophy not fatalist or determinist as it might at first appear to be.

> And I declare my faith:
> I mock Plotinus' thought
> And cry in Plato's teeth,
> Death and life were not
> Till man made up the whole,
> Made lock, stock and barrel
> Out of his bitter soul.
>
> (*CP*, p. 223)

Mechanical predestination will not suffice for Yeats, and in his detailed description of the Four Faculties he shows they are escape routes that Man can choose in order to avoid it. For example, there is a False Mask and a True Mask, a True Creative Mind and a False Creative Mind from which Man can make a judgement. And the Body of Fate embraces such happenings as changes in the human body like old age, and includes details from his environment. Ellmann points out in his brilliant analysis of *VIS*[3] that quaternaries such as the Four Faculties have often appeared before, with variations according to their time and place: the Four Zoas of Blake, the four humours of medicine in the Middle Ages, the four elements of Magic, etc. By means of the Four Faculties, an act of choice is possible, although the soul is undoubtedly committed to a cycle of lives. The paradox of the soul being free, yet not free, of living in time and out of it is accepted by both Yeats and Eliot, and may be clarified by an examination of their poetry, in which it is itself the very heart.

In the third section of *VIS*, which deals with life after death, the soul, through reliving its earthly life, gradually reaches a blessed state after many incarnations. Man's soul in eternity is his Daimon or Daemon, a name employed and accepted in the religious hierarchy for many centuries, from Plato on. (It may be advisable to point out that the daemon, or intermediary between Man and the Divine Being should not be confused with demon, the malignant spirit of Judaic and Christian theology.) Again we can see Yeats's interpretation of Heraclitus's phrase, 'we live their death and we die their life', referring to the never-ending circle of souls descending to death and rebirth. For Yeats an important addition in this section is his belief that it is possible for the souls of the dead to communicate, through *Anima Mundi*, with writers and artists. In an earlier essay, Yeats describes how he came to believe this: 'In sleep or waking came images which one was to discover presently in some book one had never read . . . I came to believe in a great memory passing on from generation to generation.'

Yeats's verse cannot be fully appreciated without an understanding of how by myth he was searching for a unity, yet various literary critics have described *VIS* in abusive terms: 'a philosophic jungle'; 'enormous cranky, pseudo philosophy'; 'home-made, gimcrack'. In a very perceptive essay, George Orwell pointed out that 'Yeats's philosophy has some very sinister implications . . . Translated into political terms, Yeats's tendency is Fascist . . . He is a great hater of democracy, of the modern world, science, machinery, the concept of progress – above all, of the idea of human equality.'[4] In all this, Yeats echoes the right-wing thought of the 1920s and 1930s: only by a pattern of creative order can the disorder the modern world imposes on us be combated; and, as Eliot wrote of James Joyce's *Ulysses*, there is no better way of achieving this than through mythological discourse, which by tradition veils its subtleties. What-ever one's political beliefs may be, and however difficult the discrep-ancies and contradictions of the path taken in *VIS* may seem, it is ultimately the summation of Yeats's philosophic thought, and there-fore vital to a full understanding of how his poetry was nourished.

Notes

1. I.A. Richards, *Science and Poetry* (London: Kegan Paul, 1924; repr. 1926).
2. T.S. Eliot, *After Strange Gods* (London: Faber and Faber, 1934).
3. Richard Ellmann, *Yeats: the Man and the Masks* (1948, rev. 1979; Har-mondsworth: Penguin, 1987).
4. George Orwell, *Collected Essays, Journalism and Letters*, eds Sonia Orwell and Ian Angus (London: Secker and Warburg, 1968), II, pp. 271–6.

Part Two
Critical Survey

Introduction

Yeats begins as an Irish poet of the Celtic Revival – a narrow nationalist furrow – and ends as an internationally known figure. But we could argue against this that the early poems are in English not Gaelic and are therefore already looking out of Ireland for an English audience which would soon be found outside the narrow base of Dublin and his circle of friends. Similarly one can observe that even the great poems of Yeats the sage and Nobel prize-winner of the later years are also based in or subtly allude to the original matrix in which the poet's materials and verse-forms were first tentatively tried out and then established. 'What can I but enumerate old themes?' says Yeats towards the end of his life in 1939.

While attempting to follow this progress in the poetry I have also been conscious of the need to substantiate the poet's great claim for his generation

> We were the last romantics – chose for theme
> Traditional sanctity and loveliness:
> Whatever's written in what poets name
> The book of the people. . . .
>
> ('Coole Park and Ballylee, 1931')

This means keeping in mind that the early poems come at the end of the nineteenth-century developments of Romanticism, and that, paradoxically, the later poems are written at the beginning of the modern period and are contemporary with Pound and Eliot. Yeats, as is well known (see pp. 148–9), worked with Pound as his secretary during 1913–15, and one of the effects of this apprenticeship of the older to the younger poet was Yeats's attempt to change his style from a tired rhetoric to more colloquial expression. But, again, note how even the greatest of the new 'modern' poems harks back to the themes and even the verse movement of Shelley and Keats. His anthology *The Oxford Book of Modern Verse*,[1] often dismissed as perverse in respect of the purpose for which it was intended, is helpful in documenting the context in which Yeats was writing, since the kind of modernism which he thought fit to include illuminates his own work.

A note on texts

The early poems were often much altered in later editions, and this is why the Variorum Edition of Yeats exists; in particular Yeats felt the need to toughen up the diction of his poetry, and to energize the soft and gentle rhythms of the verse. The poems printed here are from the final version of the *Collected Poems* (*CP*), for ease of reference; nevertheless, it is worth trying to hunt out the texts in the early volumes in order to study the alterations, perhaps the most notorious being to 'The Lamentation of the Old Pensioner' (*CP*, p. 52).

There are at least three ways of thinking about these alterations. If you were trying to place Yeats historically in the 1880s and 1890s you would need to consider the original texts. Secondly, from a purely aesthetic point of view, some people prefer the early versions, arguing that though Yeats thought he had improved his work, he had in fact *spoilt* his poems by these alterations. Finally, standing back from the text and thinking generally about cultural history, it is possible to take the line that the alterations are useful in showing the shift of sensibility between the nineteenth and twentieth centuries.

Early Yeats

The first three poems are chosen to illustrate both the variety and the skill of the young poet and his typical subject-matter.

The Stolen Child

Where dips the rocky highland
Of Sleuth Wood in the lake,
There lies a leafy island
Where flapping herons wake
The drowsy water-rats;
There we've hid our faery vats,
Full of berries
And of reddest stolen cherries.
Come away, O human child!
To the waters and the wild
With a faery, hand in hand,
For the world's more full of weeping than you can understand.

Where the wave of moonlight glosses
The dim grey sands with light,
Far off by furthest Rosses
We foot it all the night,
Weaving olden dances,
Mingling hands and mingling glances
Till the moon has taken flight;
To and fro we leap
And chase the frothy bubbles,
While the world is full of troubles
And is anxious in its sleep.
Come away, O human child!
To the waters and the wild
With a faery, hand in hand,
For the world's more full of weeping than you can understand.

Where the wandering water gushes
From the hills above Glen-Car,
In pools among the rushes
That scarce could bathe a star,
We seek for slumbering trout
And whispering in their ears
Give them unquiet dreams;

Leaning softly out
From ferns that drop their tears
Over the young streams.
Come away, O human child!
To the waters and the wild
With a faery, hand in hand,
For the world's more full of weeping than you can understand.

Away with us he's going,
The solemn-eyed:
He'll hear no more the lowing
Of the calves on the warm hillside
Or the kettle on the hob
Sing peace into his breast,
Or see the brown mice bob
Round and round the oatmeal-chest.
For he comes, the human child,
To the waters and the wild
With a faery, hand in hand,
From a world more full of weeping than he can understand.

(*CP*, p. 20)

PUBLICATION   The poem first appeared in the *Irish Monthly*, in December 1886, and later in the volume *The Wanderings of Oisin and Other Poems* (1889). In the *Collected Poems* (*CP*) it appears in the section called 'Crossways'.

LOCATION AND CONTEXT   Yeats is very specific about this, explaining in a note to the poem: 'The places mentioned are round about Sligo. Further Rosses is a very noted fairy locality. There is a little point of rocks where, if anyone falls asleep, there is danger of their waking silly, the fairies having carried off their souls.' (See map on p. 194.)

A few poems written earlier than this had had an Indian context. However, from the beginning of 1886 Yeats had begun to take Irish culture seriously, and 'The Stolen Child' is one of the first to have an Irish setting. In so doing it represents the assertion of Irish themes and subject-matter as serious subjects for poetry, that is, not as a joke, but as a kind of political statement. To emphasize this point, it is worth mentioning that the poem was also published in anthologies produced at this time to awaken consciousness of Irishness.

FAERY SONG   The theme of the Changeling, the strange baby which the faeries place in the human cradle, is well known. What is odd and unusual about this poem is the point of view; you might say that it is an example of a supposed faery literature about the destiny awaiting the *human* child who is taken in exchange. Poets writing about faeries present no problem to the reader, thanks to Shakespeare's *A Midsummer Night's Dream*. Earlier in the nineteenth century, thanks to Coleridge's doctrine of the 'suspension of disbelief', there was no difficulty about the appearance of such subject-matter in a Protestant and scientific culture; later in the same century one could talk about Symbolism with reference to a poem of this kind, once again denying the literal 'truth' of what is being discussed. Today we could still read the poem in the same detached way, even if we now might want to think that Yeats is showing a coded sympathy for a suppressed or alien people or their subculture; such an assumption implying that of course the poet does not believe a word of his poem to be *true*. However, I'm afraid this will not do, and this poem is the first example I shall give of Yeats's pulling the rug from underneath the accepted liberal beliefs of the English reader: unfortunately for us he has seen the faeries and believes in them literally, as this slightly later letter illustrates:

> Last night I had a rather interesting magical adventure. I went to a great fairy locality – a cave by the Rosses sands – with an Uncle & a cousin who is believed by the neighbours & herself to have narrowly escaped capture by that dim kingdom once. I made a magical circle & invoked the fairys. My uncle – a hard headed man of about 47 – heard presently voices like those of boys shouting & distant music but saw nothing. My cousin however saw a bright light & multitudes of little forms clad in crimson as well as hearing the music & then the far voices. Once their was a great sound as of little people cheering & stamping with their feet away in the heart of the rock. The queen of the troop came then – I could see her – & held a long conversation with us & finally wrote in the sand 'be careful & do not seek to know too much about us'. She told us before she wrote this however a great deal about the economy of the dim kingdom. . . .
>
> (*Letters*, 1, p. 321)[2]

The reference to 'the economy' is unexpected and returns us to the harsh world of the 1890s, where George Bernard Shaw and the Fabians were hard at work, trying to reorganize such matters.

COMMENT   The nineteenth-century ideals for poetry were derived from William Wordsworth's pronouncements at the beginning of the century. Put very simply, Poetry was to be 'the spontaneous overflow of powerful feelings', and forms of verse which were near

81

to the supposed taste of the 'people' were to be preferred (e.g. Wordsworth's own *Lyrical Ballads*). This programme is still there in Yeats's contemporaries, for instance in Thomas Hardy, who was in so much else his opposite.

'The Stolen Child' can be seen therefore not just as a song but as a perfect example of such a lyrical ballad. Notice too the refrain (refrains like this will linger to the end of Yeats's career), and the contrast of the ideas with the words used within the poem. On the one hand the world is said to be so full of weeping that the child must escape from it, but that awful 'world of weeping' is never described. Instead the faeries do not seem to want to live, or to take the child, under the earth, where they are traditionally located, or to sing the delights of another world. They offer normally *hidden* scenes of this world, particularly of the natural world out of doors, as if they are merely nature spirits. Yet the world that the child is leaving – see the last stanza – is an indoor world already invaded by nature, although it is domesticated; the sibilant whisperings of the faeries in the first three stanzas are replaced by 'bumpy' words like 'kettle' and 'bob'; the brown mice are vivid images of life to set against the world of illusion which the faeries traditionally offer; indeed those mice are almost Keatsian in their tactile reality as they 'bob' around 'the oatmeal chest'. This language shows that the fairies are ambiguous in their attitude in that final stanza, and allows us to see that they have deceived the child, that is, the poet allows his or perhaps our attitude rather than the faeries' to break through and come to the fore. The world of reality that the child is leaving is in fact pleasant and peaceful, and it is the faery world of 'the waters and the wild' which seems ominously threatening. Perhaps the poem's success depends upon these unresolved ambiguities.

REVIEWS, ETC. This poem was noticed early in Yeats's career. It was well reviewed, and became so well known, that, like 'The Lake Isle of Innisfree', he was unable to subject it to later revision. Yeats's own self-criticism is interesting. While correcting his poems for publication in 1888, he said:

> I have noticed some things about my poetry, I did not know before, in this process of correction, for instance that it is almost all a flight into fairyland, from the real world, and a summons to that flight. The Chorus to the 'stollen child' [*sic*] sums it up – That it is not the poetry of insight and knowledge but of long-ing and complaint – the cry of the heart against necessity. I hope some day to alter that and write poetry of insight and knowledge. . . .
>
> (*Letters*, 1: 54–5)

Cuchulain's Fight with the Sea

A man came slowly from the setting sun,
To Emer, raddling raiment in her dun,
And said, 'I am that swineherd whom you bid
Go watch the road between the wood and tide,
But now I have no need to watch it more.'

Then Emer cast the web upon the floor,
And raising arms all raddled with the dye,
Parted her lips with a loud sudden cry.

That swineherd stared upon her face and said,
'No man alive, no man among the dead,
Has won the gold his cars of battle bring.'

'But if your master comes home triumphing
Why must you blench and shake from foot to crown?'

Thereon he shook the more and cast him down
Upon the web-heaped floor, and cried his word:
'With him is one sweet-throated like a bird.'

'You dare me to my face,' and thereupon
She smote with raddled fist, and where her son
Herded the cattle came with stumbling feet,
And cried with angry voice, 'It is not meet
To idle life away, a common herd.'

'I have long waited, mother, for that word:
But wherefore now?'

        'There is a man to die;
You have the heaviest arm under the sky.'

'Whether under its daylight or its stars
My father stands amid his battle-cars.'

'But you have grown to be the taller man.'

'Yet somewhere under starlight or the sun
My father stands.'

        'Aged, worn out with wars
On foot, on horseback or in battle-cars.'

'I only ask what way my journey lies,
For He who made you bitter made you wise.'

'The Red Branch camp in a great company
Between wood's rim and the horses of the sea.
Go there, and light a camp-fire at wood's rim;
But tell your name and lineage to him
Whose blade compels, and wait till they have found
Some feasting man that the same oath has bound.'

Among those feasting men Cuchulain dwelt,
And his young sweetheart close beside him knelt,
Stared on the mournful wonder of his eyes,
Even as Spring upon the ancient skies,
And pondered on the glory of his days;
And all around the harp-string told his praise,
And Conchubar, the Red Branch king of kings,
With his own fingers touched the brazen strings.

At last Cuchulain spake, 'Some man has made
His evening fire amid the leafy shade.
I have often heard him singing to and fro,
I have often heard the sweet sound of his bow.
Seek out what man he is.'

          One went and came.
'He bade me let all know he gives his name
At the sword-point, and waits till we have found
Some feasting man that the same oath has bound.'

Cuchulain cried, 'I am the only man
Of all this host so bound from childhood on.'

After short fighting in the leafy shade,
He spake to the young man, 'Is there no maid
Who loves you, no white arms to wrap you round,
Or do you long for the dim sleepy ground,
That you have come and dared me to my face?'

'The dooms of men are in God's hidden place.'

'Your head a while seemed like a woman's head
That I loved once.'

         Again the fighting sped,
But now the war-rage in Cuchulain woke,
And through that new blade's guard the old blade broke,
And pierced him.
         'Speak before your breath is done.'

'Cuchulain I, mighty Cuchulain's son.'

'I put you from your pain. I can no more.'

While day its burden on to evening bore,
With head bowed on his knees Cuchulain stayed;
Then Conchubar sent that sweet-throated maid,
And she, to win him, his grey hair caressed;
In vain her arms, in vain her soft white breast.
Then Conchubar, the subtlest of all men,
Ranking his Druids round him ten by ten,
Spake thus: 'Cuchulain will dwell there and brood
For three days more in dreadful quietude,
And then arise, and raving slay us all.
Chaunt in his ear delusions magical,
That he may fight the horses of the sea.'
The Druids took thcm to their mystery,
And chaunted for three days.
                                    Cuchulain stirred,
Stared on the horses of the sea, and heard
The cars of battle and his own name cried;
And fought with the invulnerable tide.

(CP, p. 37)

PUBLICATION   The poem was first published as 'The Death of Cuchullin' in *United Ireland*, 11 June 1892.

CONTEXT AND SOURCES   Yeats supplied the following note: 'Cuchullin (pronounced Cuhoolin) was the great warrior of the Conorian cycle. My poem is founded on a West of Ireland legend given by Curtin in 'Myths and Folklore of Ireland'. The bardic tale of the death of Cuchullin is very different.' The Irish sagas are based on oral sources and Yeats has every right to make his own adaptation from differing originals.

STORY   This story haunted Yeats all his life and he returned to it in dramatic works on several occasions, for instance in *On Baile's Strand* and *The Death of Cuchulain*.

Emer, who is Cuchulain's wife, exacts her revenge on Cuchulain by employing a son of his by another woman, whom he does not recognize until it is too late. This part of the story is very like that of Arnold's 'Sohrab and Rustum', a very popular poem in the Victorian period.

NARRATIVE   This poem represents the second skill of the young poet: that of telling a story as succinctly and tautly as possible. He had written a very long narrative poem in the 1880s, called *The Wanderings of Oisin*, which was very much indebted to the Pre-Raphaelites. In this poem too there is a debt to William Morris, but more to the tense verse of *The Defence of Guenevere*, which provided an antidote to the rather lax verse movement of the later nineteenth century. The speeches show a tendency to dramatize the event and to reduce the plain narrative to a minimum.

TEXTUAL CHANGES   As noted above, one of the difficulties in discussing Yeats's early poetry is that he frequently revised it so much – the text in the *Collected Poems* (printed here) is almost a new poem.

For example, the early version of lines 80–6 was:

> Go, cast on him delusions magical,
> That he may fight the waves of the loud sea.'
> Near to Cuchullin, round a quicken tree,
> The Druids chanted, swaying in their hands
> Tall wands of alder and white quicken wands.
>
> In three days' time he stood up with a moan,
> And went down to the long sands alone,
> For four days warred he with the bitter tide,
> And the waves flowed above him and he died.

The changes from this to the *CP* text were not always appreciated by Yeats's early admirers who had of course grown up with the first versions. For example, Joseph Hone, Yeats's biographer, says:

> In this case Yeats did not make a new poem but contented himself with re-writing about half the lines. 'To Emer, raddling raiment in her dun' is better than 'Forgael's daughter, Emer, in her dun', but taken as a whole there is a good deal to be said for the first version. . . . The second [version of the last line] is fine too, but has not the same sense of water flowing on and on that is heard in the other. 'And the waves flowed above him and he died' holds the invulnerability of the sea, and the majesty, peace and finality of death. That it should be lost would be a tragedy.[3]

The Players Ask for a Blessing on the Psalteries and on Themselves

Three Voices [*together*]. Hurry to bless the hands that play,
The mouths that speak, the notes and strings,
O masters of the glittering town!
O! lay the shrilly trumpet down,
Though drunken with the flags that sway
Over the ramparts and the towers,
And with the waving of your wings.

First Voice. Maybe they linger by the way.
One gathers up his purple gown;
One leans and mutters by the wall –
He dreads the weight of mortal hours.

Second Voice. O no, O no! they hurry down
Like plovers that have heard the call.

Third Voice. O kinsmen of the Three in One,
O kinsmen, bless the hands that play.
The notes they waken shall live on
When all this heavy history's done;
Our hands, our hands must ebb away.

Three Voices (together). The proud and careless notes live on,
But bless our hands that ebb away.

(*CP*, p. 93)

PUBLICATION   The poem was first published in *In the Seven Woods*
(1903). This book was produced at the Dun Emer Press – later the
Cuala Press – which was founded in 1903 by Yeats's sister Elizabeth
(Lolly) Yeats. Such private presses owed much to the influence of
William Morris, who had founded the Kelmscott Press; Lily, Yeats's
other sister, had worked with May Morris as an embroideress.

THE PSALTERY   Morris had also been interested in Early Music,
and had encouraged Arnold Dolmetsch, who tried to revive the
playing of medieval instruments. Hence the Psaltery. As can be seen
from the illustration (see p. 116), Dolmetsch's psaltery had a different
shape from the usual trapezoidal dulcimer.
    Yeats was interested in the idea of poetry as accompanied speech
(not song), and wrote an essay on the Psaltery:

> Since I was a boy I have always longed to hear poems spoken to a
> harp, as I imagined Homer to have spoken his, for it is not
> natural to enjoy an art only when one is by oneself. . . .
>
> (*E&I*, pp. 13–27)

Yeats's own efforts at such performance were not particularly successful, and he was often mocked for the monotony of his heavily
accented declamation; but it is an interesting development of the
Romantic desire for a truly primitive form of expression, and in the
emphasis on oral culture Yeats was ahead of his time (see below, pp.
115–17).

DRAMATIC FORM   As it stands, this poem has the form of a short
play for declamation or possibly for singing; or it could be thought
of as the prologue to a play. At this time Yeats was involved in the
organization and management of the Abbey Theatre, Dublin, for

which he wrote many plays. His theatrical ideas were unusual, in that his plays often began and ended with a song and the unfolding and folding of a cloth (to represent the curtain in normal theatre). In a later example, 'Two Songs from a Play' are the two poems which enclose the play *The Resurrection*. This poem was written for recitation by the Abbey Players, and the musicians were Arnold Dolmetsch and his company.

COMMENT   The poem is an invocation to the angels to come down from 'the glittering town' of Heaven and to bless the hands of the players. The simplicity of the poem reinforces the idea of the Middle Ages as the notional time in which all this takes place. The almost childish view of the corporeality of the angels (there is humour here, too) reminds us of the fairies encountered earlier in 'The Stolen Child'. However, there is no reason to attribute to Yeats any literal belief in Christianity – the Three in One seems almost magical in its numeracy, rather than awe-inspiring in its theology.

Although it appears to be a very short poem, 'The Players Ask for a Blessing' is lengthened out by Yeats's poetic skill. There are only six rhymes employed in the whole twenty lines, and the many repetitions – 'hands' (5), 'notes' (3) , 'bless' (3), 'hurry' (2), 'kinsmen' (2), 'ebb away' (2) 'play' (2), and of course 'O' (6) – reinforce the circularity of ideas and the notion of a musical performance in which the same notes are frequently repeated. The angels, seeming perhaps as solid as those on a Christmas card, are reprimanded for drunkenness, a state induced it seems by the waving of flags and wings – or perhaps this kind of humour is an apt rebuke by the players, whose own lives are transitory, to the stupified eternity of the angels. 'Eternity' leads us naturally to a consideration of the thought of the poem if 'thought' be the correct word to use here. The players wish their art to live on 'When all this heavy history's done . . .' One of the angels is reluctant to exchange eternity for 'the weight of mortal hours'. Though the idea of the immortality of art is an old Romantic theme, the curious literalness of its appearance here may prepare us for 'Sailing to Byzantium', where Yeats will ask 'the singing masters of his soul' to gather him 'into the artifice of eternity'; the angels and the Three in One will be replaced by stranger spiritual manifestations.

Poems 1910–20

The next three poems show a widening of Yeats's interests and a change to writing in a tougher and harsher diction: this can be seen by comparing the 'The Magi' with 'The Second Coming', though even the earlier poem has some unexpected lines. The dream of Irish freedom is overtaken by the events of the historical struggle, culminating in the Rebellion of 1916, though it is arguable whether Yeats fully understood or sympathized with it.

The Magi

Now as at all times I can see in the mind's eye,
In their stiff, painted clothes, the pale unsatisfied ones
Appear and disappear in the blue depth of the sky
With all their ancient faces like rain-beaten stones,
And all their helms of silver hovering side by side,
And all their eyes still fixed, hoping to find once more,
Being by Calvary's turbulence unsatisfied,
The uncontrollable mystery on the bestial floor.

(*CP*, p. 141)

PUBLICATION   The poem was written in 1913; it was first published in *Poetry Chicago* in May 1914, and later in *Responsibilities* (1914).

SOURCES AND CONTEXT   In a note published with the poem which follows in *CP* – 'The Dolls' – Yeats tells us: 'I looked up one day into the blue of the sky, and suddenly imagined, as if lost in the blue of the sky, stiff figures in procession. I remembered that they were the habitual image suggested by blue sky, and looking for a second fable called them 'The Magi'. . . .' As so often in studying Yeats, one feels constrained rather than helped by the note, which seems to muddy what might be an easy poem at first reading, and to control what one is allowed to feel. The poem becomes weirdly personal in the light of the note, and gives one cause to wonder what strange mental states Yeats evidently thought were universal – to whom else I wonder does a blue sky habitually suggest the Magi? As with the faeries and the angels whom we have previously encountered, problems arise – how literally are we supposed to take all this? 'In the mind's eye' helps us to rationalize the poem, but 'now as at all times' is more worrying. Yeats seems to have encountered a vision which is outside his control, and in some sense independent of

> Did she in touching that lone wing
> Recall the years before her mind
> Became a bitter, an abstract thing,
> Her thought some popular enmity:
> Blind and leader of the blind
> Drinking the foul ditch where they lie?
>
> When long ago I saw her ride
> Under Ben Bulben to the meet,
> The beauty of her country-side
> With all youth's lonely wildness stirred,
> She seemed to have grown clean and sweet
> Like any rock-bred, sea-borne bird:
>
> Sea-borne, or balanced on the air
> When first it sprang out of the nest
> Upon some lofty rock to stare
> Upon the cloudy canopy,
> While under its storm-beaten breast
> Cried out the hollows of the sea.

(CP, p. 206)

PUBLICATION   The poem was written in January 1919 and first published in *The Dial* (November 1920). In 1921 it found its place in *Michael Robartes and the Dancer*, a volume containing several political poems relating to recent events in Ireland, including 'Easter 1916' in which the heroine of this poem also appears.

CONTEXT   The person in the poem is Constance Markievicz (née Gore-Booth), a member of the Anglo-Irish aristocracy (see pp. 136–7). Yeats had met Constance in London in 1893 and then stayed at her family's country-house, Lissadell (see p. 175), in 1894, where he also met her sister Eva. This visit is commemorated in the elegy 'In Memory of Eva Gore-Booth and Con Markiewicz' [*sic*] (*CP*, p. 263). Constance's riding to hounds is also remembered from this time. Both sisters, possibly fired by Yeats's talk of Irish nationalism, threw themselves into literary and political activity. Constance helped to organize the Easter Rising (which the British authorities regarded as the Irish rebellion) of 1916. She was therefore sentenced to death with the others who had survived the fighting; then she was reprieved and imprisoned in Holloway Gaol – this is the scene of Yeats's poem. Later she became a member of the first Dáil Éireann and a Cabinet Minister. Yeats, coming to them as an outsider, idealized the Gore-Booth girls as representatives of the aristocracy and seems to have had difficulty in accommodating himself to their later political activities, which were as intense as those of Maud Gonne. He preferred to remember the sisters as they were: 'Your sister and yourself', he wrote to Eva in 1916 after the Rising, 'two beautiful figures among the great trees of Lissadell, are among the dear memories of my youth.'

COMMENT   While such biographical information is historically important, it is amazing how little detail there is in the poem. While Yeats omits to supply particulars, it cannot be said in this case that the poem could refer to *any* female political prisoner of the time. (I suppose it could be argued that there have been many aristocratic and middle-class women in the twentieth century who have taken up political causes and been forced into the humiliation of imprisonment, but I don't think that this is the point of Yeats's poem.)

But what surprises the modern reader, conditioned by the praise of freedom-fighting, and the injustice of such political imprisonings as revealed, for instance, by Amnesty International, is that this does not seem to even begin to be a poem of protest at the imprisonment. Nor does Yeats praise the woman's political involvement. (One might have expected the *earlier* Yeats to admire her for literally carrying out the programme of Irish freedom for which he and his friends had prepared the way.) But no: Yeats seems to vacillate. This was not how it was all supposed to happen. Fanaticism is not to be admired in a person of noble mind; Yeats has been surprised by the blood-sacrifice of the Easter Rising, and is unable to sympathize with Constance's involvement with the rabble. She has moved out of the aristocratic world in which Yeats has mentally 'placed' her. There is also a hint of what we would call patriarchal attitudes in the poem: women are better employed in more traditional activities, such as looking beautiful on horseback.

Having discussed all this by way of dealing with what Yeats does *not* say, it is worth reading the poem slowly and carefully to understand what it *does* say, and how beautifully it is crafted and structured. The first stanza begins simply and concentrates upon the appearance of an actual seagull: it is not a symbol when it first enters the prisoner's cell. It is marvellous that the woman, who had no patience, has been changed so much by imprisonment that one of the least tameable of wild creatures can now come so close to her. The word 'touch' generates the second stanza, and the second idea: that the gull unites her with the memory of her youth. The poet, almost in an aside from the poem, lashes out at the degrading nature of political activity and its lack of wider vision ('blind'). The third stanza elaborates the contrast with her youth, both in its aristocratic and lonely aspects, culminating in a reference back to the seagull which is seen as a symbol of it – she was 'clean and sweet' like the bird.

At this point any other poet would have given up and drawn a

93

line; the poem seems to be *complete*: the reason for the gull's appearance at the beginning is now clear. A circle has been described, and the gull is established as a symbol, obviously alluding to freedom and therefore making the requisite faint protest against imprisonment; it would have been a neat little poem.

But Yeats concludes the third stanza with a colon: 'sea-borne' links through to an unexpected fourth stanza showing the gull in its typical activity. But every detail of its action is also symbolic; it leaves its nest on the rock to ride '*balanced* on the air', and its eyes are fixed on the clouds (i.e. it is not 'blind' but looking to some higher ideal). Underneath the seagull rages the sea of politics and fanaticism. The truly aristocratic virtue of detachment from such transitory worldly activity is what is to be admired.

CONCLUSION   This is hardly advice which the subject of the poem was likely to take; indeed, one wonders what she made of it! But it foreshadows Yeats's own movement of mind as we approach the 1920s – away from the confused hurly-burly of the active life towards the contemplative ideal, the life of the sage who looks down from above on human history, as from the top of a tower. Nevertheless, 'On a Political Prisoner' is a surprising, if not a shocking title for a Yeats poem, compared to what has gone before. Again, this modern-sounding title is evidence that we have moved into the Modern period.

The Second Coming

Turning and turning in the widening gyre
The falcon cannot hear the falconer;
Things fall apart; the centre cannot hold;
Mere anarchy is loosed upon the world,
The blood-dimmed tide is loosed, and everywhere
The ceremony of innocence is drowned;
The best lack all conviction, while the worst
Are full of passionate intensity.

Surely some revelation is at hand;
Surely the Second Coming is at hand.
The Second Coming! Hardly are those words out
When a vast image out of *Spiritus Mundi*
Troubles my sight: somewhere in sands of the desert
A shape with lion body and the head of a man,
A gaze blank and pitiless as the sun,
Is moving its slow thighs, while all about it
Reel shadows of the indignant desert birds.
The darkness drops again; but now I know

That twenty centuries of stony sleep
Were vexed to nightmare by a rocking cradle,
And what rough beast, its hour come round at last,
Slouches towards Bethlehem to be born?

(*CP*, p. 210)

PUBLICATION   The poem seems to have been written in January 1919; it was first published in *The Dial* (November 1920), and then in *Michael Robartes and the Dancer* (1921). In the case of this poem the dates are very important as they influence interpretation: we need to know what political or other events Yeats is referring to at the beginning of the poem, and also, if the prophetic elements in the poem are to be taken literally, what events post-date the composition of the poem: for example, Mussolini's march on Rome, the rise of Fascism in Germany, etc. (see below, p. 140).

READING THE POEM   There are two ways of reading the poem – (a) without knowledge of Yeats's system of belief; or (b) with some knowledge of it. I suppose one must also consider the fact that at first publication, four years before *VIS*, only the first was practicable, though of course a note appended to the poem by Michael Robartes – which will be referred to later – did exist.

(a) The general reader with no knowledge of the esoteric system, but with a Christian background, would know from the title that the poem was about the second coming of Christ, which was prophesied in the New Testament, and could not conceive that it referred to anything else.

In going through the first section of the poem such a reader would probably pick up that a 'gyre' meant a circle. The falcon, a medieval tamed and trained beast (i.e. not a 'rough' one), is normally under the control of the falconer. It now appears to be moving out of hearing, and therefore, by a simple association of ideas, one arrives at 'Things fall apart; the centre cannot hold' – words that have a particular meaning in the downfall of empires. This would fit the immediate post-war situation in 1919. (In fact as Jon Stallworthy has shown in *Between the Lines*[5], the first draft of the poem had at line 3 a particular reference to the collapse of Russia in 1917 and the German advance into Eastern Europe

The germans are ( ) now to Russia come . . .

In accordance with his usual procedures, Yeats soon edited out these 'local references'.) The thought is then completed with a series of gloomy assertions, featuring words loaded with the connotations of right-wing fears – 'anarchy', 'blood' and the 'drowning' of 'the ceremony of innocence'. I suppose one might at the time have thought of the end of the tsars and the demise of Holy Russia; but, as in all oracles, the exact meaning of such a statement is universal in its implications and deliberately vague. The first section of the poem concludes with a possible echo of Shelley, who excelled at this kind of rhetoric:

> The good want power . . .
> The powerful goodness want. . . .
>
> (*Prometheus Unbound*, ll. 625–6)

The world has entered a state of dissolution.

At this point, as in a good hell-fire sermon, the reader is led to make a leap from the horror of imminent destruction to grasp at whatever straw of comfort is available from any source whatever. The Second Coming is proferred. Now the Second Coming might seem – in a state of cool reflection – to be rather over the top as the solution to a political crisis, but, as we can see from the nearly contemporary poem, *The Waste Land*, by T.S. Eliot, intellectuals were in a state of despair. And, of course, the Second Coming is to be preceded by cataclysmic events, according to the Book of Revelations; it is there too that the origin of the 'beast' is to be located: the poem relies, not on exact biblical knowledge, but on the vague memory of it in general circulation amongst those with a Christian education.

The prophecy in the second section plays upon such an educational background with hint and suggestion. Yeats begins by reiterating the word 'Surely' – a classic way of introducing something one is *not* sure of at all. The phrase 'The Second Coming' is therefore not at first delivered as an outright solution or as a threat; it seems to slip out of the poet's subconscious mind unawares, and is repeated as if to make sure that this is what has been heard, as if it was an untoward idea for this day and age. The fact that the 'vast image' 'troubles my sight' is also quite apologetically expressed, as if it was some personal annoyance which will not go away, or even as if Yeats needed to visit an oculist. It is hardly the idiom of an Old Testament prophet: Yeats has the prophecy inflicted on him, as it were, and all this makes it more believable as he sleepwalks and stumbles through it. Nor, when the image begins to crystallize, are we actually told that it is the Egyptian Sphinx – though every reader seems able to supply this information, and it happens to fit with one's general knowledge of a 'desert'. The point of this is to show how far we are taken in; Yeats clearly needs help in his trance-like state and we rush forward to eke out the prophecy for him. Of course, it is the thought of the Sphinx *moving* that is dreamlike and extremely threatening. Then the vision closes, and the oracular tone is resumed by the poet, even though 'now I know' seems odd, because the statements about Christ – 'the rocking cradle' – do not really follow from what has gone before. But the poet's final question remains threatening, because of what is now assumed to be true: it is not the vision that is questioned, but the name and nature of the beast which is open to doubt – if it is not Christ, what exactly is it that is to be unleashed?

(b) A reading with knowledge of Yeats's system of belief, on the other hand, is both helpful – because so much more can be explained – and yet, as so often when a crossword clue is solved, may take away the mystery and possibly the fascination of the poem.

Yeats appended a long note to the poem in which the fictional Michael Robartes expounds an outline scheme of historical change which anticipates the theories of *VIS* (see above pp. 67–9). If this account of the cycles of history – the 'gyres' – is followed through, then the twentieth century is going to be a crucial stage. The 'falcon', in the opening lines, was originally to have been a 'hawk' (see Stallworthy, *Between the Lines*)[6], and is associated with intellect and logic in Yeats's symbolism. 'Gyre' can mean both the flight of the falcon and the spiralling movement of history. In his note to the poem Yeats explained: 'All our scientific, democratic, fact-accumulating, heterogeneous civilisation belongs to the outward gyre . . .' The departure of the falcon, which represents these qualities, demonstrates the break-up of the present historical cycle – see the picture on p. 68.

The next lines, describing the collapse of civilization, refer specifically to the growth of materialist beliefs (not just to the Marxist Revolution in Russia), leading to a dispersal of the forces which should hold the civilization together. Though 'the blood-dimmed tide' presents no difficulties in the light of the events of 1917–19, the meaning of 'the ceremony of innocence' remains debatable within the poem: but see the famous lines in 'A Prayer for my Daughter' – the next poem in *CP* – for clarification:

> How but in custom and in ceremony
> Are innocence and beauty born?
> Ceremony's a name for the rich horn,
> And custom for the spreading laurel tree.

As in 'The Magi', a vision is granted to the seer, but the 'image out of *Spiritus Mundi*' (i.e. the vast storehouse of images which exist, according to Yeats and his teachers, independently 'of any personality or spirit') has the same effect as 'in the mind's eye' in the previous poem. You could say that Yeats cleverly pretends – to the general reader – that this 'image' is simply a casual thought which has occurred to him one day, whereas, if you understand his esoteric system of belief it must be something much more important – a true vision.

Incidentally, the source of the 'rough beast' and the desert can be more specifically located than the vague *Spiritus Mundi*, which has already been explained as the storehouse of images. It seems to have been anticipated during Yeats's apprenticeship to MacGregor Mathers; in 1887, at a meeting of the society of 'The Hermetic Students', Mathers had given him a cardboard symbol to induce a vision: 'I closed my eyes. Sight came slowly . . . but there rose before me mental images that I could not control: a desert and a black Titan raising himself up by his two hands from the middle of a heap of ancient ruins' (see p. 47). While what Yeats sees in the poem may be the Sphinx, it is also possible to read in the overtones of this earlier 'mental image'.

Finally, we may consider the 'twenty centuries'. Once again, as in the case of Christ 2,000 years ago, and 2,000 years is the length of one phase of the cycle, in deference to ancient ideas about the magic of numbers – the new age is ushered in by the new Birth. When the outward gyre reaches its termination the Christian phase will be replaced by a contrary movement; this will be the antithesis to it. But what is to be born? Perhaps, as in the Apocalypse of St John the Divine, the 'beast', the Anti-Christ. At the end of the poem the location at 'Bethlehem' deliberately parodies and outrages the Christian hope.

CONCLUSION   Only an outline of Yeats's system and its application to one poem has been given (which can be supplemented by the account in Chapters 3 and 4). The critical problem remains: to what extent does this additional information add anything to the poem? Of course, one might answer, all information improves the reader's understanding, but prophecy, in particular, is more effective if it is only imperfectly understood. The 'general readers' of this poem in the 1930s were amazed that Yeats had so clearly prophesied the rise of Fascism in Europe – and who can say that they were wrong?

Poems of the 1920s

The next two poems are taken from *The Tower* (1928), which was widely recognized as Yeats's most important volume of poems up to that time. In it his varied interests seem at last to coalesce: the Irishness, tempered by experience of the actual history of recent years; the spiritual beliefs, purged of dottiness, are announced with authority; and his love of women, now that he had married and had children, seems temporarily domesticated – vigorous attention is given to family and home. The tower of the title is both that home (see illustration, p. 100) and also Samuel Palmer's *Lonely Tower* (see illustration and discussion on pp. 51, 170–1) with all its richness of symbolism. However, as Richard Ellmann wittily puts it: 'At Thoor Ballylee in 1922 the symbolical tower seemed likely to be attacked by unsymbolical men and weapons at any moment . . .'[7] The fact that the tower had been so threatened during the Civil War brought home to Yeats that he, and Ireland, had much to lose in the present crisis of Irish history.

Meditations in Time of Civil War – Part VI

The Stare's Nest by My Window

The bees build in the crevices
Of loosening masonry, and there
The mother birds bring grubs and flies.
My wall is loosening; honey-bees,
Come build in the empty house of the stare.

We are closed in, and the key is turned
On our uncertainty; somewhere
A man is killed, or a house burned,
Yet no clear fact to be discerned:
Come build in the empty house of the stare.

A barricade of stone or of wood;
Some fourteen days of civil war;
Last night they trundled down the road
That dead young soldier in his blood:
Come build in the empty house of the stare.

We had fed the heart on fantasies,
The heart's grown brutal from the fare;

The Tower, *cover design by T. Sturge Moore.*

More substance in our enmities
Than in our love; O honey-bees,
Come build in the empty house of the stare.

(*CP*, p. 230)

PUBLICATION   This is one of seven poems written at or about
Thoor Ballylee between 1921 and 1923 – Yeats did not live there for
all this time and the house was in any case really only habitable as a
summer residence. The sequence was first published in *The Dial*
(January 1923), where the bird in this poem was a jay. The
sequence then appeared in the volumes *The Cat and the Moon* (1924)
and *The Tower* (1928).

CONTEXT   For the Civil War in Ireland, see p. 42. Yeats's general
note to the sequence explains that the republicans blew up a bridge
nearby. The poems within the sequence frequently employ the
possessive 'My' in their titles, as does this one. Later Yeats wrote a
long note (*AU* pp. 579–80) explaining that a 'stare' is the West of
Ireland name for a starling. As the title indicates, the nest was built
beside his window.

COMMENT   This is an apparently simple poem of great complexity.
Like the other poems in the sequence it is about ancestors and heirs,
about disintegration and the attempt to rebuild after a disaster. The
isolation of the tower and its occupants' lack of verifiable 'news' are
crucial to the understanding of the poem. In the absence of such
news, one relies on odd snippets of gossip which are reported
'telegraphically' in stanzas 2 and 3. Yeats, as always the master of
syntax, uses these disconnected juxtapositions to mirror the anarchy
of society: the poem is as much about Ireland as it is about the
tower.
    The honey-bees, a traditional symbol of workers who produce
'sweetness and light' (i.e. honey and wax), are summoned to reclaim
the building. 'My wall is loosening' is ambiguous; on the one hand it
could be minor structural damage which allows the bees entry: or it
could imply impending ruin so that the building will not be habitable
by humans but only by these 'natural' heirs to make their own use
of it after Yeats's demise. In the last verse, the use of 'we' and 'our'
shows Yeats's consciousness that the nationalist sentiments of his
own plays and poetry had contributed to 'fantasies' about Ireland
which are now being acted out in blood. There does not seem to
be – apart from the bees – any positive hope for the future. Notice
that the last line of each stanza, though not italicized, acts as a
refrain, and gathers meaning with each repetition; in other late
poems the refrain can sometimes work *against* the sense of the rest of
the poem.

Sailing to Byzantium

I

That is no country for old men. The young
In one another's arms, birds in the trees
– Those dying generations – at their song,
The salmon-falls, the mackerel-crowded seas,
Fish, flesh, or fowl, commend all summer long
Whatever is begotten, born, and dies.
Caught in that sensual music all neglect
Monuments of unageing intellect.

II

An aged man is but a paltry thing,
A tattered coat upon a stick, unless
Soul clap its hands and sing, and louder sing
For every tatter in its mortal dress,
Nor is there singing school but studying
Monuments of its own magnificence;
And therefore I have sailed the seas and come
To the holy city of Byzantium.

III

O sages standing in God's holy fire
As in the gold mosaic of a wall,
Come from the holy fire, perne in a gyre,
And be the singing-masters of my soul.
Consume my heart away; sick with desire
And fastened to a dying animal
It knows not what it is; and gather me
Into the artifice of eternity.

IV

Once out of nature I shall never take
My bodily form from any natural thing,
But such a form as Grecian goldsmiths make
Of hammered gold and gold enamelling
To keep a drowsy Emperor awake;
Or set upon a golden bough to sing
To lords and ladies of Byzantium
Of what is past, or passing, or to come.

(*CP*, p. 217)

PUBLICATION AND PLACING   The poem was written in the autumn of 1926. It was first published in *October Blast* (1927). In *The Tower*, it is placed first in the volume, that is, well before 'Meditations in Time of Civil War' (just discussed). In this position it complements 'All Souls' Night', which is given the place of comparable honour at the end of the volume.

CONTEXT, SOURCES, SCHOLARSHIP   The poem is based on wide reading about the city of Byzantium (Istanbul) which had fascinated Yeats from the time of his spiritualist phase. By and large Byzantine studies were not fashionable, and to a certain extent later scholarly interest is derived from the impact of Yeats's poems. It is important to understand, therefore, that Yeats had to work hard at this neglected area of scholarship. The convincing 'experience' of the city is all taken from books; although Yeats travelled extensively in 1907 and 1924, seeing the mosaics at Ravenna and Monreale in Sicily (see pp. 185–6), he never went to Byzantium in any literal sense. 'Byzantium' is a symbol, a holy city of the intellect. This is made clear in *VIS*:

> I think if I could be given a month of Antiquity and leave to spend it where I chose, I would spend it in Byzantium, a little before Justinian opened St Sophia and closed the Academy of Plato. . . .
> I think that in early Byzantium, maybe never before or since in recorded history, religious, aesthetic and practical life were one, that architect and artificers . . . spoke to the multitude and the few alike. . . .

He went on to praise the total effect of this upon the beholder, which is 'an incredible splendour like that which we see pass under our closed lids as we lie between sleep and waking, no representation of a living world but the dream of a somnambulist'. The poem gave Yeats the opportunity to make a summative statement about his own life and its direction: 'Now I am trying to write about the state of my soul, for it is right for an old man to make his soul, and some of my thoughts upon that subject I have put into a poem called 'Sailing to Byzantium' . . . I symbolise the search for the spiritual life by a journey to that city' (draft BBC script, 1931).

COMMENT   Before going through the poem I should like to recommend that the new reader looks at the 'Ode to a Nightingale' by John Keats, or at least recalls the stanza:

> Thou wast not born for death, immortal Bird!
> No hungry generations tread thee down;
> The voice I hear this passing night was heard
> In ancient days by emperor and clown. . . .
>   The same that oft-times hath
> Charm'd magic casements, opening on the foam
> Of perilous seas, in faery lands forlorn.

In interpreting this poem it is usually assumed that Keats's living nightingale is credited with immortality (because the song of the nightingale remains always the same); this in turn symbolizes the immortality of art. It is also worth recalling that Hans Andersen wrote a story about 'The Emperor's Nightingale' – here, besides the true nightingale, we find a description of an artificial singing version of the bird.

The first stanza of Yeats's poem has been extensively altered from an early version in which it was made abundantly clear that the 'country' referred to was Ireland, but also included references to the legendary 'country of the young' (for a full discussion of these important alterations, see Jon Stallworthy *Between the Lines*[8]). Originally, too, there was a merchant and a collection of mariners in the second stanza, who were undertaking, at some point near the conclusion of the first millenium, a real voyage to Byzantium. As we have seen in the composition of other poems, for example, 'The Second Coming', such specific references are soon left behind by Yeats, who wishes to make a general point about the transmigration of the soul, not about social conditions in the Eastern Mediterranean during the ninth century.

So we are now given, in the final version, a first stanza which is packed with images of youth and generation. But, going back to the first line again, 'that' country is unsuitable 'for old men', and is rejected. The wreck of the body, described at the beginning of the second stanza, can liberate the soul, recalling:

> The soul's dark cottage, battered and decayed,
> Lets in new light through chinks that time has made;
> Stronger by weakness, wiser men become,
> As they draw near to their eternal home.
> Leaving the old, both worlds at once they view,
> That stand upon the threshold of the new.
> (Edmund Waller, 'On the Foregoing Divine Poems')

The activity of the soul is traditionally singing, and for this it is necessary to find a singing-school: 'therefore' the voyage to Byzantium.

The poem becomes much more difficult to follow. At the beginning of the third stanza the poet has arrived in the city, and sees the sages, who resemble the figures in a mosaic, standing in the holy fire; now this could be, as in traditional ideas about the destiny of the soul, purgatorial, but I think here is simply a state of intensity of being (one recalls that at the height of the aesthetic movement Pater asked the devotee of Art 'to burn always with this hard gem-like flame, to maintain this ecstasy'). 'Perne in a gyre'– literally referring to a bobbin within a helical track, and recalling the recurrent symbol of the historical cycle, is particularly obscure, and seems to invade the consciousness of the general reader with an example of esoteric belief: but the strange words also add to the magic of the moment, so their obscurity may be intentional, as the aspirant 'conjures' the sages to come from the fire and initiate him 'into the artifice of eternity'. There his heart and animal body will be purged away. The new transformation is unexpected.

It is the strange word 'artifice' which introduces a counter-theme. The soul is able to choose its new form, and Yeats asks to be changed into what looks like a clockwork bird, an automaton – note that no specific reference to nightingale is given. In the final lines the magical 'golden bough' is introduced; this had been a kind of password which enabled Aeneas to penetrate the recesses of the Underworld. (It seems to me that a complicated series of references to Virgil and Dante, both Underworld poets, has been going on behind the poem and surfaces at this point.) The poet is then able to sing of all aspects of Time, which are presumably present in the state of eternity.

The last stanza seems a strange ending to the quest of the soul. Yeats's friend Sturge Moore, who had praised the first three stanzas, objected to the logic of the fourth: 'such a goldsmith's bird is as much nature as a man's body'. This criticism led Yeats to try to clarify the matter in the later poem 'Byzantium'.

Last Poems, the 1930s

Many of Yeats's last poems avoid the difficulties which characterize the poems of the 1920s: he continued to write prolifically into old age, and produced long sequences of ballads, often harking back to the themes of his earlier poetry, but presenting the material in an altogether more direct and approachable way. Such ballads are characterized by the subtle use of the refrain.

The O'Rahilly

Sing of the O'Rahilly,
Do not deny his right;
Sing a 'the' before his name;
Allow that he, despite
All those learned historians,
Established it for good;
He wrote out that word himself,
He christened himself with blood.
> *How goes the weather?*

Sing of the O'Rahilly
That had such little sense
He told Pearse and Connolly
He'd gone to great expense
Keeping all the Kerry men
Out of that crazy fight;
That he might be there himself
Had travelled half the night.
> *How goes the weather?*

'Am I such a craven that
I should not get the word
But for what some travelling man
Had heard I had not heard?
Then on Pearse and Connolly
He fixed a bitter look:
'Because I helped to wind the clock
I come to hear it strike.'
> *How goes the weather?*

What remains to sing about
But of the death he met

Stretched under a doorway
Somewhere off Henry Street;
They that found him found upon
The door above his head
'Here died the O'Rahilly.
R.I.P.' writ in blood.
                    How goes the weather?

                                        (*CP*, p. 354)

PUBLICATION   The ballad was first published in *New Poems*
(1938).

THE STORY   The O'Rahilly (pronounced O'Reilly) was the head
of the clan in Co. Kerry, and one of the heroes of the 1916 Easter
Rising. Although he regarded the proposed rising as foolhardy, and
had therefore told the 'Kerry men' not to take part in it, he himself
arrived in Dublin at the last minute and was gunned down in Henry
Street next to the General Post Office. For other poems about the
Easter Rising, see pp. 144–7.

COMMENT   Though the poem lacks the sophisticated agonizing of,
say, 'Easter 1916', as if Yeats, now at a distance from events, can
simplify them in memory, the simplicity is deceptive. In the first
place this is not Yeats writing as himself: he is putting on an act. The
extremely melodramatic style of presentation is that of the Victorian
street-ballad – once again, the Wordsworthian ideal, this time of the
lyrical ballad, continues to haunt Yeats. (Cf. 'The Stolen Child'.)
This is to be a poem for the people. But the refrain is ambiguous: in
an earlier version it was 'Praise the Proud'. '*How goes the weather?*' is
presumably oppositional, since it implies 'How goes it with Ireland
now that the heroic age is past?' It is significant that Yeats praises
what others might see as a crazy example of heroism: but the
O'Rahilly had preserved his honour and that of his clan. This praise
of the beauty of foolishness ties in with the 'fools' and 'madmen' who
inhabit many of the later poems; see, for example, 'Why should not
old men be mad?'. Such poems as these must have been shocking to
those who had grown up with the beautiful poems of the early Yeats,
since they seemed to show a coarsening of that early style.

The Circus Animals' Desertion

I

I sought a theme and sought for it in vain,
I sought it daily for six weeks or so.
Maybe at last, being but a broken man,
I must be satisfied with my heart, although

107

Winter and summer till old age began
My circus animals were all on show,
Those stilted boys, that burnished chariot,
Lion and woman and the Lord knows what.

II

What can I but enumerate old themes?
First that sea-rider Oisin led by the nose
Through three enchanted islands, allegorical dreams,
Vain gaiety, vain battle, vain repose,
Themes of the embittered heart, or so it seems,
That might adorn old songs or courtly shows;
But what cared I that set him on to ride,
I, starved for the bosom of his faery bride?

And then a counter-truth filled out its play,
The Countess Cathleen was the name I gave it;
She, pity-crazed, had given her soul away,
But masterful Heaven had intervened to save it.
I thought my dear must her own soul destroy,
So did fanaticism and hate enslave it,
And this brought forth a dream and soon enough
This dream itself had all my thought and love.

And when the Fool and Blind Man stole the bread
Cuchulain fought the ungovernable sea;
Heart-mysteries there, and yet when all is said
It was the dream itself enchanted me:
Character isolated by a deed
To engross the present and dominate memory.
Players and painted stage took all my love,
And not those things that they were emblems of.

III

Those masterful images because complete
Grew in pure mind, but out of what began?
A mound of refuse or the sweepings of a street,
Old kettles, old bottles, and a broken can,
Old iron, old bones, old rags, that raving slut
Who keeps the till. Now that my ladder's gone,
I must lie down where all the ladders start,
In the foul rag-and-bone shop of the heart.

(*CP*, p. 391)

PUBLICATION   The poem was published in *Atlantic Monthly* (January 1939), and then in *Last Poems and Two Plays* (1939).

CONTEXT   This is one of several valedictory poems in which Yeats reviewed his work, and I have chosen it because of its appealing honesty. The poem recalls in particular the Cuchulain story, and questions whether or not the creation and the dressing-up of such mythological figures for the stage had been self-deception.

COMMENT   The first section is almost charming in its admission of failure. Once again the syntax is brilliant at mirroring the movement of thought. The 'stilted boys' are presumably the Gaelic heroes of Yeats's poems and plays, and the chariot may be connected with Fergus or Cuchulain. These circus animals are then unveiled in the second section as Yeats's 'old themes', and he proceeds to list some of his early work. His first long poem had been 'The Wanderings of Oisin', a richly allegorical work, in which Yeats now thinks he had missed the point. *The Countess Kathleen* (1899) was a parable about Ireland, in which the heroine had tried to sell her soul in order to feed the starving poor; but the poet slips from the fiction to the person who had acted the part: Maud Gonne had also sold her soul to 'fanaticism'. Finally, the Fool and the Blind Man are characters in *On Baile's Strand*, a play of 1904, which covered the same story as 'Cuchulain's Fight with the Sea'. But the last two lines make clear that he had been unable to see through the play-acting to the reality – another confession of self-deception, and perhaps a waste of talent.

Finally, in lines of an amazing clatter of consonantal discord, the poet acknowledges that, in the end, the source of all this, the raw material of life, was the opposite of fairy-tale and romance. They began, and he ends, without the stilts and ladders of the mythological circus, 'in the foul rag-and-bone shop of the heart', all pretence being done away with. This poem had been intended by Yeats to stand as the penultimate poem in *Last Poems* – to be followed by the last little squib of 'Politics' – but the present order of *Collected Poems* was imposed by his publishers.

Notes

1. W.B. Yeats, *The Oxford Book of Modern Verse* (Oxford: OUP, 1936).
2. *The Collected Letters of W.B. Yeats*, Vol.1: 1865–95 John Kelly and Eric Domville (Oxford: The Clarendon Press, 1986) (see p. 204).
3. Joseph Hone, *W.B. Yeats: 1865–1939* (London: Macmillan, 1942; 2nd edn 1965, repr. 1989), pp. 119–20.
4. Richard Ellmann, *Yeats the Man and the Masks* (1948, rev. 1979; Harmondsworth: Penguin, 1987), p. 203.
5. Jon Stallworthy, *Between the Lines* (Oxford: Clarendon Press, 1963).
6. Ibid., pp. 18–21.
7. Richard Ellmann, *The Identity of Yeats* (London: Faber and Faber, 1954), p. 244.
8. Stallworthy, op. cit., pp. 87–136.

Part Three
Reference Section

Yeats's family, friends and acquaintances

> Think where man's glory most begins and ends,
> And say my glory was I had such friends.
>
> (*CP*, p. 370)

Many of Yeats's acquaintances were remarkable people in their own right. Some came to prominence in the movement to secure Irish freedom, and perhaps obtained a 'glory' that they would not have achieved in other, less volatile, times. Others are really only important because they knew Yeats, and he gave them a kind of immortality in his poems.

Some of his friends, like Maud Gonne and Robert Gregory, are transformed into symbol and myth. Their characters and actions are larger than life – like the heroes and heroines of Greek mythology in the clarity of their affirmation of truth through example. They are also figures created by Yeats from his inner self, and often become the anti-mask which he so constantly sought.

> Poet's imaginings
> And memories of love,
> Memories of the words of women,
> All those things whereof
> Man makes a superhuman
> Mirror-resembling dream.
>
> ('The Tower, III', *CP*, pp. 223–4)

It is his realization of these ideal figures in their loneliness, courage and pride which accounts for so much of his verse. By *Last Poems*, most of his friends belong to the heroic past, for which the present is no compensation for Yeats. Their attitude to life was positive, and lived with nobility and joy. By revealing them to us, Yeats is declaring his own belief in the Platonic truth which their lives embody.

JAMES CONNOLLY, 1868–1916   James Connolly was born in Ulster, the son of a farm labourer; he lived in Scotland during his boyhood; married, returned to Ireland in 1896 and founded the Irish Socialist Republican Party. An internationally minded Labour leader, he was seven years in the United States. On his return he founded the Irish Labour Party, and was one of the signatories of the Proclamation of the Irish Republic, 1916. He was in charge of operations at the GPO in the Rising, and twice wounded; so he

112

faced the firing squad propped up in a chair on account of a gangrened leg.

He first met Yeats in 1897 with Maud Gonne (see below), in connection with the anti-Jubilee demonstrations, when he addressed meetings. He was a member of the Memorial Committee, which included Yeats, at the 1898 Wolfe Tone Centenary Celebrations. For references to him in Yeats's poems, see 'Pádraic Pearse' below.

(Note: 'The player Connolly' mentioned in 'Three Songs to One Burden', III, (*CP*, p. 371) is not James Connolly, but a young actor from the Abbey Theatre whom Yeats knew, and who, as the poem says, was the first man to be killed in the Rising.)

ROBERT CORBET, DIED 1872   The poet's great-uncle, and the owner of Sandymount Castle (see below p. 161). Yeats liked to think of him as one of his ancestors who belonged to the Protestant landed gentry, and who had the characteristics of that class. In 'Are you Content?' (*CP*, p. 370) Yeats asks his ancestors, including Corbet, to judge what he has done.

Corbet was an amiable and sociable man who in his youth had been a soldier; latterly he was interested in the arts and in landscaping his small estate in Sandymount. He became an unsuccessful stockbroker, more interested in gardening than business; so he found himself in financial difficulties, and quietly drowned himself by stepping overboard from the Dublin–Holyhead boat when out to sea.

EAMON DE VALERA, 1882–1975   Eamon de Valera was born in New York of a Spanish father and an Irish mother. After his father's death he was sent, at the age of three, to his mother's family in Ireland, where he was educated in school and university; later he became a mathematics teacher and university lecturer, with a passionate interest in Gaelic literature. In 1916, aged thirty-three, he was Adjutant of the Dublin Brigade of the Volunteers in the Easter Rising. His death sentence was commuted to life imprisonment, as was that of Cosgrave and Constance de Markievicz (see below pp. 136-7). In 1919 de Valera was elected President of Sinn Féin; he opposed the Treaty (1921) whereby the Irish Free State was recognized (less the Six Counties in the north) as a Dominion in the British Commonwealth. When the Dáil ratified it, de Valera resigned, as his party wished for an autonomous Republic with no oath of allegiance to the British monarchy. He was President of Sinn Féin in the Civil War, June 1922–May 1923. At the election in February 1932, he and Fianna Fail were returned to office (Yeats did not vote for him) and the Oath of Allegiance was abolished. Subsequently he was An Taoiseach (prime minister) for several terms of office, and President of Ireland 1959–1973.

Yeats met him in New York in 1920 and thought him 'a living argument rather than a living man. All propaganda, no human life . . .' In 1932 he interviewed him about the importance of the Government not stopping the subsidy to the Abbey Theatre. On that occasion he was impressed by his 'simplicity and honesty', though he differed in opinion from him.

'Parnell's Funeral' (*CP*, p. 319) is a bitter political poem in which Yeats curses those who brought Parnell's downfall. In the second part, he lists de Valera, Cosgrave and even O'Duffy, as contemporary politicians who have none of Parnell's virtues and heroic qualities; if they had Parnell's 'heart' there would have been no Civil War in Ireland, and O'Higgins would not have been assassinated.

> Had de Valera eaten Parnell's heart
> No loose-lipped demagogue had won the day,
> No civil rancour torn the land apart.

In 'The Statesman's Holiday' (*CP*, p. 389), a very slight poem, de Valera is listed with such diverse leaders as F.E. Smith (later Lord Birkenhead), who in 1921 refused to negotiate with the leaders of southern Ireland; General Sir Hubert Gough, who was in what was called the Curragh mutiny of 1913; George II of Greece, who was exiled from his country; and Lord Nuffield (then William Morris), who 'made the motors' – all famous, but not free from worry nor leading the happy life of the retired statesman who has become a wandering balladist playing upon a one-stringed lute, a better trade than politics.

EDWIN ELLIS, 1848–1916   The son of a printer who worked with Isaac Pitman on his system of phonotype, a poet and painter, and a friend of Yeats's father. From 1889 Ellis collaborated with Yeats on the three-volume edition of *The Works of William Blake, Poetic, Symbolic and Critical*, published by Quaritch in 1893.

In May 1900 Yeats wrote in his own copy of the Blake edition:

The writing of this book is mainly Ellis's, the thinking is as much mine as his. The biography is by him. He rewrote and trebled in size a biography of mine. The greater part of the 'symbolic system' is my writing; the rest of the book was written by Ellis working over short accounts of the books by me.

Much of the editing of this work is inaccurate and it is full of misprints; nevertheless, Yeats was the first editor to tackle Blake on his own level, with regard to the interpretation of the symbolism, and so the edition is of unique value. Kathleen Raine, in her introduction to *Blake and Tradition*,[1] makes the following observation:

> There must be few books on Blake, good or bad, which I have not since read, including Ellis and Yeats's monumental commentary, as obscure to me at first reading as Blake himself. Yet I then sensed, and have since come to be certain that, for all its inaccuracies in those mechanical matters to which the modern academic world attaches such inordinate importance, of all his commentators Ellis and Yeats (or was it above all Yeats?) most nearly shared Blake's essential premises.

FLORENCE FARR (MRS EMERY), 1860–1917   Yeats met Florence Farr in 1890, after a performance of a play she had been acting in at the Club House, Bedford Park (see below pp. 177–9). He was fascinated: 'Her speech was music, the poetry acquired a nobility, a passionate austerity . . .' A year later he persuaded his friend Arnold Dolmetsch, a famous maker of harpsichords and lutes, to make a psaltery with twelve strings for her.

> When Florence who died a Buddhist nun,
> Took up the psaltery which Dolmetsch made.

With the aid of this instrument, which was a sort of simplified lute, she half-spoke, half-sang Yeats's verse, an art which he called 'cantilating'. From Yeats's essay, 'Speaking to the Psaltery' (*E&I*, pp. 13–28), one can see exactly what he intended. But there were many critics who were not impressed by these performances; one of these was Bernard Shaw, who said that cantilating was nothing less than 'nerve-destroying crooning like the maunderings of an idiot banshee'. The triangular relationship between the three is amusingly recounted by a friend, Clifford Bax, who edited *Florence Farr, Bernard Shaw and W.B. Yeats*.[2]

Florence Emery was also an important committee member of the Order of the Golden Dawn at the time of the expulsion from the temple of MacGregor Mathers. So it is perhaps surprising that Yeats, who was also on the committee, should later have forgotten the row they had in 1900 when he puts Florence Emery and MacGregor Mathers together in 'All Souls' Night' (*CP*, p. 256), among his friends who have died. However, there is no doubt of the warmth of the two splendid verses to Florence Emery compared with the grudging acknowledgement to Mathers. The second verse to her is the core of the poem, which was later the 'Epilogue to "A Vision"'.

In 1912 she went to Ceylon where she became Principal of Ramanathan College, a Vedanist seminary for girls, and translated Tamil poetry, studying under a swami. She died of cancer in 1917,

Florence Farr with her Dolmetsch psaltery which she used to accompany her speaking of verse.

after many 'foul years' of the disease, having previously written to Yeats, using words which stayed with him: 'I am always glad to hear of someone making a brave end. I came here to make mine brave and I seem to have started another incarnation.'

ISEULT GONNE (MRS FRANCIS STUART), 1894–1954   In the summer of 1910, when Yeats went to stay with Maud Gonne at her house in Normandy, he met her daughter Iseult, who was at a convent school nearby. She was beautiful, sensitive and intelligent; for example, she was so interested in Yeats's reading a translation of Tagore's poems that she asked him to get her a Bengali grammar in order that she might read the poems in the original. In 1912 Yeats paid a second visit in the summer, during which Iseult's graceful dancing on the seashore inspired him to write 'To a Child Dancing in the Wind' (*CP*, p. 136). Neither this nor 'Two Years Later' (*CP*, p. 137) is particularly distinguished verse; in fact the poems might have been written by any minor Georgian poet, especially the latter with its clichéd theme of youth and age. In 1916, during the war, Yeats again returned in the summer to Normandy, where Maud Gonne was nursing the wounded in a hospital. He read her 'Easter 1916' on the beach of Calvados, but she thought the poem did not do justice to the martyrs of the Rising. Iseult acted as his secretary throughout the summer, and very attractive she must have been to him. 'Men improve with the Years' (*CP*, p. 152) tries to work out a *modus vivendi* in their relationship: a triton is safe enough – top half man, lower half fish. But the solution is not so simple. Can he really be 'delighted' with just wisdom?

> O would that we had met
> When I had my burning youth!

This is the same sentiment as he expressed some years later in 'Politics' (*CP*, p. 392), another slight poem. Later in the year, Iseult, now aged twenty-two, arrived in London, where Yeats felt responsible for her. 'Presences' (*CP*, p. 174), indicates his state of mind, which is hardly suitable for responsibility for anybody. Norman Jeffares[3] points out that 'To a Child Dancing in the Wind', 'Two Years Later' and 'Presences' all contrive to contrast Iseult's youthful innocence with Maud Gonne when young, and this is the obvious trend of Yeats's thought. More and more Iseult comes to represent what her mother had been to him.

In 1917 he again returned to Normandy in the spring. On this occasion he proposed marriage to Iseult more than once; but she refused 'Uncle Willie', as she called him. Later in the year he found her a job as assistant librarian in the School of Oriental Languages in London, and on 21 October he married Miss Hyde-Lees. A few days after his marriage he wrote 'Owen Aherne and his Dancers' (*CP*, p. 247), in which the duologue between I and the Heart reveals Yeats's realization of the inappropriateness of the whole affair with Iseult. The verse has a new strength in comparison with the washy lyrics about Iseult.

> The Heart behind its rib laughed out. 'You have called me
>   mad', it said,
> 'Because I made you turn away and run from that young
>   child;
> How could she mate with fifty years that was so wildly bred?
> Let the cage bird and the cage bird mate and the wild bird
>   mate in the wild.'

But in 'Two Songs of a Fool' (*CP*, p. 190) he still shows responsibility for Iseult, the hare, although he is now married to the 'speckled cat'. (Note that many poems in *CP* are not placed in the order they were written: for example, this poem is dated 1918.)

'O let her choose a young man now and all for his wild sake', says the Heart. She chose to marry, in the 1920s, an erratic, unsettled adventurer, one Francis Stuart, and when Yeats met her, at Glendalough in 1929, she had a child of 'about three'. (She parted from her husband some years later.) In *Last Poems* Yeats remembers

> A girl that knew all Dante once
> Live to bear children to a dunce;
>
> (*CP*, p. 388)

None of the poems relating directly to Iseult is more than a charming lyric in either *Responsibilities* or *The Wild Swans at Coole*. But the whole affair is of interest, if only to show how much we owe to Mrs Yeats.

MAUD GONNE (MADAME GONNE MACBRIDE), 1866–1953   Maud Gonne's autobiography, *A Servant of the Queen* (1938), referring not to Queen Victoria but to Cathleen ni Houlihan, gives much of her background, though little about Yeats for the first 250 pages. Professor Jeffares, in *W.B. Yeats: Man and Poet*, devotes more words to her than to any other friend of the poet. Yeats was twenty-three when he met her at the family house in Bedford Park; he had never seen in a 'living woman so great beauty' – complexion like 'the bloom of apples', divine stature (six feet tall), graceful movement, charm and vitality. She brought into his life 'an overpowering tumult', by which he meant he was wildly in love with her. Until 1903, when she married John MacBride, Yeats had hoped he would marry her and repeatedly proposed marriage to her. He seems to have been for a long time unaware that she had been the mistress of a French politician, Lucien Millevoye, and had had two children by him.

Her sole purpose in life was concentrated in the attainment of an Irish nation. She came from the same Anglo-Irish stock as Constance Gore-Booth, and she also rejected all that that social group stood for, with a compulsive energy. Among other projects, she travelled throughout Ireland to help evicted tenants against landlords; organized the Friends of Irish Freedom, a revolutionary group in Paris, against England; lectured to Young Ireland Societies; helped to promote the Wolfe Tone Centenary celebrations; and established Inghinnide na hÉireann (Daughters of Ireland). But she was not content with just lecturing: any methods to rid Ireland of its English oppressors were to be encouraged. Yeats often allied himself with the proud and strong hero as a type, but he was not then in favour of violence. Maud Gonne made a cult of violence into which she swept him, culminating in the Jubilee riots of 1897 in Dublin. I do not think the ferocity of these has been sufficiently commented upon. On the night of the celebrations, Yeats was at her side in the National Club in Rutland Square (now Parnell Square), outside of which hung a huge screen on which were large photographs of eviction scenes and of men who had been executed or had died in the cause of Irish freedom. Electric cables were cut to prevent Unionist shops having loyalist lighting displays; a coffin with black flags and the words 'British Empire' on it, accompanied by a brass band playing the Dead March, was thrown into the Liffey on the orders of James Connolly, who thought the police were about to seize it; huge crowds assembled in the evening outside the National Club, arrests were made, and the police charged; after which it was discovered that an old woman had been killed. When Maud Gonne went out, a voice cried out: 'This is your work, Miss Gonne, I hope you are satisfied.' The news of the old woman's death spread, and that night £2,000-worth of plate-glass windows were broken – in fact, every window in Dublin with Jubilee decorations.

In the next year Yeats travelled with her on a lecture tour in England and Scotland to promote the 1898 Wolfe Tone Association and Irish nationalist celebrations. He afterwards declared they were the worst months of his life, and henceforward he refused to be drawn into her political schemes. In 1900, during Queen Victoria's visit to Dublin, in reply to a Dublin Unionists' gathering of 12,000 children in a grandstand, from which they might cheer the passing Queen, Maud Gonne marched another 40,000 children out to a field at Drumcondra where, in the presence of priests, they swore an undying hatred for England until freedom had been won. 'How many of these children will carry bomb or rifle when a little over thirty?' Yeats asked. The Easter Rising in 1916 was to answer his question.

No poet has celebrated a woman's beauty to the extent Yeats did in his lyric verse about Maud Gonne. From his second book to *Last Poems* she becomes the Rose, Helen of Troy (the Ledaean Body), Cathleen ni Houlihan, Pallas Athene, and Deirdre. The following list gives some idea of the references to her, either in poems directly addressed to her, or in others about her, and shows how many references there are in a single volume; but even this list is not complete. (The *CP* page reference is given for each poem.)

The Rose (1893)
'The Rose of the World' (p. 41);
'The Pity of Love' (p. 45);
'The Sorrow of Love' (p. 45);
'When you are Old' (p. 46);
'The White Birds' (p. 46);
'The Countess Cathleen in Paradise' (p. 48);
'The Two Trees' (p. 54).

'A symbol of spiritual love and supreme beauty' is how Yeats describes the Rose, and he also combines it with themes concerned with ancient Irish heroes, so it comes to mean both Maud Gonne and Ireland. 'The Rose of the World' is a typical Pre-Raphaelite poem, showing a view in which sex and religion are inextricably mixed in unrequited love, similar in many ways to Rossetti's 'The Blessed Damozel'; filled with dreamy, sleepy imagery, 'pale waters', 'passing stars', 'dim abode', and archaic diction like 'betide'. This poem culminates in an image of Maud Gonne 'lingering' by God's throne, which AE described as a 'ridiculous' view of experience.

The Wind among the Reeds (1899)
'He hears the Cry of the Sedge' (p. 75);
'He thinks of those who have Spoken Evil of his Beloved' (p. 75);
'The Secret Rose' (p. 77);
'The Poet pleads with the Elemental Powers (p. 80).

The themes of the sacredness of passion and of the Rose have not changed since *The Rose*, nor has the diction.

In the Seven Woods (1904)
'In the Seven Woods (p. 85);
'The Arrow (p. 85);
'The Folly of Being Comforted' (p. 86);
'Never Give all the Heart' (p. 87);
'Adam's Curse' (p. 88);
'Red Hanrahan's Song about Ireland' (p. 90);
'O Do Not Love Too Long' (p. 93).

Yeats has arrived at the Coole period, and through the influence of

Maud Gonne

the environment there and all that it stood for, has managed to put away

> The unavailing outcries and the old bitterness
> That empty the heart.
>
> ('In the Seven Woods' *CP*, p. 85)

This does not refer to Maud Gonne's marriage, for the poem was written in August 1902, but to the eleven years of loving her. These are beginning to have their effect, especially in 'The Folly of Being Comforted'.

Between 1899 and 1910, Yeats was occupied with the Abbey Theatre, writing and producing his plays, so there are only fourteen poems in *In the Seven Woods*, one a ballad. Those concerned with Maud Gonne are therefore over half the total.

The Green Helmet (1910)
'A Woman Homer Sung' (p. 100);
'Words' (p. 100);
'No Second Troy' (p. 101);
'Reconciliation' (p. 102);
'King and No King' (p. 102);
'Peace' (p. 103);
'Against Unworthy Praise' (p. 103).

After Maud Gonne's marriage and his struggles in the Abbey Theatre, Yeats was bitter and distressed. However, his verse takes on a new strength; no longer the vague twilight suggestions of the previous volumes, but taut, lambent statements, often in three- or four-stressed lines, with controlled rhythms to match. In 'Words' he realizes it is Maud Gonne who has made him into a poet whose words now obey his call. But, fortunately, she did not understand them, otherwise he might have 'thrown poor words away' and been content to marry her. 'No Second Troy' (1908) consists of four rhetorical questions that are absolutely sure in their strong rhythmical variation and diction; in fact, as Louis MacNeice pointed out, they are 'counterpointed' like Gerard Manley Hopkins's verse. How wrong were contemporary critics not to sense this development in Yeats's work, instead of condemning him as a poet who had said all he had to say in his previous lyric verse.

Responsibilities (1914)
Untitled prefatory poem (p. 113);
'When Helen Lived' (p. 124);
'Fallen Majesty' (p. 138);
'Friends' (p. 139);
'The Cold Heaven' (p. 140);
'That the Night Come' (p. 140).

Henceforth the number of poems about Maud Gonne decreases.

The 'barren passion' of line 19 of the Untitled prefatory poem is bitter, as are many memories of his unrequired love:

> And what of her that took
> All till my youth was gone
> With scarce a pitying look?
> How could I praise that one?

('Friends' CP, p. 139)

Ultimately, however, the memory is therapeutically bitter-sweet. The one superbly constructed sentence of 'That the Night Come' is dramatically right for the terse passion it expresses. In 'The Cold Heaven', a boreal celebration of Maude Gonne's marriage, Yeats recalls what she meant to him. The poem's long complex rhythms, counterpointing the alexandrines, are a preview of what is to come in his mature verse.

The Wild Swans at Coole (1919)
'The Wild Swans at Coole' (p. 147);
'The Living Beauty' (p. 156);
'Her Praise' (p. 168);
'The People' (p. 169);
'His Phoenix' (p. 170);
'A Thought from Propertius' (p. 172).

Yeats is now recalling Maud Gonne in small parts of the poems: in the bitterness of verse 3 of 'The Wild Swans'; in realizing he is growing old in 'The Living Beauty' (1915), another poem with a splendidly counterpointed long sentence; and in the refrain of 'His Phoenix'. 'The People' sums up the wasted years in Dublin politics with Maud Gonne, when he might have been writing verse in the Urbino-like setting of Coole Park.

Michael Robartes and the Dancer (1921)
'A Prayer for my Daughter' (p. 211).

Suddenly he comes to the conclusion that political opinions destroy a woman, and states it with one of the rhetorical questions that he now can manage so well:

> An intellectual hatred is the worst,
> So let her think opinions are accursed.
> Have I not seen the loveliest woman born
> Out of the mouth of Plenty's horn,
> Because of her opinionated mind
> Barter that horn and every good
> By quiet natures understood
> For an old bellows full of angry wind?

('Friends' CP, p. 139)

But it is really not so sudden. Ten years previously he had written to

Synge: 'Women, because the main event of their lives has been a giving themselves and giving birth give all to an opinion as if it were a terrible stone doll.' Both Maud Gonne and Constance Markievicz had found themselves in Holloway prison, and as they grew old their bitterness and hatred hardened them. A few years later Seán O'Casey describes Maud Gonne, now in her sixties, at a meeting at which he was required to tell a hostile audience why he wrote critically of the Irish in *The Plough and the Stars* (1926):

> She was clad in a classical way, with a veil of dark blue over her head, the ends flowing down over her shoulders. She turned slowly, only once, to glance at him [O'Casey] and Seán saw, not her who was beautiful, and had the walk of a queen, but the poor old woman, whose voice was querulous, from whom came many words that were bitter, and but few kind. . . . This was she for whom Yeats had woven so many beautiful cloths of embroidered poetry. She, too, was changed, changed utterly, for no ring of glory now surrounded that wrinkled, querulous face. Shadows now were all its marking, shadows where the flesh had swelled or where the flesh had sagged. This is she who, as Yeats declared,
>
> *Hurled the little streets upon the great.*
>
> She had never done that, for her knowledge of the ways of the little streets was scanty, interesting her only when they issued from their dim places headed by a green flag. She never seemed to have understood Yeats the poet. Indeed, she could not, having little of the poet in herself, so that she never felt the lure of melody. . . . Here she sat now, silent, strong; waiting her turn to say more bitter words against the one who refused to make her dying dream his own.

The Tower (1928)
'Among School Children' (p. 242)
'A Man Young and Old' (p. 249).

Yeats, now sixty years of age, looks on the children in the 'long schoolroom', and is reminded of his own schooldays and of a story that Maud Gonne told him about hers. Was she similar to these children? Then he sees in his mind her 'present image', and so to the picture of every mother dreaming of her own children – a bitter thought to imagine them at sixty years old. In 'A Man Young and Old' the image of stone again appears when he thinks of her. It is the regret of an old man; but is also the start of Yeats's great creative period.

The Winding Stair (1933)
'Quarrel in Old Age' (p. 286).

Beyond the 'distorting days' of 1931, when he temporarily quarrelled with her, he remembers her youth and beauty once again.

Last Poems (1936–39)
'Beautiful Lofty Things' (p. 348);
'A Bronze Head' (p. 382).

The former will be discussed in this section with reference to the other heroic characters mentioned (O'Leary, Lady Gregory, J.B. Yeats, Standish O'Grady.) Here he remembers Maud Gonne as Pallas Athene, but evidently in her role as a goddess of war, rather than as patron of the arts or possessor of all wisdom and knowledge. As a virgin divinity she was inaccessible to the passion of love. Maud Gonne certainly fulfilled the second state with regard to Yeats. 'A Bronze Head' refers to the bronze-painted plaster bust of her, now in the Municipal Gallery, Dublin. The poem once again declares her superhuman qualities. In actuality, the bust shows a tight-lipped old woman, with eyes downcast, almost as if she was determined not to communicate with the sculptor, so evident is her withdrawal.

LADY GREGORY, 1852–1932   Born Augusta Persse, a Connacht-woman of the Protestant landed class from nearby Roxborough House, she had a culturally impoverished childhood, without many books, but was fortunately introduced to Irish myth and history, and taught some Gaelic by Mary Sheridan, who for forty years was nurse to her family. At the age of twenty-eight she married Sir William Gregory, the Governor of Ceylon, aged sixty-three, who owned Coole Park. Twelve years later he died, and as a widow – like Queen Victoria she always dressed in black – she devoted herself to making Coole a place where writers could gather and discuss, or work in peace undisturbed.

Before her marriage, the drawing room at Coole had had no books in it. But she gradually slipped into its 'idle elegance' certain very personal books. Her literary friends, who gave their works, included Wilfrid Blunt, AE, Masefield, Douglas Hyde, George Moore, Synge, Seán O'Casey and Theodore Roosevelt. And, of course, a shelf-load of all but the earliest Yeats, who dedicated some of his books to her, and wrote poems in that very room. Round this room were manuscripts and letters in various caskets and boxes: a poem written out for her by Robert Browning at Christmas 1884, letters from Thomas Hardy, Bernard Shaw, Henry James, Bret Harte and Mark Twain.

The walls of the breakfast room were lined with engravings of eighteenth- and nineteenth-century friends of the Gregorys; there was one especially fine engraving of Sir Joshua Reynolds's portrait of Edmund Burke. Under this was a letter from Burke to a Robert

Gregory, urging him to consider the natives first in India. How much must Yeats have been influenced by Lady Gregory's attitude to these portraits as she looked up at them with 'increase of pride in the ancestral eye and hand that chose these memorials of high company to bring to his home, to put before the eyes of his successors'. In *The Oxford Book of Modern Verse* (1936) Yeats significantly includes both the Coole Park poems among his own work which he selects.

Yeats's love and admiration for Lady Gregory and all she stood for at Coole are interwoven into the fabric of his verse for many years.

> If you, that have grown old, were the first dead,
> Neither catalpa tree nor scented lime
> Should hear my living feet, nor would I tread
> Where we wrought that shall break the teeth of Time.
> Let the new faces play what tricks they will
> In the old rooms; night can outbalance day,
> Our shadows rove the garden gravel still,
> The living seem more shadowy than they.

These lines, published in *The Tower* (1928; *CP*, p. 238), were written in 1912. Earlier, in 'A Friend's Illness' (*The Green Helmet*, 1910; *CP*, p. 109) and in 'Friends' (*Responsibilities*, 1914; *CP*, p. 139) he acknowledges that Lady Gregory enabled him to write verse, or, as he puts it,

> So changed me that I live
> Labouring in ecstasy.

In collaboration with Yeats she wrote *Cathleen ni Houlihan* and *The Pot of Broth*; her own output included numerous folk-tales, more than twenty-five plays, editing an *Autobiography* (1894) of Sir William Gregory; *Our Irish Theatre* (1913); *Hugh Lane's Life and Achievements* (1921); her own *Journals 1916–1930*; and *Coole* (1931). Her collections of Irish tales are the best of many translations from the Gaelic, and should not be missed by anyone wishing to enjoy reading the background to the myth used by Yeats; they include *Gods and Fighting Men: the story of the Túatha de Danaan and of the Fianna of Ireland; A Book of Saints and Wonders; Cuchulain of Muirthemne*; these, and her other books, were republished in the 1970s. These tales, sometimes taken from the songs and stories of travelling men and beggars at Coole, or from the cottagers in the Kiltartan district (while Yeats, not speaking Gaelic, sat on the wall outside) are miraculously welded to the earlier scholarly translations of Standish O'Grady or Douglas Hyde.

Seán O'Casey, in his autobiography, *Inishfallen, Fare 'Thee Well*[4] also describes her when he met her in the early 1920s; she was then over seventy:

> A sturdy, stout little figure soberly clad in solemn black, made gay with a touch of something white under a long, soft, black silk veil that covered her grey hair and flowed gracefully behind half-way down her back. . . . Her face was a rugged one, hard, as that of a peasant, curiously lit with an odd humour in the bright eyes and the curving wrinkles crowding around the corners of the firm little mouth. She looked like an old, elegant nun of a new order, a blend of the Lord Jesus Christ and of Puck, an order that Ireland had never known before, and wasn't likely to know again for a long time to come.

He goes on to describe his visit to Coole in much detail.[5]

Lady Gregory was the modern example of the Protestant from the Irish landed class who was 'inevitably on the side of the people', and this often meant she was against England. After she had lost her fight to get the pictures of her nephew, Hugh Lane, for Dublin, Yeats showed his admiration for the patrician virtues based on honour which he knew she had:

> Bred to a harder thing
> Than Triumph, turn away
> And like a laughing string
> Whereon mad fingers play
> Amid a place of stone,
> Be secret and exult,
> Because of all things known
> That is most difficult.

(CP, p. 122)

In the Civil War in the 1920s, Roxborough House, her old home, was burnt to the ground. Soon the fine beech trees had been cut down, the river was choked by weeds and the garden became a wilderness. After a visit, Lady Gregory said she felt like Oisin on his return from Almhuin, 'for as he was the last of the Fianna, so am I of my generation the brothers, the sisters; and now the homestead that had sheltered us all a deserted disconsolate ruin'. Throughout 1931 she suffered much pain from a malignant cancer, which she bore courageously, and was angry with Yeats for recording her illness in 'Coole Park and Ballylee, 1931':

> Sound of a stick upon the floor, a sound
> From somebody that toils from chair to chair;
> Beloved books that famous hands have bound,
> Old marble heads, old pictures everywhere;

127

> Great rooms where travelled men and children found
> Content or joy; a last inheritor
> Where none has reigned that lacked a name and fame
> Or out of folly into folly came.

She died in May 1932, aged eighty. Her name lives on in Yeats's verse, and in her own work.

MAJOR ROBERT GREGORY, MC (*LÉGION D'HONNEUR*), 1881– 1918   Lady Gregory's only son, born in London, was a classical scholar at Harrow School, learnt Gaelic at Coole, and became an excellent stage designer for Yeats's plays at the Abbey Theatre. He was married and had three children.

On 23 January 1918 Major Robert Gregory of the Royal Flying Corps (as the RAF was then called) was shot down when returning to base in Northern Italy. The following sixteen lines are not an implicit lament for a personal friend, but the presentation of Robert Gregory, who speaks as a prototype fulfilling everything which Yeats most admired.

An Irish Airman Foresees his Death

> I know that I shall meet my fate
> Somewhere among the clouds above;
> Those that I fight I do not hate,
> Those that I guard I do not love;
> My country is Kiltartan Cross,
> My countrymen Kiltartan's poor,
> No likely end could bring them loss
> Or leave them happier than before.
> Nor law, nor duty bade me fight,
> Nor public men, nor cheering crowds,
> A lonely impulse of delight
> Drove to this tumult in the clouds;
> I balanced all, brought all to mind,
> The years to come seemed waste of breath,
> A waste of breath the years behind
> In balance with this life, this death.

(*CP*, p. 152)

To start with, Gregory possessed psychic second sight which gave him a premonition of his death – a faculty Yeats believed in and admired. As a reason for fighting he gave no shallow political emotions, neither hating the Germans nor loving the English. This was an astonishing view for First World War times, when most young Englishmen thought it their duty to die for their country. Gregory's roots were specifically in his demesne at Kiltartan, where he realized the poor would not benefit whether the war was lost or won, and he was sufficiently aloof to be uninfluenced by cheering crowds or political demagogues. This solitary detachment could be consummated in the 'tumult of the clouds', the lofty height from which he could view the conflict in its true perspective. He had thought it out, and been struck by the paradox of death in life, which alone could bring him fulfilment. So he made his decision with cold, dispassionate bravery, knowing the consequences.

Despite his love for Kiltartan as his 'country', Gregory had spent much of his youth in England and France, having been educated at Harrow School, Oxford University and the Slade School of Art. His all-roundness at sports is not mentioned in this poem, as in 'In Memory of Major Robert Gregory', the long elegy. But sooner or later, his sporting talents had to be brought to terms with his ability as an artist; by the age of thirty-seven, when he died, his versatility had evidently precluded his becoming a dedicated painter, if either the quality or quantity of his work is any indication. It is doubtful if he ever would have been a successful painter, and this is what Yeats sensed: so the implications of the last four lines of the poem. As in 'Ego Dominus Tuus' and 'A Dialogue of Self and Soul', there is a conflict in the same personality between the subjective vision of the artist and the antiself or objective viewpoint of the sportsman-soldier. This inevitably leads to the paradox of death in life, in the last line of the poem, which Gregory determines to resolve in the only possible way – by heroic death in the clouds: the joy and loneliness of the heron (see p. 199).

It is a magnificent short poem, showing Yeats's development as a poet in verse entirely matched to the Ireland of his day, rather than verse belonging to a Celtic dream world. A strong statement is secured by the many rhetorical repetitions:

> Those that I fight I do not hate,
> Those that I guard I do not love;
> My country is Kiltartan Cross,
> My countrymen Kiltartan's poor,

which mount until the climax of

> A lonely impulse of delight
> Drove to this tumult in the clouds;

with its sudden trochaic foot on 'Drove' itself urging forward the internal rhythms. The four-footed lines, nearly all end-stopped with tight rhymes, give the poem an inexorable finality, like death itself; and as two-thirds of the words are monosyllabic, this proud simplicity makes it hang in the memory.

Two other poems beside 'An Irish Airman Foresees his Death'

refer to Gregory's death, 'In Memory of Major Robert Gregory' (*CP*, p. 148) and 'Shepherd and Goatherd' (*CP*, p. 159).[6] Both are very different from the two great English classical elegies, in which the poet immediately calls upon the reader to weep for the sad death. Consider Shelley's *Adonais*, on the death of Keats:

> I weep for Adonais – he is dead!
> O, weep for Adonais! though our tears
> Thaw not the frost which binds so dear a head!

or Milton's *Lycidas* who

> Must not flote upon his watry bier
> Unwept, and welter to the parching wind
> Without the meed of some melodious tear.

In 'Shepherd and Goatherd' Yeats is restrained and, according to Henn[7], 'the Shepherd is Yeats in youth, the Goatherd himself in age', though obviously at another level the poem is referring to Robert Gregory's characteristics. 'In Memory of Major Robert Gregory' is more concerned with showing Robert as the twentieth-century example of the universal man, in the footsteps of Sir Philip Sidney, the perfect Renaissance man.

> Soldier, scholar, horseman, he
> As 'twere all life's epitome.

DR DOUGLAS HYDE, 1860–1949   The son of the Protestant rector of Frenchpark, County Roscommon, Douglas Hyde met Yeats when he was an undergraduate at Trinity College. There he learnt Gaelic and wrote folk-tales and verse in that language. He possessed a gentle temperament, was diplomatic, and had no enemies. He visited Coole when Yeats was there in the summer of 1899, having previously published *A History of Gaelic Literature* (1892) and been Founder and first President of the Gaelic League (1893). (See *AU Dramatis Personae*, pp. 216–19, for Yeats's account of meetings with him.) The sonnet, 'At the Abbey Theatre' (*The Green Helmet*, 1910; *CP*, p. 107) was written at a time when Yeats was disillusioned with the audiences' reactions to some of the plays produced at the Abbey Theatre. He thinks that Douglas Hyde, whose pseudonym was An Craoibhin Aoibhinn (pronounced Crievin Eving), the Gaelic for 'the delightful little branch', being closer to the countryfolk, may be able to explain the reasons for the fickleness and ignorance of the mob. From 1908 to 1932, Hyde was Professor of Modern Irish at University College, Dublin; Senator (1932–37) and then, by unanimous consent of all parties, first President of Eire (1939–45).

Yeats seemed to envy his ability to write fresh Gaelic verse, and wrote of him: 'He had the folk mind as no modern man had it . . .

He wrote in joy and at great speed because emotion brought the appropriate word. Nothing in that language of his was abstract, nothing worn out.'

AUGUSTUS JOHN (OM, RA), 1878–1961   A Welshman, with a striking appearance – Viking yellow hair and vivid blue eyes – Augustus John trained at the Slade School of Art, where as a student, he showed superb skills of draughtsmanship. He became a brilliant portraitist in the grand manner, with colour tonally high and a somewhat Impressionist handling of paint. He travelled much in a rather gypsy fashion. Yeats met him at Coole in 1907, when he sat for his portrait; when it was finished Yeats did not much like it on account of its heavy shading and his untidy appearance, with windswept hair, which he thought was not typical. The portrait reveals him as no longer the dreamer of Celtic twilight, but the fighter for the Abbey Theatre and man of the world. Yeats describes this visit by Augustus John to Coole, in a letter to Florence Farr, which, as well as revealing some of John's characteristics shows Yeats's sense of humour and his extraordinary spelling.

Coole Park,
Gort. Co. Galway.

My dear Florence Emery:

Agustus John has just left and I have time for letters. He has done numberless portraits of me to work up into an etching – all powerful ugly gypsey things. He behaved very well here, did the most wonderful acrobatic things on the floor and climbed to the top of the highest tree in the garden [the Autograph Tree, see Gazetteer, Coole Park] and did not talk much about his two wives and his seven children. Lady Gregory was always afraid some caller would say 'How many children' 'Seven' 'You must have married very young' 'About four years'. 'Twins I suppose' 'Oh no but –' and then all out. He wore hair down to his shoulders and an early victorian coat with a green velvet collar. Robert watched him with ever visible admiration and dicipleship.

In June 1930 John painted another portrait of Yeats, seated with hat on lap, legs wrapped in a fur rug, in the open air at Renvyle, on the edge of the Atlantic in Connemara. This fine portrait is poorly reproduced as a frontispiece to *AU*, disgracefully cut down at the top and bottom, so that the artist's careful relationship of figure to landscape is distorted, making Yeats look shorter than he really was.

LIONEL JOHNSON, 1867–1902   In 'Modern Poetry' (*E&I*, p. 491), Yeats describes the Rhymers Club of poets who in the 1890s used to meet at 'The Cheshire Cheese', just off Fleet Street, to read and discuss their verse. One of these was Lionel Pigot Johnson, a Catholic convert, 'determined, erect, his few words dogmatic, almost a dwarf but beautifully made, his features cut in ivory'. He had had a classical education (Winchester College and Oxford), was of Irish extraction, a minor poet but major critic, interested in the Irish Literary Renaissance and Celtic legend. Between 1890 and 1895 Yeats got to know him well, dedicating *The Rose* (1893) to him. No doubt Yeats envied his scholarship and his assured manner when dealing with people. But there was a conflict in Lionel Johnson's life, which was to be his undoing, a struggle to achieve a Unity of Being in a world which shunned the artist. He wished to be a solitary man, yet had not the strength to be; to make his life a ritual devoted to art, yet he could not separate art from life satisfactorily. But he certainly did not hold with 'Art for art's sake' as a doctrine. 'I have spent years in trying to understand what is meant by that imbecile phrase', he told the Irish Literary Society in 1894. His lack of inner strength lead to mental instability, to insomnia, and then to a chronic alcoholism resulting in his early death. Yeats remembers him in 'The Grey Rock':

> Since, tavern comrades, you have died,
> Maybe your images have stood,
> Mere bone and muscle thrown aside,
> Before that roomful or as good.
> You had to face your ends when young –
> 'Twas wine or women, or some curse –
> But never made a poorer song
> That you might have a heavier purse,
> Nor gave loud service to a cause
> That you might have a troop of friends.
> You kept the Muses' sterner laws,
> And unrepenting faced your ends,
> And therefore earned the right – and yet
> Dowson and Johnson most I praise –
> To troop with those the world's forgot,
> And copy their proud steady gaze.

> (*CP*, p. 115)

Later in life, Yeats discovered that Johnson had never met the people he claimed to have done, that

he never met anybody, because he got up at nightfall, got drunk at a public-house or worked half the night, sat the other half, a glass of whisky at his elbow, staring at the brown corduroy curtains that protected from dust the books that lined his walls, imagining the puppets that were the true companions of his mind.

He died in hospital after he had slipped on the polished floor of an inn, while trying to sit on a chair, fracturing his skull. In 'The Tragic Generation' (*AU*, IV), Yeats wonders why so many of these poets of the 1890s made such a mess of their lives, and he comes to the conclusion that 'souls turned from practical ends become contemplative but not yet ready for the impress of the divine will, an unendurable burden'.

Johnson receives a tribute in 'In Memory of Major Robert Gregory' (*CP*, p. 148), along with Synge and George Pollexfen, thereby witnessing to the deep influence which these three had on Yeats's life.

> They were my close companions many a year,
> A portion of my mind and life, as it were,

Yet he also had Johnson in mind in a later poem:

> What portion in the world can the artist have
> Who has awakened from the common dream
> But dissipation and despair?
>
> ('Ego Dominus Tuus', *CP*, p. 180)

Ellman is perhaps less than fair when he writes of the nineties: 'The last decade of the century is thronged by extravagant *poseurs*.'[8] Beardsley's graphic brilliance of line in his black and white drawings dominated the nineties, and Johnson, as well as being an excellent literary critic, wrote lyric verse which Yeats thought worthy to be included in *The Oxford Book of Modern Verse*, singular though his selection sometimes was. Yeats, shy and diffident as a young man, felt inferior to Johnson when he first met him. In 'The Grey Rock' he acknowledges the real integrity of these men who, like himself, were dedicated poets.

SIR HUGH LANE, 1875–1915   Hugh Lane was born at Ballybrack, County Cork, the son of a penniless parson who had married Adelaide Persse, Lady Gregory's sister. His parents separated and it was left to Lady Gregory to plan his future. She arranged for him to be trained at Colnaghi, the Fine Art dealers in Old Bond Street, London. In a short time he had shown much talent and had started his own gallery, where he was able to sell Old Masters and to buy French Impressionists. Soon he was arranging exhibitions of the work of Irish artists, including Jack Yeats, in Dublin and London. In 1908 he became the founder of a Gallery of Modern Art in Dublin, bequeathing 154 works, but specifying that a special gallery should be built to house them. Lady Gregory, in her *Journals, 1916–1930*,[9] writes thus of Lane, her favourite nephew:

His career was meteoric; it reads like a Balzac novel. Spending nothing on himself (except perhaps on his clothes, for I always remember him as immaculately dressed), lunching on a bun and cup of tea, living in his lovely house in Chelsea, he would not afford a fire in his bedroom, though downstairs there would be hanging a noble Titian ... one of the most lovely Goyas in existence, and other pictures worth thousands of pounds – nor would he afford himself a taxi. In 1909 he was knighted.

This description of him goes some way to explain Yeats's phrases about Parnell, Lady Gregory and Lane – 'All that delirium of the brave', that frenzied excitement in living, that quality of 'passionate serving'. This contrasted with the mediocrity of Dublin Corporation, which refused to provide money to house thirty-nine of his best pictures, including Renoir's magnificent *Les Parapluies*. Lane in consequence left them to the National Gallery, London. However, in subsequent years, relations with Dublin improved, and as most of his collection in London, including the Renoir, was being housed in cellars, Lane wrote a codicil to his will in February 1915, reversing his decision to bequeath the pictures to London, and giving them to Dublin instead. Unfortunately, he failed to get a witness to his signature. Coming back from the United States in May of that year, he was drowned in the *Lusitania* (the liner torpedoed by a German submarine).

Yeats saw Lane as a proud man, arrogant to his enemies, and defeated by the meanness of popular passions. Like Parnell he was hounded by men of small minds who placed little value on what he stood for; thus he was a heroic figure. So in 'An Appointment' (*Responsibilities; CP*, p. 141), Yeats shows his contempt for the representatives of petty bureaucracy. Meanwhile, as Lane's Trustee, Lady Gregory was labouring to get the pictures back to Dublin, but English lawyers eventually declared that the unwitnessed codicil was legally valueless. (Not until 1959 was agreement reached: the collection now is half in Dublin and half in London, exchanges taking place, though it is still owned by the National Gallery, London.) In five poems (*CP*, pp. 119–23) Yeats sears the hated bourgeoisie who have opposed his heroic figures. 'To a Wealthy Man who promised a Second Subscription to the Dublin Municipal Gallery if it were proved the People wanted Pictures' makes it clear that Yeats thinks that in aesthetic matters the people have to be led. He is no believer in democracy in art, and cites the work of three autocratic Italian Renaissance rulers, including Guidobaldo da Montefeltro, of Urbino (see below, pp. 183–5). 'September 1913' compares the Ireland of the 1798 rebellion with the contemporary dried-up state, in Yeats's white-hot rhetoric, which upset so many of the Irish political leaders of the time.

Was it for this the wild geese spread
The grey wing upon every tide;
For this that all that blood was shed,
For this Edward Fitzgerald died,
And Robert Emmet and Wolfe Tone,
All that delirium of the brave?
Romantic Ireland's dead and gone,
It's with O'Leary in the grave.

(*CP*, p. 120)

'To a Friend whose Work has come to Nothing' is addressed to Lady Gregory, after her failure over the pictures. 'Paudeen', like all these poems, has a reference to loneliness and solitariness as an integral part of heroic strength – the curlew in this poem; the wild geese, the Irish exiles after the Boyne, in 'September 1913'; the eagle's nest in 'To a Wealthy Man. . .'.

'To a Shade' sums up the achievements of Parnell, Lane and Lady Gregory in giving to 'their children's children loftier thought'. Yeats outlines the background to these poems in a note (*CP*, pp. 529–31). Lady Gregory may have failed in her task, but at least she failed triumphantly, and Hugh Lane has achieved an immortality in these poems which he would not otherwise have gained.

MAJOR JOHN MACBRIDE 1865–1916   Described by Hone[10] as 'a red-headed, high-spirited Celt', he was born at Westport, County Mayo; when a boy, joined the IRB, was second-in-command of the Irish Transvaal Brigade against the British in the Boer War; married Maud Gonne in 1903; legally separated from her two years later. He knew nothing of the preparations for the Easter Rising, but when the GPO was fortified he immediately offered his services to Thomas MacDonagh at his post; in fact he was possibly the only leader who had been under fire before. After the Rising he was courtmartialled and shot.

Yeats had first proposed marriage to Maud Gonne in 1891, and when he received news in the United States of her marriage to John MacBride, he was overwhelmingly shocked, especially as both he and her friends thought it a most unsuitable match – which it certainly was. But after MacBride's execution by the firing squad in 1916, Yeats includes him with the heroes to be remembered, even though he was 'a drunken, vainglorious lout' who had done Yeats 'most bitter wrong'.

He, too, has resigned his part
In the casual comedy;
He too, has been changed in his turn,
Transformed utterly:
A terrible beauty is born.

(*CP*, p. 203)

135

THOMAS MACDONAGH, 1878–1916   In 'Easter 1916' (*CP*, p. 202) MacDonagh is the first of the four heroes; and is mentioned also in verse two of 'Sixteen Dead Men' (*CP*, p. 205). He was born in County Tipperary, his father a schoolteacher, his mother English. When in his early twenties he lived more than a year in Paris, and spoke fluent French. He was on the staff at St Enda's (see below, p. 144) from 1908 and therefore Gaelic speaking. He became a University College lecturer; wrote *Literature in Ireland*; and was married, with two children. A leader of the IRB and one of the signatories of the Proclamation, he was executed with the others – a tragic loss of a poet, scholar and musician, just 'coming into his force'.

Yeats first met MacDonagh in 1909 and thought him 'a man with some literary faculty which will probably come to nothing through lack of culture and encouragement' ('Estrangement', *AU*, p. 488). At the time, 'The Green Helmet' period, Yeats was bitter about Ireland, and this is scant praise for MacDonagh; however, he does go on to say, 'in England this man would have become remarkable in some way'.

COUNTESS DE MARKIEVICZ, 1868–1927   Constance, the elder of the two Gore-Booth sisters whom Yeats visited at Lissadell House (see below, pp. 175–6), married in 1900 a Polish artist: Count Casimir de Markievicz. A daughter, Maeve (born in 1901), was brought up by her grandmother, Lady Gore-Booth, and saw her mother so little she did not recognize her in 1921. Constance was temperamentally a rebel against the Anglo-Irish landed class into which she had been born, and always backed the underdog with passionate and fiery intensity. She devoted her life from 1908 to the welfare of the Irish poor and the freeing of Ireland from English rule. Later, she supported James Connolly in the transport workers' strike in 1913; and in the Easter Rising of 1916 was second-in-command at the post on St Stephen's Green. She was sentenced to death for her part in the Rising, but the sentence was commuted to life imprisonment ('On a Political Prisoner', *CP*, p. 206 see p. 91).

She was released in 1917 and for the next ten years, until her death, she played a part in Irish politics. She was Secretary for Labour in the Dáil cabinet in 1920; backed the Republicans ('Irregulars') in 1922; and eventually supported de Valera on how a settlement should be made with England: she was therefore opposed to Yeats. In addition, Yeats was appalled at her downfall, as he thought, from the beautiful and courageous rider with the County Sligo Harriers to the conspirator among ignorant men. The Easter Rising may have 'changed, changed utterly' her as well as the other leaders, but in her case he regrets it as a betrayal of her tradition:

That woman's days were spent
In ignorant good-will,
Her nights in argument
Until her voice grew shrill.
What voice more sweet than hers
When, young and beautiful,
She rode to harriers?

She died in a hospital in a slum quarter of Dublin, at her own wish, among the poor, thousands of whom followed her coffin at a public funeral. There is a limestone bust of her on St Stephen's Green. Of two biographies,[11] the first, by Anne Marreco, *The Rebel Countess*, is inclined to gloss over her faults; the second, by Seán O'Faoláin, *Constance Markievicz*, is more objective.

JOHN MASEFIELD (OM), 1878–1967   Masefield first met Yeats in the 1890s when he used to attend the 'Monday evenings' at Woburn Buildings (see below, pp. 179–81). But he had seen much of life before that, having left school at the age of fifteen to become an apprentice on a windjammer which sailed round Cape Horn; subsequently he was for three years in New York. He was invited to Coole by Lady Gregory, who liked him as a person but was not impressed by his poetic talents. His full and successful life as poet, editor, critic, novelist and autobiographer is well known. In 1930 he became Poet Laureate on the death of Robert Bridges; in 1935 he was awarded the Order of Merit.

Masefield's *Some Memories of W.B. Yeats*[12] is the best account of the Woburn Buildings house and its visitors. When the Yeatses were at Broad Street, Oxford (see below, p. 181), Masefield lived on Boar's Hill nearby, and used to visit them and invite them to his home. He and his wife also visited the Yeatses at Riversdale, Rathfarnham, for the Irish poet's seventieth birthday party (13 June 1935). In 1963, at the age of eighty-five, he went to London to protest against the possible demolition of 18 Woburn Buildings, but was reassured that the interior of Yeats's sitting-room would be preserved as far as possible, despite extensions to an hotel. His final tribute, 'On what he was', are lines full of warmth, written in the Georgian poetic style one associates with Masefield. Very different was W.H. Auden's 'In Memory of W.B. Yeats' (1940), in which such lines as 'for poetry makes nothing happen', a sentiment far removed from Yeats's philosophy, though integral to Auden's, are typical of Auden's egocentric approach throughout the poem. Similarly, we are shocked by Auden's 'You were silly like us', for Yeats may have been silly, but never like Auden. On the other hand, Masefield's sensitive relevance sounds a sympathetic note, though Yeats would not have agreed that beauty was one of the mainsprings of his poetry:

137

He died far from the trotting of the donkeys
With the turf-creels; far from the smell of peat,
And Sligo pier, where the ear-ringed pilots talked;
Far from those sea-marks which henceforth all seamen
Will note with thought of him.
　　　　By the bright sea
He changed this life, beside a dancing-floor
Where beauty is created day by day.

SAMUEL LIDDELL (LATER MACGREGOR MATHERS), 1854–1918
'A well-read man, keen of visage, who talked in a deep voice and pre-
tended to know more than he did' is how Hone[13] describes Mathers.
Yeats, in 'The Trembling of the Veil. Four Years 1887–1891' (*AU*),
says he had 'much learning but little scholarship, much imagination
and imperfect taste'. When Yeats first saw Mathers he was copying
ancient manuscripts from occult books in the British Museum Reading Room, and later, after being introduced, he told Yeats of the
Order of the Golden Dawn and the temple of the Order he had
founded in London (see above, p. 47). Mathers was the author of *The
Kabbalah Unveiled* (1887) in which he tried to prove that the learning
the Jews had received from Moses passed down in Jewish tradition,
and had, through white magic, influenced Egyptian occult thought
and, later, Pythagoras – an enthusiastic but inaccurate estimate.

Yeats met Mathers twice in Paris, where he had gone to live: in
1894 and two years later to discuss with him a proposal for an
Order of Celtic Mysteries. In 1900 they had a quarrel about the
organization and control of the Order of the Golden Dawn in which
Yeats and Florence Emery were the equivalent of committee members, and thereafter Yeats never saw Mathers again. He died in
Paris and was survived by his wife who was clairvoyante and the
sister of Henri Bergson, the philosopher. The extent of his influence
on Yeats's thought was considerable, so he was included with
Florence Emery and W.T. Horton, a fellow adept, in 'All Souls
Night' (*CP*, p. 256).

SEÁN O'CASEY, 1880–1964　　There are no direct or indirect references to O'Casey in *CP*, but his views of Yeats and Lady Gregory in
the six volumes of his *Autobiography* show how he appreciated their
personal virtues and the excellence of their work, although he
himself came from a totally different background.

He was born in a Dublin tenement, of Protestant parents, and
had a rough early life earning just enough money to keep himself
alive in a variety of jobs. After initial failures he got *The Shadow of a
Gunman* (1923) accepted by the Abbey Theatre, and afterwards *Juno
and the Paycock* (1924): both tragi-comedies of slum life, with witty,

shrewd dialogue, strong characterization, and much sardonic criticism of Irish weaknesses. On account of the last characteristic they were not popular with Irish audiences, and riots, similar to those during Synge's *Playboy of the Western World*, took place in the theatre. Lady Gregory and Yeats backed him fully, and in his autobiography, *Inishfallen, Fare Thee Well*[14] there are warm references to Lady Gregory (see above, p. 127): 'I owe a great deal to you, Lady Gregory, to Mr Yeats, and to Mr Robinson [the Director of the Abbey Theatre], but to you above all. It was you said to me, "Mr O'Casey, your gift is characterization", and so I threw away my theories, worked at characters, and *The Shadow of a Gunman* is the result.' Unfortunately, Yeats and Lady Gregory refused to have O'Casey's *The Silver Tassie* for the Abbey Theatre, a decision they afterwards regretted, as did O'Casey who refused to see Lady Gregory in London some years later (1929).

Fundamentally, O'Casey was a rebel, as was Lady Gregory, and he had faith in life, as had Yeats.

GENERAL EOIN O'DUFFY, 1892–1944   After Eamon de Valera and Fianna Fail (the Republican party) had won the election in the Irish Free State in February 1932, certain members of the IRA were released from prison. But they were suspected of having Communist sympathies, and indeed some of them had been to Moscow. To counteract this, in common with right-wing examples in Germany and Italy, a movement grew in the country to oppose these tendencies. It had as many as 30,000 members, who wore blue shirts, drilled and saluted in a Fascist manner. Its leader was General Eoin O'Duffy, who for twelve years had been Police Commissioner of the Irish Free State government before being dismissed by de Valera. O'Duffy openly sought the end of parliamentary democracy (which he called an English growth), and described Hitler and Mussolini as great leaders. Then he formed a National Guard, blue-shirted, which, incidentally, received the backing of the Church. By 1938 de Valera's law courts had imprisoned many of the Blueshirts as well as IRA officers, and the former movement fizzled out, O'Duffy going off to Spain to support Franco in the Spanish Civil War in a manner which can only be described as farcical. Many Blueshirts were shot by Franco's Moors (i.e. their own side), in their only battle. 'What am I to tell the mothers of Ireland?', wailed O'Duffy. Thereafter his Irish volunteers were restricted to ceremonial duties. (For more information, see Maurice Manning, *The Blueshirts*.)[15]

In 1933 Yeats was momentarily interested in the movement. A Blueshirt friend, Captain Dermot MacManus, who often visited Riversdale, brought with him once, and once only, General O'Duffy, with whom Yeats on this occasion talked philosophy, which O'Duffy would certainly not have understood. But Yeats wrote for him at his request 'Three Songs to the Same Tune' (*CP*, p. 320), which he rewrote when he discovered that the new party's ideals were not his, as Hone[16] says, 'increasing their fantasy, their extravagance, so that no party could sing them'. And it would certainly not have been possible to march to them, even in their revised version, 'Three Marching Songs' (*CP*, p. 377).

Other than wanting a political party which had a disciplined way of life, Yeats realized in his old age that he had had enough of politics. He makes this position absolutely clear in a letter to a friend:

> Do not try to make a politician out of me, even in Ireland I shall never I think be that again – as my sense of reality deepens & I think it does with age, my horror at the cruelty of governments grows greater . . . Communist, fascist, nationalist, clerical, anti-clerical are all responsible according to the number of their victims. I have not been silent, I have used the only vehicle I possess – verse. If you have my poems by you look up a poem called 'The Second Coming'. It was written some sixteen or seventeen years ago & foretold what is happening. . . . I am not callous, every nerve trembles with horror at what is happening in Europe 'the ceremony of innocence is drowned'.

However, the Fascist label stuck to Yeats, and Edward Norman, author of *A History of Modern Ireland*, stated without any further qualification: 'And the Blueshirts had, predictably, got the support of those who watched over Ireland's culture. Yeats was a firm supporter.' Dr Norman must be thinking of those beautiful sky-blue shirts which Yeats often wore, as Richard Ellmann says, not for political but aesthetic reasons.

STANDISH O'GRADY, 1846–1928   From the Protestant landed class, O'Grady was educated at Trinity College, Dublin. He wrote a *History of Ireland* (1878–80), mostly about the old Irish heroes, Finn, Oisín and Cuchulain, with very little history. However, he was the real creator of the Gaelic revival, his translations of the Irish legends bringing the Celtic past to the ordinary reader for the first time. Similarly, such books as his *Early Bardic History* (1879) influenced the Celtic revival.

Louis MacNeice (*The Poetry of W.B. Yeats*) points out an important difference between the Irish and the English in their attitude to their folk legends; and MacNeice, with his split Irish and English background, understands both peoples. He thinks that these imaginative periods from folk times

> are not in fact separated from modern Ireland by the same great gulf that separates modern England from the Round Table.

Ireland has remained a far more primitive country in which the primitive saga-virtues still awake echoes among the people at large. It is not a mere affectation that a statue of Cuchulain stands in the Dublin Post Office as a memorial to the 1916 rebels.[18]

Furthermore, there are countless native legends in Ireland, whereas King Arthur seems to be the sole English one. Also, long ancestral memories, so common in Ireland, are virtually unknown in England: for example, I once talked with an Irish countrywoman about Oliver Cromwell as if he had been living recently.

According to AE, O'Grady was 'the most conscientious and honourable man in public life in Ireland', and John Quinn ranks him with Douglas Hyde as being one of only three people in the Dublin literary world 'who did not say anything malicious about others'. So the position of O'Grady as the third of the Olympians in 'Beautiful Lofty Things' (*CP*, p. 348), is not strange. In each case Yeats remembers the person by his bearing at one particular moment, and especially in the position of his or her head, implying pride, control, inner strength and magnanimity. The fact that Yeats is able to exalt such banal subjects as waiting for a local train or speech-making at a banquet, shows how marvellously by *Last Poems* he is able to manage his verse. In *AU* (p. 422), Yeats gives an account of Standish O'Grady speaking at a dinner given for the poet. Like the rest of the guests, O'Grady had had plenty to drink, yet he never betrayed it, for he spoke with style and wit, in a low, sweet voice, with noble gesture.

> Standish O'Grady supporting himself between the tables
> Speaking to a drunken audience high nonsensical words.

KEVIN O'HIGGINS, 1892–1927   Kevin O'Higgins was born in County Leix. After taking his BA at University College, Dublin, he became a lawyer, and later a minister in the first Free State Government under Cosgrave, in 1922. The country was then in a state of civil war, guerrilla forces of the IRA being in arms against government troops. But the Government somehow managed to preserve the upper hand, and the Senate, with Yeats as a member (see Gazetteer, 'Dublin. Merrion Square', p. 164), was convened at the end of the year, although the rebels declared they would shoot all senators at sight. Yeats's friend, Senator Oliver Gogarty, was taken off by armed men, but managed to escape by jumping at night into the swollen waters of the Liffey; and the houses of thirty-seven senators were burnt to the ground, including Renvyle, Gogarty's house in Connemara, where Yeats had been staying when Augustus John painted his portrait. In May 1923 there was a cease-

141

fire and the government started on constructive plans for the future. O'Higgins was the outstanding minister of this Government and showed statesmanlike judgement in trying for a *rapprochement* between Ulster and the Free State; he also made a major contribution to the drafting of the Statute of Westminster at the Imperial Conference (1926).

He was altogether exceptional: an honest, liberal-minded politician, who fearlessly spoke out and would act if he thought it right, whatever the cost. Winston Churchill described him as 'a figure from the Antique, cast in bronze'. Yeats knew him well as a personal friend; he and his wife often visited Mr and Mrs O'Higgins's house in Dublin. He also admired O'Higgins's writing and speeches in the Dáil, which he thought resembled those of Burke in the eighteenth-century tradition. On 10 August 1927, as O'Higgins walked to Mass, he was brutally assassinated by terrorists. The whole of Ireland and, of course, Yeats, were profoundly shocked by this savage murder of a man who showed such promise for the future. 'Death' (*CP*, p. 264), directly deals with O'Higgins's heroic qualities in the face of death, the sibilants hissing his disdain:

> A great man in his pride
> Confronting murderous men
> Casts derision upon
> Supersession of breath.

Some years later, as Yeats walks round the Municipal Gallery, he comments on O'Higgins's portrait among those of the makers of modern Ireland (*CP*, p. 368). 'Blood and the Moon' (*CP*, p. 267), is influenced by O'Higgins's murder in glorifying the tower and the winding-stair, those symbols which Yeats uses not only for himself but also for the four Anglo-Irish writers, Goldsmith, Swift, Berkeley and Burke, whose qualities he most admires. He was not listed by Yeats with de Valera and Cosgrave, those politicians who were unable to 'eat' Parnell's heart, that is to say, take on some of the great qualities of Parnell (*CP*, p. 320). O'Higgins, the 'sole statesman' would not have died had they inherited some of Parnell's virtues.

JOHN O'LEARY, 1830–1907   Born in County Tipperary, O'Leary became a medical student at Trinity College, where he joined the revolutionary Fenian Brotherhood, and edited *The Irish People*, the official IRB newspaper from 1863–65. In 1865, after being convicted of treason and felony, he was sentenced to twenty years' penal servitude in England, but was released in 1871 on condition that he did not return to Ireland for fifteen years. On his return after his exile, he met Yeats and seemed venerable to the young poet, although he cannot have been more than in his middle fifties. A wonderful friendship grew up between the two, despite their difference in age. O'Leary respected Yeats's integrity; Yeats acknowledged that 'from O'Leary's conversation and from the Irish books he lent or gave me has come all I have set my hand to since'. The poems of Thomas Davis (1814–45) and other patriotic literature of the eighteenth and nineteenth centuries were chief among these.

> Nor may I less be counted one
> With Davis, Mangan, Ferguson,
> Because, to him who ponders well,
> My rhymes more than their rhyming tell
> Of things discovered in the deep
> Where only body's laid asleep.
>
> (*CP*, p. 56)

Thus in 'To Ireland in the coming times' Yeats allies himself with the Irish patriot poets, but also adds, in the last couplet, his indebtedness to magic, of which O'Leary disapproved. So Yeats wrote to him to allay his suspicions: 'If I had not made magic my constant study I could not have written a single word of my Blake books, nor would The Countess Cathleen have ever come to exist. The mystical life is the centre of all that I do and all that I think and all that I write.'

O'Leary possessed a generosity of spirit, bred in suffering, which Yeats immediately recognized as the opposite of an ambitious politician. A venerable and bearded sage, he was the subject of more than one portrait by J.B. Yeats. His ancient Roman virtue and moral integrity appealed to Yeats, who saw him as the personification of god-like nobleness: one of the heroic, lonely figures, first in the ranks of the Olympians – 'Beautiful lofty things: O'Leary's noble head.'

In 1889 he helped Yeats by being chiefly responsible for obtaining subscribers to enable him to have *The Wanderings of Oisín* published. Two years later, Yeats was sharing lodgings with him in Dublin when the news of Parnell's death in Brighton reached them; at that time O'Leary was President of the newly formed Irish Literary Society (see *AU*, pp. 209ff.) He was President of the Supreme Council of the IRB until his death, on St Patrick's Day 1907. Six years later Yeats thought of it as the end of an era:

> Romantic Ireland's dead and gone,
> It's with O'Leary in the grave.
>
> ('September 1913', *CP*, p. 120)

PÁDRAIC PEARSE, 1880–1916   Pearse's father was a Devon man

143

who had settled in Dublin as a monumental mason, and married an Irish country-woman. Pádraic, the eldest of four children, became a member of the Irish Bar, an enthusiastic supporter of the Gaelic League, a fine Gaelic scholar, a passionate orator, and founder (1908) and headmaster of St Enda's School for boys, one of the few lay schools in the country, and one which Yeats visited. He seems to have been dedicated from his early years to the freeing of Ireland from the English, and his life showed certain austere features fitting this dedication. In his lectures to American audiences when he was touring the United States in 1932–33, Yeats spoke of Pádraic Pearse and his younger brother, William:

> Three or four years after the betrayal of Parnell two little boys, sons of a Dublin stone mason, knelt down beside their beds and prayed that they might sacrifice their lives for Ireland. In their early twenties, I saw them occasionally: they would come to the Abbey Theatre for some reason or other. I think they hired it for some concert or public meetings.

More likely it was hired for political meetings, as Pádraic rarely relaxed socially or visited a theatre, never drank alcohol or smoked, and was unmarried.

His desire for a Blood Sacrifice was to be consummated sooner than anyone expected. In 1913 the Irish Volunteers were formed after a large meeting in Dublin, the committee including Pearse and The O'Rahilly (see above p. 106). Soon 10,000 had enrolled, among them Eamon de Valera, a mathematics teacher. The movement went from strength to strength, despite not receiving official backing from the IRB; and the Gaelic League became political as well as literary (see Gazetteer, Dublin, Trinity College (p. 162) for Pearse and Yeats speaking at the Antient Concert Rooms in 1914). In April 1916, after a meeting in Liberty Hall, Dublin, the Volunteers, led by Pearse as Commander-in-Chief, issued a Manifesto, obviously written by him, to the people of Ireland declaring a Provisional Government of the Irish Republic 'as a Sovereign Independent State'. On Easter Monday, about sixty armed Volunteers entered the General Post Office, ejected the staff and civilians who happened to be there and fortified the building. At the same time, other strategic positions in the city were occupied. The week of the Rising has been well documented and photographed: *Protest in Arms* by Edgar Holt, and *Easter Rebellion* by Max Caulfield both give admirable accounts.[19] After five days, about 2,000 rebels, armed only with rifles, had held at bay nearly ten times that number of British troops armed with machine-guns, artillery and a gun-boat. But the Rising was not generally popular, on account of the material damage done to the city, and on the Thursday, Pearse, who was holding out in the GPO, realized that it was doomed. At the end of the week the rebels capitulated. There followed, from 3 May to 12 May, a protracted series of courts martial which produced a violent revulsion of feeling as two or three of the leaders were executed each day. Pearse knew that they would be more powerful in death than life and declared at his trial: 'We seem to have lost, but we have not lost; we have kept faith with the past and handed on a tradition to the future.'

Yeats was in England at the time, and wrote at once to Lady Gregory at Coole: 'I have little doubt there have been many miscarriages of justice. ... I am trying to write a poem on the men executed "terrible beauty has been born again" ... I had no idea that any public event could so deeply move me and I am very despondent about the future.' He was then more than fifty years old, and had obviously never lost that awareness of responsibility which he had had as a young man after the Jubilee riots, in which Maud Gonne was involved. In 'The Man and the Echo', written many years later, Yeats emphasizes this point:

> All that I have said and done,
> Now that I am old and ill,
> Turns into a question till
> I lie awake night after night
> And never get the answers right.

> (*CP*, p. 393)

In September, he finished 'Easter 1916' (*CP*, p. 202), the first of the four poems of homage to the Easter martyrs. He starts by thinking of how he met these men in ordinary life in Dublin and spoke 'polite meaningless' words to them. Then, abruptly, he changes the tone, switching to the incantatory refrain of the poem:

> All changed, changed utterly:
> A terrible beauty is born.

He later used this powerful oxymoron 'terrible beauty' when he was commenting upon a short story of Oscar Wilde's, which he quotes in its original form, before Wilde lengthened it, in *The Trembling of the Veil*, iv (*AU*). In both this poem and the Wilde story there is a narrative of tragic action, having its tragedy in the ambiguity of its motivation, concerned with death, and set in a street. Yet the meaning of 'terrible' is not altogether clear, for the word has become threadbare through colloquial usage – a long way from the soul-searing *terribilità* of Dante's vision. In the second stanza of 'Easter 1916', Yeats outlines the characteristics of the four leaders whom he knew. In the third he compares the rock-like integrity of their hearts with the mutations of natural phenomena. The 'terrible beauty' is the result of their singleness of purpose and dedication – especially in the case of Pearse – which changes them utterly. They become terrifyingly strange and cold in their beautiful unity of mind and action with regard to their consecrated task.

> Hearts with one purpose alone
> Through summer and winter seem
> Enchanted to a stone
> To trouble the living stream.

Natural life, 'the living stream', changes by the minute; but not these passionate, devoted men and women. He accounts for this in one of the many memorable poetic phrases which make 'Easter 1916' one of the greatest poems of this century:

> And what if excess of love
> Bewildered them till they died?

He answers with the final prophetic refrain, uttered with granite certainty:

> I write it out in a verse –
> MacDonagh and MacBride
> And Connolly and Pearse,
> Now and in time to be,
> Wherever green is worn,
> Are changed, changed utterly:
> A terrible beauty is born.

In the short, ballad-type poem, 'Sixteen Dead Men' (*CP*, p. 205), he is again concerned with the correctness of the timing of the Rising. But he decides that heroes are men who would not consider the matter in the same light as we who 'meddle with give and take', for they converse 'bone to bone' – an image like that of stone which Yeats constantly uses for hard, essential matters. 'The Rose Tree' (*CP*, p. 206), written in 1920, is introduced as a duologue between Pearse and Connolly. The politicians (de Valera and Lloyd George?) have caused the Rose Tree to wither, and there is bitterness in the final verse of the poem.

The ennoblement of the heroes of the Rising rings out in Yeats's verse until 'Last Poems'. As we have noticed (p. 106), the detail of 'The O'Rahilly' (*CP*, p. 354) – his not being told of the Rising, his arrival in Dublin, his mortal wound from which he wrote his signature in blood – is told with a ballad simplicity which is very moving, because the miracle of transmutation in sacrifice is still the key:

What remains to sing about
But of the death he met
Stretched under a doorway
Somewhere off Henry Street;
They that found him found upon
The door above his head
'Here died the O'Rahilly.
R.I.P.' writ in blood.
>   *How goes the weather?*

The refrain, conventionally used by seamen upon the ship's bridge before a possible storm, implies heroic action, but also may be taken like Plato's ghost's question, 'What then?', to express doubt in the future of the political climate.

Finally, in 'The Statues' (*CP*, p. 375), the heroic Pearse is chosen as the supreme prototype of action rather than thought. 'Few men have passed from thought to action with so deadly a thoroughness and sincerity.' Yeats takes classical statuary as philosophy in action, governed as it is by measurement in which every feature is planned with Pythagorean wisdom, though now submerged in the dark sea of the modern world. In the final stanza, Greek myth and Irish legend are combined, and time is foreshortened.

Yeats saw the Easter Rising not as the work of politicians, but of heroes who in the moment of death transcended all their intellectual limitations and found themselves complete. As Cuchulain, fastened to a pillar when dying, was surrounded by the spirit presences of Ireland, so with the martyrs of the Rising. This was not the intellectual nationalism of the politician but the moment of fulfilment of the hero, and that for Yeats was sole reality.

Some had no thought of victory
But had gone out to die
That Ireland's mind be greater,
Her heart mount up on high;
And yet who knows what's yet to come?
For Patrick Pearse had said
That in every generation
Must Ireland's blood be shed.
From mountain to mountain ride the fierce horsemen.

>   (*CP*, p. 373)

GEORGE POLLEXFEN, 1839–1910, ALFRED POLLEXFEN, 1854–1916, and WILLIAM POLLEXFEN, 1811–90   Pollexfen was Yeats's mother's maiden name. George was the bachelor uncle with whom he used to stay at Sligo from childhood on for many summers (*AU*, pp. 67–74) – in fact until he was invited to Coole by Lady Gregory in 1896. Uncle George had been a fine amateur rider, and still kept a racehorse, but he had given up riding by the time Yeats was a young man, and the eccentric, unbalanced strain in the Pollexfens had started to appear in his acute hypochondria and the wilful discomfort of his living conditions, despite his being a rich man. He was always interested in astrology and the Cabbalah, as well as horoscopes which he could cast; all this much absorbed Yeats when he visited him Verse 5 of 'In Memory of Major Robert Gregory' (*CP*, p. 149), written in 1918, mentions George Pollexfen's decline from equestrian activity to a 'sluggish and contemplative' life.

'In Memory of Alfred Pollexfen' (*CP*, p. 176), written three years earlier, and a somewhat undistinguished poem, is an early indication of Yeats's ancestor worship, particularly for the Pollexfen relatives at Sligo: Old William Pollexfen and his sons – John, 'the sailor John' referred to, George and Alfred, his younger brother. The poem is written in four-footed lines, which were to become a constant feature of Yeats's later verse, with a rhyme scheme which was much more skilfully concealed by enjambement and internal rhythms than this is:

> And Masons drove from miles away
> To scatter the Acacia spray
> Upon a melancholy man
> Who had ended where his breath began.

These lines refer to George's funeral, which Yeats also describes in 'Reveries over Childhood and Youth' (*AU*, pp. 67–74). He was much moved by the simplicity of the ceremony, although there were 2,000 people present and it was the largest funeral at Sligo in living memory. Many freemasons cast 'acacia spray' in the tomb in St John's churchyard, with the words, 'Alas my brother so mote it be'; and after it Yeats wrote to Lady Gregory comparing the ceremony with Synge's recent funeral, attended 'by none . . . after some two or three, but enemies or conventional images of gloom'.

George left £50,000 to his brothers and sisters, all of whom were well-off, but none to any of Yeats's relations, much to the disappointment of Yeats's father, who was his brother-in-law and oldest friend, and much in need of money at the time.

EZRA POUND, 1885–1972 Pound first met Yeats in London in 1908 and declared him to be the only contemporary poet worthy of serious study, regarding him as a bridge between the Symbolists and Mallarmé. He often went to Yeats's Monday evenings at Woburn Buildings in the winter of 1912–13 (see below, pp. 179–81). Having persuaded Yeats to contribute to *Poetry*, October 1912, he made changes as editor, in the poem 'Fallen Majesty' (*CP*, p. 138), which Yeats sent (see Ellmann, *Eminent Domain*)[20]. Yeats visited

Pound at Stone Cottage (see p. 182) during the winters of 1913, 1914 and 1915. In Pound's *Pisan Cantos*, Canto LXXXIII refers to this:

> so that I recalled the noise in the chimney
>   as it were the wind in the chimney
>   but was in reality Uncle William
> downstairs composing.
>   . . .
>   at Stone cottage in Sussex by the waste moor

Pound edited Professor Ernest Fenellosa's translations of the Japanese Noh plays, which were to have much influence on Yeats's playwriting. In April 1914 he married Dorothy Shakespear, the daughter of Olivia Shakespear. He was best man to Yeats at his wedding in London. He met Yeats again in Paris, 1922; in Sicily, 1925; in Rapallo, 1928, 1929–30 and 1934; and once more in London in 1938.

After Synge's death, Pound took his place as Yeats's major friend. Though he was twenty years younger, and referred to Yeats as 'Uncle William' or 'Old Billyum', the relationship was on equal terms, each taking notice of the other's suggestions, despite Pound being poetically more experimental than Yeats, and therefore less apt to take advice. Canto LXXXIII was never seen by Yeats, but he would have liked

>   the sage
>   delighteth in water
>   the humane man has amity with the hills

>   as the grass grows by the weirs
>   thought Uncle William . . .

JOHN QUINN, 1870–1924   There is no direct or indirect reference to Quinn in *CP*, but for many years he was a friend and patron in New York of Yeats and his brother Jack, of AE, Douglas Hyde and Lady Gregory. The son of Irish immigrant parents, he became a very rich man through a successful practice as a financial lawyer in New York. He arranged Yeats's 1903 lecture tour in the United States and helped him financially, buying some of the manuscripts of his work and his brother's pictures. He also supported J. B. Yeats in the United States by finding him rich sitters for portraits; and he played a leading part in the Irish Literary Society in New York. He visited Coole in 1903 and 1904, and, after his return to New York, his unpublished letters to Lady Gregory reveal the deep intimacy of their friendship.

He was somewhat dictatorial in manner; but was generous, well-read and able to hold his own in literary and philosophic discussions with AE and Yeats. He had a fine sense of worthwhile painting,

149

even if in an avant-garde style, and owned many fine modern pictures. He was invaluable to Yeats, Eliot, James Joyce and Jack Yeats as a patron.

MARGOT RUDDOCK, 1907–1951   Margot Ruddock first met Yeats in 1934; she was an actress and a poet engaged in establishing a theatre for poetic drama, in which T.S. Eliot was interested; she also knew Purohit Swami, who taught her. In 1935 she frequently met Yeats and corresponded with him about her poetry until he went to Majorca (see below, pp. 187–9).

While he was in Palma with the Swami, Margot Ruddock suddenly appeared, having had a mental breakdown in London caused by spiritual problems and domestic worries. For some years when under stress she had shown signs of schizophrenia. Yeats describes her arrival in a letter to Olivia Shakespear:

> She walked in at 6.30 [a.m.], her luggage in her hand, and, when she had been given breakfast, she said she had come to find out if her verse was any good. I had known her for some years and had told her to stop writing as her technique was getting worse. I was amazed by the tragic significance of some fragment and said so. She went out in pouring rain, thought, as she said afterwards, that if she killed herself her verse would live instead of her, went to the shore to jump in, then thought she loved life and began to dance. ... Next day she went to Barcelona and there went mad.... The British Consul at Barcelona appealed to me, so George and I went there, found her with recovered sanity sitting up in bed at a clinic writing an account of her madness.

'A Crazed Girl' describes the incident:

> That crazed girl improvising her music,
> Her poetry, dancing upon the shore,
> Her soul in division from itself
> Climbing, falling she knew not where,
> Hiding amid the cargo of a steamship,
> Her knee-cap broken, that girl I declare
> A beautiful lofty thing, or a thing
> Heroically lost, heroically found.
>
> No matter what disaster occurred
> She stood in desperate music wound,
> Wound, wound, and she made in her triumph
> Where the bales and baskets lay
> No common intelligible sound
> But sang, 'O sea-starved, hungry sea.'

(CP, p. 348)

The octave of this sonnet in tetrameters has all the details of her behaviour, then the unexpected and sudden declaration:

> A beautiful lofty thing, or a thing
> Heroically lost, heroically found.

Why does Yeats group her as a 'beautiful lofty thing' with his other personal friends? What qualities had she in common with Lady Gregory and Maud Gonne, the two women he includes in 'Beautiful Lofty Things' (*CP*, p. 348)? Fundamentally it must have been her heroic courage, which saved her from grave despair and melancholy, for the sestet of the sonnet enlarges on these qualities. As a young dancer she also had beauty, wildness and grace – further qualifications for inclusion. The phrase 'O sea-starved, hungry sea' is difficult. Perhaps she is identifying herself with the sea, which in her mind is itself 'starved' by its own shortcomings and loneliness.

In 1937, after she had recovered, Yeats arranged for her to be the chief speaker in three BBC broadcasts of his poems, because she possessed one quality which he much valued – the ability to pass naturally from speech to song for the refrain of these poems. Hand-drums were used to accentuate rhythms, and the refrains were most moving when sung by her unaccompanied voice, especially in 'Sweet Dancer' (*CP*, p. 340), which he wrote for her. This is an infinitely sad poem in two seven-line stanzas, with grave, slow rhythms, describing the melancholy scene as men come to take her away. Yeats shows his admiration for her, and regret that it should have happened: regret being the more important reaction, because he was worried he might have caused her final breakdown. Soon after the broadcast she was taken to a mental home, where she died in 1951. If you look at 'The Man and the Echo', you will find that Yeats's conscience, when he is an old man near to death, is much troubled by his often telling Margot Ruddock to concentrate on her poetic technique, and eventually, in Majorca, suggesting to her she should stop writing.

> Did words of mine put too great strain
> On that woman's reeling brain?
>
> (*CP*, p. 393)

GEORGE RUSSELL, 1867–1935   An Ulsterman, Russell, who was known as AE, was a fellow student of Yeats at the Metropolitan School of Art in Dublin in 1884. Later he became a painter of mystical landscapes, rather like inferior Corots; a poet with a genuine visionary bias, but lacking precision or vitality, with a somewhat loose and archaic diction, not unlike *The Wind in the Reeds* period of Yeats; and an active supporter of the Irish Literary Renaissance. Yeats dedicated his prose romance *The Secret Rose* to AE in 1897. He was interested in theosophy, though not in magic, anticipating Yeats in investigating Indian thought. From 1910 he was editor of the *The Irish Statesman*, for which he refused to publish 'Leda and the Swan' (*CP*, p. 241), as it might be misunderstood. He was a prolific essayist, and he also worked for the Irish Agricultural Organization Society, organizing cooperative dairies and rural banks.

AE was a most likeable and magnanimous man who lived nearly all his life in Dublin and used to hold weekly 'evenings' for discussion. These were similar to Yeats's in Merrion Square, but attended by a rival literary clique, which James Joyce's Stephen Daedalus irreverently referred to as 'The yogibogeybox in Dawson Chambers'. He was Yeats's oldest friend, but they frequently quarrelled, for they were poles apart in character, as Mrs Yeats realized when she spoke of him as 'the nearest to a saint you or I will ever meet'. He died of cancer; Yeats attended his funeral in Dublin.

JUNZO SATO, 1897–   In March 1920, Junzo Sato, a young Japanese diplomat, was attending a business course at Portland, Oregon. As a member of the Yeats Society of Japan he had enjoyed reading Yeats's poetry, and was therefore delighted when he had an opportunity to hear the poet lecture on the Irish Literary Renaissance. His own words, quoted by Shotaro Oshimo in *W.B. Yeats and Japan*[21], reveal his next step:

> I wished to express in some way how deeply moved I was. And after reflecting all night, I decided to present Yeats with my favourite short sword, forged by Bishū Isafuné Motoshigé. For it seemed to me that there was nothing more suitable than this sword as a present to Yeats, who had a keen appreciation of and an ardent longing for Japanese art.

Yeats accepted the 550-year-old Sato family sword (reciprocating by giving Junzo Sato a copy of his *Complete Works*, and later dedicating *The Resurrection* to him).

This perfect weapon of Motoshigé's (Yeats misspells his name) became for Yeats an emblem of Self (*Ille*) when rejecting a life of mysticism. *A Dialogue of Self and Soul* (*CP*, p. 265), at the climax of the 'Tower' period, is Yeats's affirmation of life lived to the full, which he describes in a letter: 'I am writing a new tower poem . . . which is a choice of rebirth rather than deliverance from birth. I make my Japanese sword and its silk covering my symbol of life.' 'Symbols' (*CP*, p. 270) is but a shorthand of the same theme. For the *samurai* and Yeats, the sword was more than just a razor-sharp weapon; it possessed a spiritual quality. In Japanese poetry it was often a symbol of determination to fight for a noble cause. Thus the splendidly positive declaration by *My Self* in the poem, almost as if he had the sacred sword in front of him while he speaks:

I am content to follow to its source
Every event in action or in thought;
Measure the lot; forgive myself the lot!
When such as I cast out remorse
So great a sweetness flows into the breast
We must laugh and we must sing,
We are blest by everything,
Everything we look upon is blest.

OLIVIA SHAKESPEAR ('DIANA VERNON'), 1863–1938   From 1894 until her death Yeats wrote fuller letters to Olivia Shakespear than to any of his friends, male or female, discussing in detail what he was reading, the poems he was writing, his reactions to personal and political events, and constantly seeking her advice. Many of the letters are quoted in Wade's edition but after her death when Ezra Pound, her son-in-law, returned many, Yeats burnt them. Nevertheless, from those we have, it is possible to fill in the gist of her responses; and remarkably intelligent she was in her critical comments, and well-read in English, French and Italian literature – apart from being a novelist herself. From her photograph and from the descriptions of those who knew her, there is no doubt of her serene beauty, which reflected a gentle, contemplative and still temperament.

She was the cousin of Lionel Johnson, the Rhymer, who had introduced her to Yeats in 1894. At that time he was still involved in his unrequited affair with Maud Gonne, and this led him to embark on a relationship with 'Diana Vernon', as he called Olivia Shakespear, until her husband, an aged solicitor, died. 'The Lover Mourns for the Loss of Love' (*CP*, p. 68) is a short, explicit statement of the situation. 'He Bids his Beloved Be at Peace' (*CP*, p. 69), reveals more sensuality than some of his contemporary love poems (Professor Jeffares says he has counted twenty-three references to the hair of the beloved in these poems). 'The Travail of Passion' (*CP*, p. 78), with its Rossetti-like imagery, has another of these hirsute attributions. He includes Olivia Shakespear ('Diana Vernon') in a trio with Lady Gregory and Maud Gonne in 'Friends':

> Three women that have wrought
> What joy is in my days. . . .
>
> (*CP*, p. 139)

In December 1929 he met her in London after a gap of some months, and then wrote 'After Long Silence' (*CP*, p. 301). After her death he wrote to Dorothy Wellesley: 'For more than forty years she has been the centre of my life in London, and during all that time we have never had a quarrel, sadness sometimes, but never a difference.'

153

ARTHUR SYMONS 1865–1945 A poet, playwright and critic, Symons introduced Yeats to the French Symbolist school; in fact he wrote a very important book, *The Symbolist Movement in Literature* (1899), in which Yeats had a hand. After the friendship between Yeats and Lionel Johnson had lessened, Symons became Yeats's closest friend, being an especially sympathetic listener. A most important influence on Yeats in the nineties, he encouraged him in his use of symbolism, a process already started in *The Wanderings of Oisin*. A member of the Rhymers Club, he visited the Aran Islands and Coole Park with Yeats in 1896. There is no specific reference to him in *CP*.

J.M. SYNGE, 1871–1909 Although Synge, born in County Dublin, educated Trinity College, was one of Yeats's nearest friends from 1896 until his death from cancer in 1909, their common interest was drama rather than poetry. The notorious riots provoked by *The Playboy of the Western World* in 1907 at the Abbey Theatre were the climax of the Dublin reaction to Synge's criticism of the weaknesses in Irish character: these had been expressed in *In the Shadow of the Glen*, an earlier play. Yeats's memories of this occasion gave birth to the bitter, epigrammatic, 'On those that hated "The Playboy of the Western World", 1907' (*CP*, p. 124), in which he scorns the emasculated reaction to the play: also to the section of 'Beautiful Lofty Things' (*CP*, p. 348), when he remembers his father addressing the audience after the play. Synge was thought by the '*Playboy*' audience to be unpatriotic and a blasphemer:

> 'Is it killed your father?'
> 'With the help of God I did, surely, and that the Holy Immaculate Mother may intercede for his soul.'

And, incredible though it now seems, the spark which started the fiery riot, after which the actors could not be heard for the rest of the play, was the line: 'a drift of chosen females in their shifts' – a shift being a chemise which it was then considered obscene to mention. These developments in the history of the Irish theatre are outside the scope of this book, but it is impossible to excise such incidents, for they build up the picture of that 'rooted', 'solitary', and 'enquiring' man John Synge as an heroic figure so much admired by Yeats for his courage to expose unpleasant traits of personality, and weaknesses in Irish life, often with savage humour.

When they first met in Paris in the 1890s, Yeats advised Synge to leave and go to the Aran Islands: 'Live as one of the people themselves; express a life that has never found expression.' Synge took his advice, so totally altering the direction of his career, and the journey became for Yeats an archetype like that of Dante and Bunyan – a spiritual journey through life in which Synge found fulfilment:

> And that enquiring man John Synge comes next,
> That dying chose the living world for text
> And never could have rested in the tomb
> But that, long travelling, he had come
> Towards nightfall upon certain set apart
> In a most desolate stony place,
> Towards nightfall upon a race
> Passionate and simple like his heart.
>
> (*CP*, p. 149)

The discovery by Synge of the tough peasantry and their violent lives was to influence Yeats in turn. Henceforward disillusion and violence figure in his own verse, and sometimes sections of his poems such as 'The Hour before Dawn':

> The beggar in a rage began
> Upon his hunkers in the hole,
> 'It's plain that you are no right man
> To mock at everything I love
> As if it were not worth the doing.
>
> (*CP*, p. 130)

or 'The Three Hermits', might be Synge's own:

> While he'd rummaged rags and hair,
> Caught and cracked his flea, the third,
> Giddy with his hundredth year,
> Sang unnoticed like a bird.
>
> (*CP*, p. 127)

In such poems Yeats has left the aesthetes in the Pre-Raphaelite room, where he sat dreaming in the 'aureate' Celtic twilight, for the beggars in the fresh Easter wind. The 'Crazy Jane' poems and many of *Last Poems* demonstrate the influence of Synge's thought on Yeats's verse. In 'The Municipal Gallery Revisited' he writes his final tribute:

> John Synge, I and Augusta Gregory, thought
> All that we did, all that we said or sang
> Must come from contact with the soil, from that
> Contact everything Antaeus-like grew strong.
> We three alone in modern times had brought
> Everything down to that sole test again,
> Dream of the noble and the beggar-man.
>
> (*CP* p. 369)

Synge exemplified for Yeats his theory of the mask, perhaps was even his own mask, his Anti-Self. For Synge, the gentle, shy and sick man, created and perfected his art so that it revealed life in its

155

brutality and harshness – the opposite of all he was in daily life: one aspect of the 'double soul' discussed by Ellmann in *Yeats: The Man and the Masks*.[23] See also 'The Mask' (*CP*, p. 106), written not long after Synge's death, and showing, in its conversation between the lovers, the difficulty in revealing true identity behind the mask.

Yeats chose eight of Synge's poems for the *Oxford Book of Modern Verse*, after having referred very briefly to Synge's verse in his introduction – a 'perverse judgement' as T.R. Henn calls it in his excellent chapter on Yeats and Synge in *The Lonely Tower*; for there is no doubt that Synge's poetry is inferior to his plays. It is the years at the Abbey Theatre which Yeats thinks should be remembered: 'I think when Lady Gregory's name and John Synge's name are spoken by future generations, my name, if remembered, will come up in the talk, and that if my name is spoken first their names will come in their turn because of the years we worked together' ('The Bounty of Sweden' *AU*, p. 553).

DOROTHY WELLESLEY (LADY GERALD WELLESLEY), 1889–1956   For details of her house and Yeats's visits to it during the last four years of his life, see below, pp. 182–3. Like Lady Gregory she gave Yeats friendship, through which he was able to discuss, either at Penns or by letter, his poetry and hers. The relationship was one of master to pupil, and she as a minor poet benefited from his advice, while he thrived on the peaceful setting which enabled him to write. Kathleen Raine sums up the relationship between them, in her Introduction to *Letters on Poetry from W.B. Yeats to Dorothy Wellesley*:

> The letters throw light upon the aims Yeats set himself as a poet during the last years of his life, the years in which he wrote his play *Purgatory* (he knew it for a masterpiece) and his last volume of poems, some of them his finest. They remind us that the soil from which great poetry grows is remote from these aridities which occupy the pens of critics; the beauty of woman, the charm of her house and her companionship, friendship, dreams and kindness, these nourish immortal poetry.[24]

JACK BUTLER YEATS, 1871–1957   Six years younger than the poet, he also spent his childhood in Sligo. Unlike his elder brother, he had a cheerful, open disposition which enabled him to get on with people easily, and especially with his Pollexfen grandfather, whose favourite he was. Sligo with its ships, fairs, races and circuses, and the variety of men and women associated with them, was an inspiration for his drawing from 1887 until he started his career as an art student in London, following in the footsteps of his father. 'In half of the pictures he paints today I recognize faces that I have met at Rosses or the Sligo quays', wrote the poet in *AU*.

By 1910 he was happily married and had had seventeen exhibitions, with patrons including Lady Gregory and Robert Gregory, John Quinn and John Masefield, who shared his enjoyment of the vigorous life and also his delight in story-telling. Before 1905, when he left watercolours for oil painting, his best work had been illustrations to *The Aran Islands*, and the record of a tour which he made with J.M. Synge in Connemara. His strength of line was especially suitable for drawing the peasants leading their hard life on poor land along the shores of the wild ocean.

His later work, after 1924, which does not reproduce well in black and white, became much more romantic, freer with broader pigments, and outlines receding, at times almost abstract Impressionist. He also wrote numerous plays, novels and articles. In 1948 he told a friend: 'In writing, as in my painting, my inspiration has always been affection wide, devious, and, sometimes, handsome . . . in every book there is somewhere in it a memory of Sligo . . . to which lovely place the beak of my ship ever returns.'

The wild faces of horsemen, the quiet dignity of tinkers and wanderers, set against tumultuous skies which flash and dance with colour, are transformed in his imagination; and that, after all, is what his brother achieved in poetry which often had that very subject matter.

JOHN BUTLER YEATS, 1839–1922   The poet's father was brought up in a large family at Tullylish in Ulster, where his father was the 'red-headed' Rector. His early days were happy, except for the horrors of a private school in the Isle of Man, from which he returned home only for six weeks in the summer. His life there was redeemed by the excellence of the art teacher who realized he had talent. George Pollexfen was a schoolfellow, but had none of the brilliance of J.B. who was always top of his class. Following in the family tradition, he entered Trinity College in 1857, reading Classics, and, afterwards, Law. When he married Susan Pollexfen at Sligo in 1863 the Pollexfens were pleased: a handsome young man, who might be a brilliant barrister, and who had already inherited Butler lands in County Kildare, suited them. Their hopes were dashed. Having been called to the Irish Bar in 1866, J.B. decided not to practise, but to train to be an artist in London, to the disgust of the worldly-wise and ambitious Pollexfens. His wife, doubtless influenced by her family, at first refused to follow him or even to acknowledge his existence as an artist, and with five children and no commissions for five years his lot was not enviable.

J.B.'s anxiety about the influence of the Pollexfens while Willie was in Sligo has been discussed (see above, pp. 14–16). Dreading the thought of the Pollexfen characteristics – taciturnity, melancholia and inarticulateness – coming out in Willie, J.B. removed him to London where he decided to help to educate him personally. When J.B. returned to Dublin in 1880, he was responsible for the poet attending the Metropolitan School of Art, which had a lasting effect on him, for he developed the ability to observe closely, despite his short sight, and this is a rare quality in academically trained people. As a result of help from Hugh Lane who recognized J.B.'s worth, he painted many portraits of leaders in Irish literary and political life, two of which were hung in a Royal Academy exhibition. Professor Bodkin (Honorary Professor of Art, Trinity College) thought the portraits of John O'Leary, Standish O'Grady and George Russell had 'an air of mingled intimacy and dignity that no other painter of modern times surpasses'. On J.B.'s return with his family to Bedford Park, his literary and artist friends, most of whom were minor Pre-Raphaelite painters, had some influence on the poet's thought, though by then he was trying to break away from his father. On the other hand, his younger brother Jack was even then showing signs of draughtsmanship and painterly ability which was encouraged by J.B.

Throughout his life he never made much money, as he never thought it right to live with that end in view. He was a brilliant conversationalist with great intellectual curiosity, an avid reader, totally unselfish and unambitious, but incapable of planning or organization. His delightful wry humour is illustrated in an anecdote in 'Beautiful Lofty Things':

> My father upon the Abbey stage, before him a raging crowd;
> 'This land of Saints,' and then as the applause died out,
> 'Of plaster Saints'; his beautiful mischievous head thrown back.
>
> (*CP*, p. 348)

Though as J.B. remembered this incident from the *Playboy* riots after nine years (1907) it was slightly different, yet still showing his humour.

> I began with some information about Synge which interested my listeners and then: 'Of course I know Ireland is an island of Saints, but thank God it is also an island of sinners – only unfortunately in this Country people cannot live or die except behind a curtain of deceit.' At this point the chairman and my son both called out. 'Time's up, Time's up.' I saw the lifted sign and like the devil in *Paradise Lost* I fled. The papers next morning said I was howled down. It was worse, I was pulled down.

In December 1907 he went to New York with his daughter Lily, and thereafter refused to return to Ireland, despite repeated requests from his family. He painted portraits and lectured, sometimes receiving financial help from John Quinn (see above, p. 149) as well as from the poet himself. All his life he wrote many letters, and there are said to be 5,000 as yet unpublished, apart from those in *J.B. Yeats-Letters to his Son W.B. Yeats, and Others*, edited, with a Memoir, by Joseph Hone.[25]

Notes

1. Kathleen Raine, *Blake and Tradition*, 2 vols (London: Routledge & Kegan Paul, 1969).
2. Clifford Bax (ed.), *Florence Farr, Bernard Shaw and W.B. Yeats* (Dublin: Cuala Press, 1941).
3. A. Norman Jeffares, *W.B. Yeats: Man and Poet* (London: Routledge & Kegan Paul, 1949), p. 190.
4. Seán O'Casey, *Inishfallen, Fare Thee Well* (London: Macmillan, 1949).
5. Ibid., pp. 127–254.
6. For a detailed study of these poems, see Frank Kermode, *The Romantic Image* (London: Routledge & Kegan Paul, 1957), pp. 30–42.
7. T.R. Henn, *The Lonely Tower: Studies in the Poetry of W.B. Yeats* (London: Methuen, 1950; 2nd edn 1965).
8. Richard Ellmann, *Yeats: the Man and the Masks* (1948, rev. 1979; Harmondsworth: Penguin, 1987), p. 75.
9. Lady Gregory, *Journals 1916–1930* ed. Lennox Robinson (1946; repr. Gerrards Cross: Colin Smythe, 1972), p. 284.
10. Joseph Hone, *W.B. Yeats: 1865–1939* (London: Macmillan, 1942; 2nd edn 1965, repr. 1989).
11. Anne Marreco, *The Rebel Countess* (London: Weidenfeld and Nicolson, 1967; paper, Corgi, 1969); Seán O'Faoláin, *Constance Markievicz* (London: Cape, 1939; paper, rev. edn, Sphere, 1967).
12. John Masefield, *Some Memories of W.B. Yeats* (Dublin: Cuala Press, 1940).
13. Hone, op. cit.
14. O'Casey, op. cit.
15. Maurice Manning, *The Blueshirts* (Canada: University of Toronto Press, 1970).
16. Hone, op. cit., p. 436.
17. Edward Norman, *A History of Modern Ireland* (1971).
18. Louis MacNeice, *The Poetry of W.B. Yeats* (Oxford, OUP, 1941), p. 74.
19. Edgar Holt, *Protest in Arms* (London: Putnam, 1960); Max Caulfield, *Easter Rebellion* (London: Muller, 1964).
20. Richard Ellmann, *Eminent Domain* (New York: OUP, 1967), p. 64.
21. Shotaro Oshimo, *W.B. Yeats and Japan* (Luzac, 1965).
22. Allan Wade (ed.) *The Letters of W.B. Yeats* (London: Hart-Davis, 1954).
23. Ellmann, op. cit., pp. 174–9 ff.
24. Kathleen Raine (ed.), *Letters on Poetry from W.B. Yeats to Dorothy Wellesley* (Oxford: OUP, 1940; reissued 1964).
25. Joseph Hone (ed.), *J.B. Yeats. Letters to his Son W.B. Yeats and Others, 1869–1922* (London: Faber and Faber, 1944).

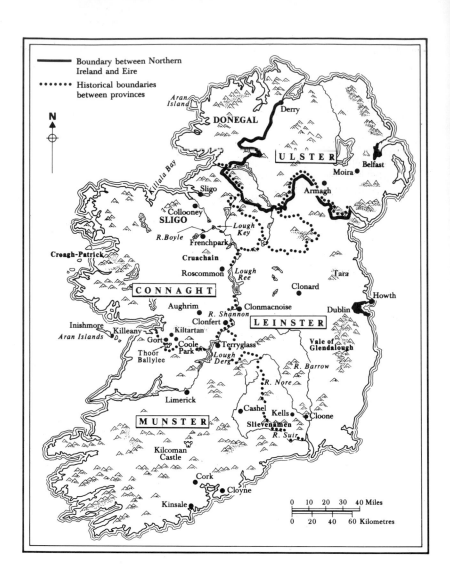

Map of Ireland.

160

Gazetteer

Ireland

SANDYMOUNT CASTLE, DUBLIN   When the poet's family were living at 'Georgeville', 1865–66, this 'castle' nearby was owned by Robert Corbet, the poet's great-uncle. J.B. Yeats had lived there when an undergraduate at Trinity College, sometimes rehearsing Greek plays in the drawingroom, and now the poet himself was wheeled in his pram in the extensive grounds. The castle was an eighteenth-century house, gothicized beyond recognition by Abbotsford-type battlements, tower and cloister. The gardens were large (five gardeners) and it was landscaped in the eighteenth-century manner by Robert Corbet, with vistas to the sea, a lake and a small deer park. After Corbet's death it was sold. The poet visited it again in 1900, but could scarcely recognize the grounds. It has now been built on, forming part of the seaside suburb of Sandymount.

GEORGEVILLE, NO. 2 SANDYMOUNT AVENUE, DUBLIN   This was where the poet was born at midnight on 13 June 1865. It is described by Hone[1] as 'a recently-built, six-roomed, semi-detached house at the head of Sandymount Avenue . . . the most genteel house in the avenue, with stone steps up to the hall door, and plate-glass windows'. Uncle Corbet was a snob and used to address letters to 'The Quarry Hole' because the house had been built on a quarry site. It is still there, though now No. 5, with its name inscribed on the stone wall.

TRINITY COLLEGE, DUBLIN   Trinity College was founded in 1592 by Queen Elizabeth I for the education of Protestants. Not until 1873 did Catholics gain completely equal privileges with Protestants. The Roll of famous Trinity men includes Jonathan Swift, Oliver Goldsmith, Edmund Burke, George Berkeley, Wolfe Tone, Henry Grattan, J.M. Synge and Oscar Wilde. The buildings, with their splendid classical façades and elaborate interior plasterwork, flanked by extensive playing-fields, occupy a large area in the very centre of Dublin. The Library houses Ireland's greatest collection of books and MSS, including the famous illuminated eighth-century gospel book, *The Book of Kells*.

The poet's great-grandfather, grandfather and father had all been undergraduates at Trinity, and it was hoped he might follow them.

But he realized his Latin and Mathematics would not be up to the standard of the entrance examination, so he went to an Art School. When he was involved in the romantic Celtic revival in the 1890s, he made long attacks on Protestant Ireland as exemplified by Trinity College, in his introduction to *A Book of Irish Verse* (1895). 'No Irishman', he wrote, 'living in Ireland has sung excellently of any but a theme from Irish experience, Irish History or Irish tradition.' Further on he pointed to Trinity College as 'an enemy of all enthusiasms; because all enthusiasms seemed her enemies she has taught her children to look neither to the world about them nor into their own souls where some dangerous fire might slumber'. He then added that the products of English universities, and of Trinity College which aped them, were ignorant of the very names of the best writers in *A Book of Irish Verse*. A decade later he had modified his views slightly, and later in life he came to admire profoundly the work and thought of Trinity College's most famous eighteenth-century graduates – Swift, Goldsmith, Berkeley and Burke.

Yeats came up against Trinity College traditions in 1914, when Pádraic Pearse, who was then considered a revolutionary, both politically and in being a Gaelic scholar, had been invited to address the Gaelic Society of the College at a commemoration of the centenary of the Irish poet Thomas Davis. The Vice-Provost, Dr Mahaffy (elected Provost in November), dissolved the Society and closed the gates of the College to them. Yeats, who was also giving a lecture on this occasion, decided he and Pearse should go ahead, so they lectured in the Antient Concert Rooms in Brunswick Street, later renamed Pearse Street.

Earlier in the same year Yeats had applied for permission to read in the library of the college. As was customary, he had to take an oath, to be read out in Latin, before the Vice-Provost, swearing not to damage the books. In due course Yeats was sent a copy of the oath with the stresses and quantities of the Latin words marked by Mahaffy, who added, according to Gogarty, 'for I have a sensitive ear'. Yeats could not read Latin, and Mahaffy's method of showing Yeats he knew this was the action of an academic snob – arrogant and insensitive.

All was forgotten by 1922 when Yeats was honoured by a D.Litt. degree from the College.

ST PATRICK'S CATHEDRAL (PROTESTANT), DUBLIN St Patrick's Cathedral is the largest Church ever built in Ireland and stands on the site of a pre-Norman Church, which legend associates with the Saint. Rebuilt in the twelfth century, most of it is thirteenth/fourteenth century, with an eight-bay nave, four-bay choir, Lady

Chapel and Baptistery. The 100-foot granite spire was built in 1750. The cathedral was much restored in 1864–69, money being given for that purpose by Sir Benjamin Lee Guinness, whose statue stands outside. It is filled with tombs of many who have served Ireland, including Jonathan Swift, Dean of the Cathedral Chapter (1713–45), and of Esther Johnson (Swift's Stella). The Latin epitaph for his wall monument was composed by Swift himself. Yeats used to 'wander and meditate' in the cathedral, or sit by this monument in the gloom, Swift for him being 'always just round the next corner'. Perhaps he thought out his famous verse based on the epitaph, with which he had difficulty before it reached its final version.

> Swift has sailed into his rest;
> Savage indignation there
> Cannot lacerate his breast.
> Imitate him if you dare,
> World-besotted traveller; he
> Served human liberty.

(CP, p. 277)

Immediately after Yeats's death in the south of France in 1939, the Dean of the Cathedral wrote to Mrs Yeats suggesting a final resting place for the poet in the cathedral – the first offer of this kind for a hundred years. But Yeats had signified he wished to be buried among his ancestors at Drumcliffe, County Sligo, so she refused the honour.

THE GENERAL POST OFFICE, O'CONNELL STREET   Amidst the general confusion of the modern city, the classical columns of the façade of the General Post Office (1814–18) by Francis Johnston, one of Ireland's finest architects, stand in lone and majestic dignity. As a result of being the headquarters of the 1916 insurgents, who proclaimed the Irish Republic there, and being bombarded again in 1922, all that survives of Johnston's work is the O'Connell Street (Sackville Street till 1916) front. In the main hall, as you buy a stamp, you pass the 1916 memorial statue, *The Death of Cuchulain* in bronze, by Oliver Sheppard, a sculptor whom Yeats knew at the Metropolitan School of Art. The analogy for Yeats between the heroic figures of the Easter Rising and those of Irish myth often occurs in his writing, and so accounts for such lines as those from 'The Statues':

> When Pearse summoned Cuchulain to his side,
> What stalked through the Post Office? . . .

The question sounds stronger if the stresses are right: the Irish pronounce it Post Óffice, whereas the English usually say Póst Office.

82 MERRION SQUARE, DUBLIN   The Yeatses and their children lived in this house from September 1922 to May 1928. It was built in the last twenty years of the eighteenth century, during the time of Grattan's Parliament that Yeats so much admired. Merrion Square, with its central garden, is the most handsome Georgian square in Dublin, second only in size to St Stephen's Green. This house, like others in the square, is of maroon-coloured brick, with a large front door, flanked by elegant Ionic pillars supporting pretty fanlight tracery. Inside there are some vast rooms, including a double drawing-room which was useful when the poet held literary evenings at which he would also read his latest work such as his play *The Resurrection*. Also, he could pace up and down whilst he dictated his Senate speeches to his wife who typed them.

Yeats was elected a member of Seanad Éireann (the Irish Senate) during this period, and as the Civil War was raging, there were guards outside the house, for many senators' houses in the country had been blown up or burnt by Irregulars. To be living in such a house, with its high rooms, marble chimneypieces and rococo plaster-work was a matter of much pride for Yeats. But when his term of office as a 'green-robed senator' was about to come to an end he realized he couldn't afford to go on living there without a senator's salary, so they moved. As it was they had to let the top storey and Cuala industries (weaving) was in the basement. Even then the size of the house must have been inconvenient for easy domesticity. V.S. Pritchett in his autobiography, *Midnight Oil*,[2] describes an afternoon call he paid on Yeats:

> The exalted voice flowed over me. The tall figure, in uncommonly delicate tweed, walked up and down, the voice becoming more resonant, as if he were on a stage. At the climax of some point about the Gaelic revival, he suddenly remembered he must make tea, in fact a new pot, because he had already been drinking some. The problem was one of emptying out the old teapot. It was a beautiful pot and he walked the room with the short steps of the aesthete, carrying it in his hand. He came toward me. He receded to the bookcase. He swung around the sofa. Suddenly, with Irish practicality, he went straight to one of the two splendid Georgian windows of the room, opened it, and out went those barren leaves with a swoosh, into Merrion Square.

RIVERSDALE, WILLBROOK, RATHFARNHAM, COUNTY DUBLIN
Yeats lived at Riversdale, a stone house with an estate of about four acres, from July 1932 until his death. Discovered by Mrs Yeats, it was ideal, with a pleasant, well-stocked garden, a walled orchard,

croquet lawn and gardener's cottage. It had a fine view of the
Dublin mountains, standing as it did a mile beyond the village of
Rathfarnham, four miles south-west of Dublin. But doubts in Yeats's
mind were evidently raised by the cynical question of Plato's ghost,
the daemon who takes part in the conversation of the soul with
itself, when death is approaching:

> All his happier dreams came true –
> A small old house, wife, daughter, son,
> Grounds where plum and cabbage grew,
> Poets and Wits about him drew;
> *'What then?' sang Plato's ghost. 'What then?'*
>
> 'The work is done', grown old he thought,
> 'According to my boyish plan;
> Let the fools rage, I swerved in naught,
> Something to perfection brought';
> *But louder sang that ghost, 'What then?'*

(CP, p. 347)

COOLE PARK, COUNTY GALWAY   For 200 years until 1932 the
Gregory family lived at Coole. This stone house, which has been
demolished, was neither grand nor imposing, a simple three-storeyed
cube of six bays with a semicircular Palladian window above a
square porch. In its setting of open parkland it had a sturdy
plainness which did not give the impression of its having been built
for defence like so many Irish houses, but rather as an accessible
dwelling where all were welcome. On the west side, Victorian bay
windows looked down to the lake; not far off was the stable block,
ruined now, but still having a magnificent dovecot in a gable which
soars above the trees. The estate is wooded and picturesque, the
Cloon river flowing under high poplars on a steep bank by the rocky
wood, Páirc-na-Carraig, through a causeway bridge of vast limestone
flags, to join a wild lake edged in brown and velvet moss. After
which it plunges underground to flow into Galway Bay twenty miles
to the west. All this under the shadow of the Dun of the legendary
King Guaire. It was here, according to ancient legend, that King
Guaire, having heard a child would be born who would be greater
than he, planned the murder of the child's mother. So King Guaire's
people 'took her and tied a heavy stone about her neck and threw
her into the deep part of the river where it rises within Coole. But
by the help of God the stone that was put about her neck did not
sink but went floating upon the water, and she came to the shore
and was saved from drowning.' The name of the child who was born
in the parish of Kiltartan was Saint Colman, afterwards famed for
his good works throughout Ireland.

165

From the days of Richard Gregory, who collected the fine library in the eighteenth century, the house was always a place of peace: the home of a Protestant family living in amity with tenants and at peace with Catholic neighbours. And thanks to Lady Gregory it was one of the few houses in Ireland unscarred by the Troubles and the Civil War in the 1920s. Yeats remembers it in 'Beautiful Lofty Things':

> Augusta Gregory seated at her great ormolu table,
> Her eightieth winter approaching: 'Yesterday he threatened
>   my life.
> I told him that nightly from six to seven I sat at this table,
> The blinds drawn up';

(CP, p. 348)

Adjoining the house was a walled garden of about three acres, planted with trees, ornamental shrubs and flowers. At the end of a flowered-bordered gravel walk, at the lower part of the garden beyond the Vineries, stood, on a simple plinth, a large bust of Maecenas brought from Italy by Richard Gregory in the 1790s. Near the middle of the garden alongside the gravel walk was a copper-beech, called the Autograph Tree, on which famous visitors were invited to inscribe their initials, whilst others were discouraged from inserting them. Although the tree was mutilated after Lady Gregory's death, it is still possible to see the initials of W.B. Yeats, his father and his brother, Jack; the lyre-cipher of John Synge, and George Bernard Shaw. Lady Gregory and her husband Sir William continually planted trees, and in 1898, at the centenary celebrations for the Rebellion of the United Irishmen, she recommended that every Nationalist should 'plant at least one tree ... and every Unionist in 1900, and every waverer or indifferent person in the year that separates them'.

It was fitting she should have arranged to meet Yeats in the centenary year to discuss the founding of the Irish National Theatre. A few days after this meeting Yeats went to Coole, which virtually became his home for many years. In 1898 he was physically sick, poor and homeless. Augusta Gregory nursed him back to health, lent him money and gave him ideal conditions in which to work. 'I found at last', he wrote, 'what I have been seeking always, a life of order, and of labour, where all outward things were the image of an inward life.' So one finds in his verse written during the next thirty years much of the imagery inspired by the experience of living at Coole: the wild swans 'mysterious, beautiful', so different from the tame and protected English kind, first as symbols of passion and beauty, then to betoken inspiration in the later poem, 'Coole Park and Ballylee, 1931':

That stormy white
But seems a concentration of the sky;
And, like the soul, it sails into the sight
And in the morning's gone, no man knows why . . .

(*CP*, p. 275)

The Seven Woods, first in their tragic sublimity reflecting the loneliness in which Yeats felt the eternity of nature, later became a mirror of his mood as he reflects on the tragedy of Coole. Even the 'Great Wind', the hurricane of 1903, which 'blew down so many trees, troubled the wild creatures and changed the look of things' became a symbol for what had happened to him after his beloved Maud Gonne had unexpectedly married. From direct experience of the Coole garden and the wood Páirc-na-Lee arose his sonnet 'In the Seven Woods' (*CP*, p. 85), in which the pigeons in the woods, and the bees in the lime-tree flowers could make him forget the bitterness of his love for Maud Gonne, as well as the futilities of the coronation festivities of Edward VII.

It was at Coole that Yeats saw the continuance of eighteenth-century traditions of courage, intellect and imagination. Whether from Swift at the beginning or Grattan at the end of the century, the pace of life induced a quietness of thought which in turn engendered a Unity of Being, as in 'Coole Park, 1929':

Great works constructed there in nature's spite
For scholars and for poets after us,
Thoughts long knitted into a single thought,
A dance-like glory that those walls begot.

(*CP*, p. 274)

Coole embodied ceremony, order and freedom, and he remembered these when in October 1937 he gave a talk for the BBC entitled 'My own poetry again': 'From my twenty-seventh year until a few years ago all my public activities were associated with a famous country house in County Galway. In that house my dear friend, that woman of genius, Lady Gregory, gathered from time to time all men of talent, all profound men, in the intellectual life of modern Ireland.'

In 1921 the excessive Irish land rates had forced the Gregory family to sell some of the land, and ultimately Coole was doomed, though there had been 'no country house in Ireland with so fine a record'. In 1927 it was sold to the Ministry of Lands and Agriculture, but Lady Gregory was allowed to live there on payment of a small rental. Yeats knew the house could not survive long: it would become, he wrote, (*EX*, p. 319) 'an office and residence for foresters, a little cheap furniture in the great rooms, a few religious oleographs its only pictures'. In 1941, after Lady Gregory's and Yeats's deaths, it was sold to a building contractor who pulled it down for the value of the stone. Nothing remains but the garden walls, the ruins of the stable block, and a few floor tiles. It is almost impossible to visualize the garden, as the great catalpa has already gone, the box hedges are eye-level, and rows of so-called Christmas trees are rising high.

THOOR BALLYLEE, GORT, COUNTY GALWAY   Sturdy, stone towers, with six-foot thick walls, built in medieval times, sometimes ruined, firmly punctuate the Irish landscape. Thoor Ballylee, within walking distance of Coole House, and once a part of the demesne, is typical. It guards a small stone bridge which was a fording place over a swift-flowing stream. The interior is simple: four storeys, each one large room, a narrow stone stair cut into the walls, and battlements as parapet. Yeats first went to Ballylee, while staying at Coole in the 1890s, and described it in 'Dust hath closed Helen's Eye', an essay published in October 1899.

> I have been lately to a little group of houses, not many enough to be called a village, in the barony of Kiltartan in County Galway, whose name, Ballylee, is known through all the west of Ireland. There is the old square castle, Ballylee, inhabited by a farmer and his wife, and a cottage where their daughter and their son-in-law live, and a little mill with an old miller, and old ash trees throwing green shadows upon a little river and great stepping-stones. I went there two or three times last year to talk to the miller about Biddy Early, a wise woman that lived in Clare some years ago, and about her saying 'There is a cure for all evil between the two mill-wheels of Ballylee', and to find out from him or another whether she meant the moss between the running waters or some other herb. I have been there this summer and I shall be there again before it is autumn, because Mary Hynes, a beautiful woman whose name is still a wonder by turf fires, died there sixty years ago; for our feet would linger where beauty has lived its life of sorrow to make us understand that it is not of the world.

When he was at Coole during many subsequent summers, he must have seen the tower and the cottages gradually becoming ruined after the farmer and his family had left them. The setting and its Gaelic associations with Mary Hynes, the local miller's daughter whom the blind poet Raftery had sung of and loved, held him fascinated. In 1917, even though the floors were rotten and there was no roof on the tower, he made a bid for the property, then owned by a government department oddly called the Congested Districts Board. As no one wanted it he managed to buy it and the two cottages for £35. Then he set to work to have repairs done, and sturdy elm furniture designed and made on the spot by a local craftsman from Gort. After Yeats's marriage in October 1917 it was important to get the work finished. But he was not able to take up residence until the summer of 1919. Even then only the ground and first floors of the tower were finished, though one of the cottages enabled him to have a study to work in. The roof was eventually cemented, despite his wish to have it covered in 'sea-green slates' which he had paid for as they had been recommended by the famous architect Sir Edwin Lutyens. But the local builder considered they would not withstand Atlantic gales, although they are certainly used in Scotland in similar circumstances. The verse (*CP*, p. 214) now carved on an outside wall of the tower remembers them. Henceforth the tower becomes a recurrent and paramount symbol in his verse as in 'A Prayer on going into my House':

> God grant a blessing on this tower and cottage
> And on my heirs, if all remain unspoiled,
> No table or chair or stool not simple enough
> For shepherd lads in Galilee; and grant
> That I myself for portions of the year
> May handle nothing and set eyes on nothing
> But what the great and passionate have used
> Throughout so many varying centuries
> We take it for the norm; . . .

(CP, p. 183)

As the tower's ground floor room was flooded when the river was high, and was always rather damp, he could live there for only very limited 'portions of the year'. Not until 1922, when the Yeatses had their Merrion Square house, was a large bedroom on the second floor completed. On one occasion when the Yeatses were living there (during the Civil War) the tower was surrounded by Irregulars who blew up part of the bridge ('The Tower', v; *CP*, pp. 229); and again, when they were not there, it was occupied temporarily by Free State soldiers.

For some years previously the symbol of the tower had been used by Yeats. Two poems written in 1915 show what it then meant to him. The first, 'Ego Dominus Tuus', is a dialogue between *Hic*, signifying the objective self, and *Ille*, the subjective self: a clash or struggle between these two, which have been termed the self and the anti-self of the same personality. Between, for example, the characteristics of the philosopher-scholar or imaginative artist and the man of action, the soldier or politician. *Hic* opens the poem:

> On the grey sand beside the shallow stream
> Under your old wind-beaten tower, where still
> A lamp burns on beside the open book
> That Michael Robartes left, you walk in the moon . . .

(CP, p. 180)

Michael Robartes is a fictional figure, the solitary scholar, perhaps one of the subjective sides of Yeats's personality. The symbol of the search for wisdom, of the lamp burning in the darkness of the night, is further developed in the second of the two poems, 'The Phases of the Moon', when Robartes says to Aherne, another fictional scholarly character, also representing a part of Yeats's subjective side:

> We are on the bridge; that shadow is the tower,
> And the light proves that he is reading still.
> He has found, after the manner of his kind,
> Mere images; chosen this place to live in
> Because, it may be, of the candle-light
> From the far tower where Milton's Platonist
> Sat late, or Shelley's visionary prince:
> The lonely light that Samuel Palmer engraved,
> An image of mysterious wisdom won by toil;
> And now he seeks in book or manuscript
> What he shall never find.
>
> (*CP*, p. 183)

Samuel Palmer (1805–81), the artist referred to in the poem, late in life took to etching on copper (not to engraving, as Yeats says), achieving some fine work when he illustrated Milton's poem 'Il Penseroso'. Yeats had copy of this etching on a wall of his room at Woburn Buildings. He must have been very fond of it, for he had it beside him when he read in the Bodleian Library, Oxford, in 1920. Palmer himself always kept a small copy of Milton's poems in his pocket and was obsessed by 'Il Penseroso', and while he was working on his etching, 'The Lonely Tower', which illustrated this poem, he wrote to a friend:

> You ask me to show you anything which especially affects my inner sympathies. Now only three days have passed since I did begin the meditation of a subject which for twenty years has affected my sympathies with sevenfold inwardness, though for the first time I seem to feel, in some sort, the power of realizing it. It is from what Edmund Burke thought the finest poem in the English language. The passage includes 'the bellman's drowsy charm'. I never artistically knew such a sacred delight as when endeavouring, in all humility, to realize, after a sort, the imagery of Milton.

The tower in Palmer's etching (see p. 51) 'on a plat of rising round', is near human habitation, the roof and gable of a cottage being visible on the skyline. Although it is night, it is not dark, for the moon and stars shine brightly, while *il penseroso* reads Plato by the light of his lamp which can be seen from far off, through the window. Two shepherds are separated by a deep chasm from the tower, but they are gazing at its light, their day's work being finished. An owl, Athene's bird of wisdom, flies toward them from the direction of the tower, above which can be seen the constellation of Ursa Major – the Bear, which the Platonist often 'outwatches'. Here is 'the image of mysterious wisdom won by toil' as seen by Samuel Palmer and so communicated to Yeats. Also mentioned is Shelley's visionary prince, named Prince Athanase, who 'sate/Apart from men as in a lonely tower'.

After the summer of 1929 the Yeatses did not live in Thoor Ballylee again, and although they owned it nothing was done to keep it in repair. Yet compared with Coole House its subsequent history is heartening. By 1952 it had really fallen into decay: Virginia Moore (in *The Unicorn*[3]) describes it as 'a barn for cattle and a rallying place for crows'. Vandals had torn planks from the oak door, and water had leaked through the roof. But then in 1961 the newly founded Kiltartan Society, aided by Bórd Fáilte Éireann (the Irish Tourist Board), started to restore it, and Mrs Yeats and her children placed it in a Trust's hands. Although all the furniture has not yet been remade the buildings are in excellent condition: weatherproof, cottages re-thatched and walls repainted. If you go there in early morning or late evening, when there are no other visitors, and stand at a window overlooking the bridge, the light from the water dances on the ceiling, and no sound breaks the silence except the stream splashing over the stones, or the wind in the big ash trees.

LOUGH KEY, COUNTY ROSCOMMON: THE CASTLE OF THE HE-ROES   One of the landscapes in Ireland which combined Christian and pagan mythology, and which much appealed to Yeats, was at Lough Key, near Boyle, County Roscommon. The shores of this romantic lough are indented with many coves, and its surface dotted with islands. On Trinity Island the White Canons had compiled the *Annals of Loch Cé* in Tudor times, and the ash trees still entwine their branches across the graves of the star-crossed lovers, Una MacDermott, daughter of the last chieftain of the Rock, and the MacCostello of Moygara. On Castle (Rock) Island, the MacDermotts had once entertained the poets of all Ireland, and there Yeats dreamed of founding a mystical cult based on druidic mysteries combined with Christianity. He relates in *The Trembling of the Veil* III (*AU*, p. 253) how the idea occurred to him:

> When staying with Hyde in Roscommon, I had driven over to Lough Kay [*sic*], hoping to find some local memory of the old story ... now called *Proud Costello, MacDermot's Daughter, and the Bitter Tongue*. I was rowed up the lake that I might find the island where he died; I had to find it from Hyde's account in the *Love-*

171

Songs of Connacht, for when I asked the boatman, he told the story of Hero and Leander, putting Hero's house on one island, and Leander's on another. Presently we stopped to eat our sandwiches at the 'Castle Rock', an island all castle. . . . The situation in the centre of the lake, that has little wood-grown islands, and is surrounded by wood-grown hills, is romantic, and at one end, and perhaps at the other too, there is a stone platform where meditative persons might pace to and fro. I planned a mystical Order which should buy or hire the castle, and keep it as a place where its members could retire for a while for contemplation, and where we might establish mysteries like those of Eleusis and Samothrace; and for ten years to come my most impassioned thought was a vain attempt to find philosophy and to create ritual for that Order. I had an unshakable conviction, arising how or whence I cannot tell, that invisible gates would open as they opened for Blake . . . and that this philosophy would find its manuals of devotion in all imaginative literature, and set before Irishmen for special manual an Irish literature, which, though made by many minds, would seem the work of a single mind, and turn our places of beauty or legendary association into holy symbols.

It was arranged that Maud Gonne should be one of the leaders of this cult and AE another. But unfortunately Maud Gonne thought it a good idea if it was organized politically so as to hasten Ireland's freedom from English domination. Yeats did not see it in this way, but as a nexus with the Irish Literary movement, and as an expression, as he says, of those symbols associated with certain holy places in Ireland, which he was in any case to develop in his verse. After some years the rites of the cult had not been worked out, and under the influence of Lady Gregory at Coole he started instead to devote his energies to the Irish National Theatre, and the writing of plays.

The whole project is very typical of Yeats's wish to find and use legendary symbols for Ireland. It is fortunate that Lady Gregory diverted his energies into play-writing, otherwise we might have been left with occult mysteries of minor importance, rather than some splendid plays which went far to incorporate the spirit of those mysteries.

KNOCKNAREA, COUNTY SLIGO   Crowned by Miosgán Meabha(Queen Maeve's cairn), Knocknarea is the most conspicuous and memorable mountain in County Sligo. It was Maeve of Connacht who, after years of bitter fighting, defeated Cuchulain and the Red Branch Knights of Ulster. Legend says that near her tomb on the mountain is a smaller tomb of Eoghan Bel, a warrior knight who was buried upright, AD 537: a gesture of heroic despair against Fate such as Cuchulain's in tying himself to a column at the moment of death, and similar to the attitude shown by the soldiers in 'The Black Tower', when they know they will continue to guard the tower although the king will never come again:

> There in the tomb stand the dead upright,
> But winds come up from the shore:
> They shake when the winds roar,
> Old bones upon the mountain shake.
>
> (*CP*, p. 396)

Yeats was haunted by the mythology connected with Knocknarea from the day when he first stayed as a small boy at 'Merville', his grandparents' house at the foot of the mountain. It was much with him when he wrote *The Wanderings of Oisin* (1886–88) within sight of the mountain at George Pollexfen's:

> Caoilte, and Conan, and Finn were there,
> When we followed a deer with our baying hounds,
> With Bran, Sceolan, and Lomair,
> And passing the Firbolgs' burial-mounds,
> Came to the cairn-heaped grassy hill
> Where passionate Maeve is stony-still . . .
>
> (*CP*, p. 409)

In fact, the 'grey cairn on the hill', on which the wind has 'thrown the thunder', was Ireland itself for Yeats: the burial mounds, the thorn-trees, the waterfalls and the *sidhe* speak to Red Hanrahan, and through him to us.

BEN BULBEN, COUNTY SLIGO   Like Knocknarea, this long, flat-topped limestone mountain (1,750 feet) with its precipice to Glencar, has long figured in Irish legend. In the best-known Irish epic tale, Diarmuid, lover of Grainne, was mortally wounded on its slopes by Finn MacCumhal's enchanted boar, after being chased by Finn throughout Ireland (see Lady Gregory, *Gods and Fighting Men*).[4] The mountain looms large in Yeats's childhood: the smoking cataract of 'The Mountain Tomb' (*CP*, p. 136), that same Glencar waterfall 'That all my childhood counted dear', in 'Towards Break of Day' (*CP* p. 208); and again when he is parodying Wordsworth in 'The Tower':

> No, not in boyhood when with rod and fly,
> Or the humbler worm, I climbed Ben Bulben's back
> And had the livelong summer day to spend.
>
> (*CP*, p. 218)

Lastly, in his final confession of faith, 'Under Ben Bulben' (*CP*, p.

397), he asks for his grave to be situated in a churchyard at the edge of the mountain.

LOUGH GILL AND INNISFREE, COUNTY SLIGO   Lough Gill, near Sligo, flanked by mountains and woods, is nearly as unspoiled today as it must have been 200 years ago. Dramatic emerald isthmuses, covered with holly, bay and arbutus trees, stretch out into the lough, which is studded with islands. Among the smallest is Innisfree (the Heather Island). Jutting out into the lough is Dooney Rock, near which the fiddler used to play and the folk danced (*CP*, p. 82). On one occasion when Yeats was staying with his uncle, George Pollexfen, in the summer of 1889, he decided he would walk round the lough, spending the night out while doing so. He gives an account of his adventures in *Reveries over Childhood and Youth* (*AU*).

The book, which inspired Yeats to think of Innisfree as a place to live in, was *Walden* by Henry Thoreau (1817–62), the American poet and philosopher, who chose Walden Pond, then a remote spot in the woods near Boston, Massachusetts, in which to live in solitude. Some of the passages which Yeats heard his father read from *Walden* explain the author's reasons: 'I went to the woods because I wished to live deliberately to front only the essential facts of life, and see if I could not learn what it had to teach, and not, when I came to die, that I had not lived.' The actual writing of the poem by Yeats was prompted by an incident which he relates in *The Trembling of the Veil* (*AU*). He was very homesick for Sligo, and as he walked through Fleet Street, London, he 'heard a little trickle of water and saw a fountain in a shop-window which balanced a little ball on its jet, and began to remember lake water. From the sudden remembrance came my poem *Innisfree*, my first lyric with anything in its rhythm of my own music.'

The poem was more popular in Yeats's lifetime than any other of his poems, so that he grew to dread being asked to recite it. Once he had to endure hearing hundreds of Boy Scouts saying it in unison, and Dorothy Wellesley records that he frowned all the time he was reciting it to her, after she had asked him to do so. Yeats never allowed Robert Louis Stevenson's words of admiration to appear in any work of his, but they can be read in Stevenson's *Letters*. From Samoa he wrote: 'It is so quaint and airy, simple, artful and eloquent to the heart.' Yeats afterwards declared the first line of the poem had an archaic diction which he would not then use, and he also disliked the inversions. Yet much critical nonsense has been written about the poem, and it seems fashionable to decry it. Stephen Spender in *The Destructive Element* says the poem 'calls up the image of a young man reclining on a yellow satin sofa',[5] presumably surrounded by his fellow-aesthetes in London. This surely is tantamount to accusing Yeats of insincerity. He really did wish to get away from 'the pavements grey', the poem being written in 1890 in his study at Bedford Park and, as Louis MacNeice points out in *The Poetry of W.B. Yeats*,[6] County Sligo is fact, not fiction.

If you ever have a chance in summer when you are in Sligo, it is worth while rowing a boat out to Innisfree and staying there for an hour or two. You will be surprised how amazingly accurate was the poet's aural memory: the wild bees hum in the heather, the low, buzzing stridulation of the crickets surrounds you, and 'peace comes dropping slow' with the sound of the gentle lapping of the lake water.

Yeats's recording of the poem, read in his unique monotonic voice, brings out the variety in the vowel music, which has been remarked on by critics, although Yeats later said that he hardly knew what a vowel was at the time he wrote the poem. John Masefield used to attend the Monday evening sessions at Woburn Buildings and often heard Yeats read. In *Some Memories of W.B. Yeats* he describes the experience: 'His reading was unlike that of any other man. He stressed the rhythm till it became almost a chant; he went with speed, marking every beat and dwelling on his vowels. That wavering ecstatic song, then heard by me for the first time, was to remain with me for years.'[7]

LISSADELL HOUSE, COUNTY SLIGO   An austere stone house in the neoclassical Grecian style, Lissadell was built during 1832–34 for Sir Robert Gore-Booth, the grandfather of Eva and Constance whom Yeats knew. It stands at the end of a long drive alongside the bay, almost on the seashore, in the woods at the foot of Ben Bulben. Its south front with the great bay windows, looks over Rosses Point across the water to Knocknarea. In 1894 Yeats visited the Gore-Booths when he was staying with his grandmother in Sligo. It is the first of those houses where he found gracious and ordered living, presided over by members of the Protestant ascendancy. Consequently it is not hard to imagine the impression left on this middle-class young man who had not been used to the style of living of the 'gentry': a hundred-foot-long gallery with columns and a floor of Kilkenny marble, with similarly magnificent rooms; this might have seemed a worthy setting for the two beautiful girls who listened to his poetry and his plans for the Irish Literary movement.

> The light of evening, Lissadell,
> Great windows open to the south. . . .
>
> (*CP*, p. 263)

A visit which he remembered over thirty years later when he wrote the elegy from which these lines are taken, after the storm-ridden and tragic lives of the two girls had ended. The house where they were brought up is now an 'image of such politics' – sadly decayed, with the surrounding woods decimated.

THE QUAYS, SLIGO   After sailing up the long, twisting estuary of the Garavogue, the moment of disembarking from their grand-father's steamship at the Quays, busy with boats, was a lifelong memory for the Yeats children. During the holidays, as Willie grew older, he would stroll along the quayside among the sailors and fishermen, sometimes hearing McCoy, a crazy ship's carpenter, as he read the Scriptures and denounced his neighbours from an old ship's boiler left on the Quay – very big, very high, the top far out of reach, and all red rust'. 'Why should not Old Men be Mad?' (*CP*, p. 388) may be using this memory as an exemplar of the inexorable whims of Fate. Yeats certainly remembered the ship's carpenter when he named his last prose work, *On the Boiler* (1938), which has a cover design, by Jack Yeats, of the bearded old man struggling to the top of the boiler to preach.

Despite his shyness, Jack as a boy mixed more with the people of the Quays than did Willie, and even on one occasion organized donkey races for the children of the sailors. In Jack's paintings the pilot with the peaked cap becomes a regular theme; in W.B. Yeats's writing the Quays epitomize the Pollexfen physical vitality and strength, which, combined with the literary and artistic gifts of the Yeatses, made the poet often think, as in 'Under Saturn' (*CP*, p. 202), of his childhood vow 'sworn in vain / Never to leave that valley his fathers called their home'.

DRUMCLIFFE   In the Drumcliffe valley, three and a half miles from Sligo, shadowed by Ben Bulben, Rector Yeats lived in the tall Rectory across the road from the plain Church (1809), whose square tower rises among the trees: the home of many of the poet's Anglo-Irish ancestors on both sides of the family, whom he sings of in 'Are you Content?'

> He that in Sligo at Drumcliff
> Set up the old stone Cross,
> That red-headed rector in County Down,
> A good man on a horse,
> Sandymount Corbets, that notable man
> Old William Pollexfen,
> The smuggler Middleton, Butlers far back,
> Half legendary men.
>
> (*CP*, p. 370)

The limestone precipices of Ben Bulben and King's Mountain form a dramatic back-drop, and, nearer, the Celtic Cross and the lower part of a Round Tower alone remain of Saint Columba's monastery.

The mythology of Ireland, Christian and pagan, is centred here. It was Yeats's wish to be buried near the Church, though the proud epitaph on his tombstone is unusually pagan. Here he would join his ancestors and the heroic figures of Irish legend.

No marble, no conventional phrase;
On limestone quarried near the spot
By his command these lines are cut:
> *Cast a cold eye*
> *On life, on death,*
> *Horseman, pass by!*

England

BEDFORD PARK, CHISWICK   From 1879–81 the Yeats family lived at 8 Woodstock Road, Bedford Park, the forerunner of all redbrick garden suburbs, then being built on the north side of the Hammersmith Road. Its consultant architect was Norman Shaw, and with its well-designed houses, pleasant winding roads and a green, lined by mature trees, it was certainly an improvement for the Yeatses on the London and Dublin terrace houses in which they had been living. Many of the inhabitants were artists and writers, and gradually Bedford Park became a self-contained residential unit, with its own cultural, religious and social activities: Chiswick School of Art, which Jack Yeats briefly attended, a new Church, and an inn with stores, as well as a club house in which plays could be performed. From the ages of nine and eight Willie and his sister Lily visited their father's friends and talked freely, with Irish accents and turns of phrase learnt from the old coachman and the stable-boy at the Pollexfens. Although they both longed to return to Sligo, the years at Bedford Park, except for the unpleasantness at school, were enjoyable.

Then J.B. Yeats led his family off to Dublin, where he tried to sell his pictures, with little success. In March 1888 he returned to live with his family at no. 3 Blenheim Road, a tall redbrick house with a large horse-chestnut tree shading the garden. The poet's mother was then suffering from the results of a stroke from which she never recovered (she died in 1900). For the period 1888–95 Yeats lived with his family; but then decided to have his own rooms in Woburn Buildings, Euston. Thanks largely to J.B. Yeats's temperament and fortunes, they had been a rootless family, except, of course, for Sligo, so Bedford Park provided a more stable existence for them. In this house Yeats met Madame Blavatsky (the founder of the Theosophical Society), MacGregor Mathers (the magician), Maud Gonne and Florence Farr. (Yeats saw Florence Farr playing the lead in May

3 Blenheim Road, Bedford Park.

1890 in a performance of *A Sicilian Idyll* at the Club House, the play being written by an Irish college friend of his father's, Dr Todhunter, who was a neighbour in Bedford Park.) But Yeats was away for long periods; in Sligo, Dublin, Paris and Coole Park; and also he was out of sympathy with many of his father's friends who, on the whole, were naturalistic as painters and realist as writers. His interest in Blake and the symbolists had moved him away from their positivist and rationalist outlook, and he found he had nothing in common with them.

> Then, too, they were very ignorant men; they read nothing, for nothing mattered but 'knowing how to paint', being in reaction against a generation that seemed to have wasted its time upon so many things. I thought myself alone in hating these young men, their contempt for the past, their monopoly of the future, but in a few months I was to discover others of my own age who thought as I did.

Thus does Yeats sum up in *AU* the painters from the Paris art schools who were the younger friends of his father. The older men whom the poet met at Bedford Park were equally limited: York Powell, Oxford Professor of History, who 'cared nothing for philosophy, nothing for economics, nothing for the policy of nations', or the painter with the model railway running round his studio or the decorative artist who had placed a great lychgate, bought from some churchyard, at the entrance of his garden. G.K. Chesterton's ridicule of 'Saffron Park', as he called it in *The Man who was Thursday* (1908), stemmed from inside knowledge, as he was married there – a ceremony all the Yeatses attended.

However, there was what the Danish architect Rasmussen calls 'a stamp of unity' about this garden suburb, and maybe as a boy Yeats benefited from an environment in which there were Morris wallpapers and de Morgan tiles. But he had outgrown it by their second stay.

18 WOBURN BUILDINGS (NOW 5 WOBURN WALK), LONDON WC1
From 1896 to 1919 Yeats occupied this terraced house near St Pancras Church, on the north side of what might now be called a 'pedestrian precinct', then a stone-flagged alley. The houses were built in the early nineteenth century, and the area had evidently come down in the world. In fact, according to Hone,[8] Yeats was known as 'the toff wot lives in the Buildings', as he was said to be the only person in the street who ever received letters. It was convenient for him as it was near the British Museum, where he was reading, and many of his friends lived nearby. Ezra Pound sometimes attended Yeats's Monday evenings, when he was at home to his

179

friends (8 p.m. until 2 a.m. or later). According to Douglas Goldring,[9] the young Pound used to dominate the room as he took it upon himself to distribute Yeats's cigarettes and Chianti, laying down the law about poetry as he did it. John Masefield, also young, but gentler mannered, describes the house in *Some Memories of W.B. Yeats*:

> On entering the house, you went along the hall to the stair, which led inwards, then curved, and brought you to the landing on which he lived. On this, the second floor, he had a biggish front sitting-room and a small back kitchen. On the floor above, he had corresponding rooms, in which he slept.
>
> His sitting-room was papered with brown paper; the window was hung with dark curtains; brown baize at one time; later a dim blue.[10]

Masefield goes on to list the pictures: a large portrait of the poet painted by his father; 'Memory Harbour' (Sligo) by Jack Yeats; Blake's first Dante engraving, 'The Whirlwind of Lovers'; some more Blake engravings, including 'The Ancient of Days'; two of the poet's own pastels of the lake and hills at Coole; and a Beardsley poster for Florence Farr's production of *The Land of Heart's Desire*. He continues:

> The table stood in the centre of the room during meals, and was then lifted to the side. At meal-times it bore upon it a little curved metal gong or striker of an unusual design (with some scarlet colour on it), which he struck to summon Mrs Old [she and her husband, a carpenter, were Yeats's landlords who looked after and 'did' for him.] After meals, the table bore dark glasses, brown or green, and a dull red-clay tobacco-jar (with an oriental dragon embossed on it), containing cigarettes. The chairs were dark, the effect of the room was sombre. After 1904–5, he added to the room a big, dark blue lectern, on which his Kelmscott Chaucer stood, between enormous candles in big blue wooden sconces. These candles stood about four feet and were as thick as a ship's oar. The dim dark blue of this lectern was the most noticeable colour in the room. He added curtains to match it.
>
> This sitting room has been described in detail because it was the most interesting room in London.[11]

After Yeats's marriage, Mrs Yeats got going on the room and obviously refurnished it in the then current taste. Swept away were the dark and sombre objects and Pre-Raphaelite blues, to be replaced by the later Voysey influence of unstained wood and earthenware bowls. In a letter to Lady Gregory, written in November 1917, Yeats describes the transformation:

I wish you could see Woburn Buildings now – nothing changed in plan but little touches here and there, and in my bedroom (the old Bathroom) with furniture of unpainted, unpolished wood such as for years I have wished for. Then there is a dinner service of great purple plates for meat, and various earthenware bowls for other purposes.

After twenty-four years Woburn Buildings was given up when the Yeatses decided to live in the summer at Thoor Ballylee. There is no doubt of the importance of this house set, as it was, in the middle of all those other influences brought in by his friends in London.

NOS 45 AND 4 BROAD STREET, OXFORD   Although both these houses were pleasant examples of late seventeenth-century town architecture, they have been demolished since the Yeatses lived in them; the first for the New Bodleian Library building, the second for a department store.

Yeats first stayed in Oxford in 1888 with his father's friend, Professor York Powell. He read in the Bodleian Library, walked much in the unspoiled Oxford countryside, and wrote to Katharine Tynan: 'One understands English poetry more from seeing a place like this. I wonder anybody does anything in Oxford but dream and remember the place is so beautiful.'

In early 1918 when Woburn Buildings had been let, Mrs Yeats found rooms in No. 45 Broad Street just over the road from the Bodleian. In October 1919 the Yeatses rented No. 4 at the other end of the street near the Cornmarket corner. It was a quieter city then, so Yeats would have had no difficulty in hearing Great Tom of Christ Church tolling the curfew on All Souls Night, when he was to remember those friends of his from the time of his first Oxford visit – Horton, Florence Farr and MacGregor Mathers, all dead by 1919.

After an extended lecture tour in the United States, in 1920, they again settled at No. 4, from where, in 1921, he wrote some of 'Meditations in Time of Civil War' (*CP*, p. 225). He used to visit Garsington Manor, Lady Ottoline Morrell's house near Oxford, the gardens of which are still much the same, though the vast industrial complex of Cowley has crept up over a lane along which Yeats and his friends used to walk back to Oxford. In the garden by the house the 'indifferent garden deities' on the terraces still stare down in stony silence, but the tiny fountain pouring from a carved stone shell into a small basin, by which Yeats must have sat, has ceased to run.

At No. 4 Yeats held his 'Monday evenings' for undergraduates and friends. After attending these, L.A.G. Strong would return to the Dragon School in North Oxford, where he was then teaching, 'exhilarated, walking on air, upheld and inspired by the knowledge, which rapidly became incredible during the week, that life could be lived on such a plane of thought and at such a pitch'.

During the winter of 1920–21, while the Black and Tans were carrying out their murderous campaign in Ireland, Yeats addressed the Oxford Union denouncing the Government's policy. He held an audience of undergraduates spellbound as he paced up and down the aisle of the Union debating hall, and for many it was an occasion they would never forget.

After a brief stay in a small rented house called Minchen's Cottage, on the main road at Shillingford, Oxfordshire, and a few months in the summer of 1921 at Thame, also in Oxfordshire, (where his son Michael was born), Yeats decided it was time to return to Ireland, and bought the house in Merrion Square. He had enjoyed his time in Oxford, especially the visits of his friends, including, among many others, Maurice Bowra, Robert Bridges and John Masefield (who lived nearby on Boar's Hill). He was not to return until May 1931 when he received a Doctorate of Letters from the University. This was his last visit to the city.

STONE COTTAGE, COLEMAN'S HATCH, HARTFIELD, SUSSEX   Pleasantly situated on a private road, Stone Cottage still overlooks a typically unspoilt heath valley in East Sussex. Now slightly enlarged since Yeats's time, nevertheless it is sturdily built of dressed stone, quarried on the spot in about 1820. When Yeats was staying nearby in 1913 with his friends the Tuckers (whose daughter married Ezra Pound), he found Stone Cottage and settled there with Pound in the autumn of that year. It was quiet and not too inaccessible – about an hour to London. There he prepared his American lecture tour, wrote and read much. He spent the winters of 1913, 1914 and 1915 there, during which time Lady Gregory sometimes came down at the weekends, bringing with her intelligent and attractive women whom she thought might be suitable for Yeats. Eventually she arrived with Miss Georgie Hyde-Lees, whom Yeats had met previously with the Tuckers. Ezra Pound was the best man at their wedding at the Register Office in Harrow Road, London, on 20 October 1917, and some days of the honeymoon were spent in Stone Cottage.

PENNS-IN-THE-ROCKS, WITHYHAM, SUSSEX   This was the home of Lady Gerald Wellesley (Dorothy Wellesley, the poet). It is an elegant, part-Georgian house of rose-red brick, set in a large garden with rocky sandstone outcrops, a lake and a small classical garden temple, much admired by Yeats. He stayed at Penns in April and May 1937 for about a week at a time, and for similar periods in March and April 1938, his last visit being in July of that year. It provided him with an aristocratic cultured setting similar to that of Coole Park; and, like Lady Gregory, Dorothy Wellesley invited mutual friends over to meet him to discuss his schemes for words and music. He once wrote to her in a thank-you letter that he 'found great peace and contentment' among beautiful things and in her company.

During his last years he was physically weak though mentally active. Dorothy Wellesley relates how they used to walk together in the old walled garden, accompanied by her Great Dane, Brutus. In 'To Dorothy Wellesley' (*Last Poems*), Brutus receives an honourable mention:

> Climb to your chamber full of books and wait,
> No book upon the knee, and no one there
> But a Great Dane that cannot bay the moon
> And now lies sunk in sleep.

(*CP*, p. 349)

Although Yeats was not especially fond of dogs, he had observed, according to Dorothy Wellesley, Brutus's 'great majesty, form and conduct' (*see Letters on Poetry from W.B. Yeats to Dorothy Wellesley*[12]):

> When Yeats seemed too tired to reach a garden seat, the three of us would walk abreast, Yeats's hand and part of his great weight supported on my right shoulder, while my left hand and shoulder was supported by the great dog. I was always afraid of a landslide, but the great hound pacing slowly beside me never let me down. The seat was reached, the end achieved, and the tremendous Dane would settle down and turn into a piece of black and white marble until, our conversation ended, he would help us back again to the house.

It was Sir William Rothenstein, RA who had originally introduced Yeats to Dorothy Wellesley, and in his autobiography, *Since Fifty*, he describes the physical appearance of the young and the old poet at Penns-in-the-Rocks: 'Dorothy, slight, fair, with deep violet eyes and auburn hair ... next to Yeats, dressed in crimson shirt, flowing coloured tie, now in his later years, brown-skinned under his crown of white hair, his dark eyes aslant, broad-shouldered and ample of form – he once so pale and lanky'.[13]

Italy

URBINO   In April 1907 Yeats joined Lady Gregory and Robert at Venice, after which they visited Florence, Milan (which he disliked), Urbino, Ferrara, and Ravenna. At Urbino he saw the great ducal palace, described by Castiglione in *The Book of the Courtier* (1528). He and Lady Gregory had read this in Thomas Hoby's translation before they went to Italy on this trip. In 'The People' Yeats describes the setting briefly:

> ... the steep street of Urbino
> To where the Duchess and her people talked
> The stately midnight through until they stood
> In their great window looking at the dawn ...
>
> (*CP*, p. 169)

Here, at the end of the fifteenth century, Duke Federico da Montefeltro had had the fortress redesigned as a palace, 'a city within a city', in 'proud, golden Urbino' as Dante described it. From the courtyard a monumental staircase ascends to the living-rooms. It was there that the Duke founded his schools of Art and Poetry, Mathematics and Humanism; the library, in its day, being more complete than that of Florence or Oxford University. In this vast, but beautifully proportioned building, dominating Urbino, flourished a vigorous intellectual life, led by Duke Federico, an honest *condottiere*, compassionate in war, a patron of the arts, well-read in the classics, educated in music, poetry, grammar, mathematics and painting; he was skilled in dancing and riding, possessing an international reputation as a fine ruler of a flourishing duchy.

In *The Courtier*, Castiglione gives a detailed and personal account, in four sections, of discussions which took place in the palace on four evenings in March 1507, presided over by the Duchess Elizabetta who was married to Guidobaldo, Federico's son. The subjects discussed cover a wide field – the responsibilities of rulers, the nature of love, the Wheel of Fortune, women's liberation, and the moral and aesthetic standards fitting to a gentleman. Some of the thirty characters who take part in the arguments show such individual traits that one feels one gets to know them by the ideas they express and the way they speak. It is therefore a surprise when, at the beginning of the fourth section, Castiglione suddenly says they are now all dead. Yeats was much moved by this. In his *Diary*, kept in 1909, he wrote:

> All Wednesday I heard Castiglione's phrase ringing in my memory, 'Never be it spoken without tears, the Duchess, too, is dead', and that phrase, which – coming where it did among the numbering of his dead – often moved me till my eyes dimmed, brought before me all his sorrow and my own, as though one saw the worth of life fade for ever.
>
> (*AU*, p. 478)

The way of life at Urbino in Duke Federico's time stood for Yeats as the keystone in a Unity of Being in which *cortesia* found its full realization. It engendered the virtues of the Renaissance idealized figure: a mixture of good scholar, soldier, classical hero, Christian believer, having a virtuous mind, a dignity, a mannered elegance and virtue in the service of his prince. And Yeats was not slow to compare this with the politicians and rich men of his contemporary Ireland. In 'To a Wealthy Man who promised a second Subscription . . .' he compares the Renaissance rulers who supported the arts with a Dublin art patron who refused to give more money for Sir Hugh Lane's new picture gallery. Duke Guidobaldo da Montefeltro is referred to

> when he made
> That grammar school of courtesies
> Where wit and beauty learned their trade
> Upon Urbino's windy hill,
>
> (*CP*, p. 119)

It was not surprising that Yeats never forgot this palace at Urbino, or his admiration for the best qualities of Renaissance rulers.

RAVENNA, SICILY AND ROME   During this visit in 1907 Yeats also visited Ravenna where he saw the superb sixth-century Byzantine mosaics. But, according to D.J. Gordon and Ian Fletcher,[14] the visit did not 'appear to have left a decisive impression on his work: his interest was concentrated on Italian painting, particularly of the Renaissance'. However, Jon Stallworthy[15] thinks that Yeats's visit to Ravenna in 1907 was the main source of his interest which culminated in the Byzantium poems. Both 1907 and 1925, when he saw more Byzantine mosaics, are important.

From December to March 1924–25 the Yeatses visited Sicily and Rome on a prolonged holiday, during which he finished *VIS*. On this holiday he examined Byzantine mosaics in Sicily and in early Christian churches in Rome, taking photographs home with him. For many years he had been reading about Byzantine art, but it must have been during these visits that he finally decided to use Byzantium as the symbol for the state in which the soul is transfigured 'out of nature'. Byzantine mosaics, from the sixth to the eleventh century, were often placed in cross-in-square churches with a central cupola or dome, and they pictured the Kosmos (paradise) at the highest point of the Church, descending to the terrestrial world at ground level. One might see in the dome a huge image of God the Father (Pantocrator) looking down on further images placed in descending order; first on Christ, the image of God, then on the saints and martyrs, then on the animal and vegetable world.

Mosaic at its best is on curved and vaulted surfaces, especially in the upper parts of a Church – flat surfaces do not reflect light as much, appearing duller. But on the curvature of domes, on the opposite sides of niches and angles, or when encased in cupolas, pendentives and vaults, the cubes of gold mosaic glitter, and the enamel sparkles. The golden ground which entirely surrounds the figures, has an aura of sanctity in this setting of brilliant reflections, and such golden grounds are common in all the great Byzantine mosaics.

> O sages standing in God's holy fire
> As in the gold mosaic of a wall,

In 'Sailing to Byzantium' (*CP*, pp. 217–18), the word 'holy' is repeated three times, twice in association with 'fire', and it is worth noting that, in the process of making the gold and enamel cubes, fire is used to purify the colour. When mosaic figures of saints are placed in a dome or cupola, as in the two Baptisteries at Ravenna, they stand frontally, as it were like spokes in a great wheel, and as one looks up at them from beneath, they appear to whirl in their circular and rhythmic relation to the other mosaics in the Church. The dome comes to possess a magical dance-like rhythm as one moves one's head up or walks forward to view the figures. Similarly, in certain mosaics in the cathedral at Monreale, Sicily, which Mrs Yeats told Jon Stallworthy had much affected Yeats, the perspective seems to be upset by the curves and angles of the tympanum, and this gives the same gyring effect, including the beholder in the movement.

Yeats also saw the Norman twelfth-century palace of La Ziza, Palermo, which has a remnant of a secular mosaic showing oriental influences, such as peacocks (emblems of immortality), in stylized trees with tendril branches, fantastic animals and archers, like a Persian tapestry. This has no parallel with religious mosaics, but its iconography may well have interested Yeats.

Finally, Professor Gordon and Dr Fletcher[16] note that the ninth-century Church of S. Prassede in Rome has 'striking counterparts of the sages in their golden fire'. This refers to the mosaics on the raised tribune (platform) in this Church. Over the grand arch, separating nave from choir, is a mosaic of the New Jerusalem of the Apocalypse; within the tribune, Christ is displayed in golden classical robes, and the saints and martyrs amidst trees of paradise, together with the twenty-four elders and the symbols of the Evangelists, all under a vaulted blue heaven. The Yeatses certainly visited this Church, and also the basilica of S. Clemente, where the vault of the tribune is covered by a twelfth-century mosaic of a great cross reaching from heaven to earth, springing from a stylized vine, together with Christ and the saints, alongside the rivers of paradise and trees with birds in the foliage. 'The hammered gold and gold enamelling', 'the sages standing in God's holy fire', the marbles on the dancing-floor (the pavement of the raised tribune) and the golden bird, 'planted on the star-lit golden bough', in the mosaics are all present in these churches.

Majorca

PALMA, MAJORCA   In December 1935, to 'escape telephones and foul weather', Yeats went by sea to Palma, accompanied by the Indian swami, Shri Purohit, whom he had met the previous year, and with whom he proposed to collaborate on a translation of the Upanishads. Purohit was a mendicant Brahmin monk, aged about fifty, a scholar and a Yogi, who for nine years had been wandering with his begging-bowl. His grandfather had been a Marátha millionaire, but Shri Purohit had renounced all worldly goods and become a Brahmin priest. Yeats had written an introduction to his autobiography, *An Indian Monk: his life and adventures* (1932).[17] In 1935, when they arrived at Palma, Yeats was suffering from the rigours of a very rough sea voyage, and Purohit from the austerities of his religious life.

For about forty years Yeats had heard AE constantly quoting from the Upanishads, using an awful translation, as Yeats says, with 'latinized words, polyglot phrases, sedentary distortions of an unnatural English', including 'muddles muddied by "Lo! Verily" and "Forsooth"', which, said Yeats, 'could not represent what grass farmers sang thousands of years ago, what their descendants sing today'. Upanishad is doctrine or wisdom of the holy books, the Vedas, sung at the feet of a holy man or Master present or in the spirit. Shri Purohit used to sing an Upanishad every morning in Sanskrit, and Yeats quickly sensed its beauty even from Purohit's translation and so collaborated with him to produce *The Ten Principal Upanishads*, published in 1937. In a letter to Dorothy Wellesley he describes their progress:

> I am delighted with my life here. I breakfast at 7.30 and write in bed until 11 or 11.30. From 3 to 4 I help Purohit Swami to translate the Upanishads. It is amusing to see his delighted astonishment when he discovers that he can call a goddess, 'this handsome girl' or even 'a pretty girl' instead of a 'maiden of surpassing loveliness'. I say to him 'think like a wise man but express yourself like the common people' and the result is that he will make the first great translation of the *Upanishads*. He takes great care of me and always walks slowly up and downstairs in front of me, very wide and impassable in his orange robe, for fear I may walk too fast for my heart.

Yeats is here being modest. It is in fact *his* translation which is the first great translation of the *Upanishads*. Whether it accurately translates the Sanskrit I do not know, but it has a simplicity and purity of diction which is similar to Eliot's in *Four Quartets* when he has similar philosophic themes to express. The Kena-Upanishad 2, is one of the shortest but shows these qualities fully:

'If you think that you know much, you know little.
If you think that you know It from study of your own mind
    or of nature, study again'.
The enquirer said: 'I do not think that I know much, I
    neither say that I know, nor say that I do not.'
The teacher answered: 'The man who claims that he knows,
        knows nothing;
but he who claims nothing, knows. The ignorant think
    that spirit lies within knowledge, the wise man
    knows It beyond knowledge.
Spirit is known through revelation. It leads to freedom.
    It leads to power.
Revelation is the conquest of death.

The living man who finds Spirit, finds Truth. But if he fail, he sinks among foul shapes. The man who can see the same Spirit in every creature, clings neither to this nor that, attains immortal life'.

These translations of the Upanishads, in superb poetic prose, have been much neglected by Yeats scholars, and, like his translation of Sophocles's *Oedipus Rex*, have not received true recognition.

During his work with the swami, Yeats's physical condition grew worse, and Mrs Yeats went out to Palma in February 1936. She found him better, but thought it would be a long convalescence, as he was suffering from nephritis, the kidney complaint from which he eventually died. He bore it with courage and humour, although it involved discomfort. Gradually his condition improved and he and the swami finished the translation, after which the swami returned to India and the Yeatses to England.

Sweden

STOCKHOLM   In his essay 'The Bounty of Sweden' (*AU*, p. 531), Yeats describes in great detail his visit to Sweden to receive the Nobel Award for Literature in 1923. The presentation ceremony took place in the Hall of the Swedish Academy on 10 December, and the dignity of the occasion, especially of 'the old King, intelligent and friendly like some country gentleman who can quote Horace and Catullus', much impressed Yeats. The whole setting reminded him of Castiglione's description of the Court of Urbino; and even the French Renaissance architectural detail of the huge eighteenth-century Royal Palace made him think of the Ulster Bank in Sligo, which he had not seen for many years, showing what an astonishing visual memory he had. He regrets that such architectural details – in this case, it was semi-circular headed windows flanked by classic pilasters – should have since been used 'for all sorts of purposes, as if they had come out of a child's box of wooden bricks'. It certainly is a decline from the Royal Palace to the small two-storeyed bank on the street corner at Sligo. Before Yeats returned, he delivered a lecture on 'The Irish Theatre', at the Swedish Royal Academy, and saw a performance of *Cathleen ni Houlihan*.

United States and Canada

Yeats embarked upon five lecture tours in the United States. The first was during 1903–04, for three months in the winter. Yeats gave thirty lectures to universities, colleges and Irish societies, and earned about $3,200; so he was able to repay Lady Gregory what he owed her. During the tour he received a cable from Maud Gonne telling him of her marriage. The second tour took place in 1911, with the Abbey Theatre company; but after the first performance at Boston, Mass., Yeats left for home, leaving Lady Gregory to manage the tour. The third tour was in February and March 1914, and the fourth in 1920 (January-May). On this occasion Yeats took his wife with him, and he met his father for the last time, in New York. While in Portland, Oregon, he was presented by Junzo Sato with his samurai's sword (see p. 152). For the last tour, which took place from October 1932 to the following January, Yeats was not accompanied by his wife, but took a friend to act as secretary and nurse. When in New York he stayed at the luxury Waldorf-Astoria hotel. He was able to make enough money to pay for improvements at Riversdale, and to endow an Irish Academy of Letters.

The strain of lecturing on tour in the United States has damaged the health of many a stronger man than Yeats, but he seems to have survived the rigours very well. He addressed audiences ranging in numbers from twenty to 2,000, and was always a cool, systematic and professional performer who was able to adapt his style appropriately. He travelled by train from the East Coast to California, and from the Gulf to Canada, lecturing in the first two tours mostly on the Irish Literary Renaissance, but later, after Synge's *Playboy of the Western World*, performed by the Abbey Players, had enraged Irish-American audiences, he read his poems and talked about them (see Henn, *The Lonely Tower*),[18] as well as showing slides illustrating Blake's *Book of Job*, and Calvert's and Palmer's etchings, including, of course, 'The Lonely Tower'. He was a great success, and John Quinn thought after one of the earlier tours that 'no Irishman since the time of Parnell's great trip' had made so 'grand an impression'. Hone describes his public speaking:

He had the lower lip which reveals the born orator and the born pugilist; a certain disdain, a certain pugnacity, is necessary both to the pugilist and the orator. In addressing large audiences he was sometimes uneasy at the start, and would stride up and down the platform in a rather surprising manner before he attained to his natural distinction of bearing, his gravity of utterance and his rhythm. His voice was musical, touched with melancholy, the tones rising and falling in a continuous flow of sound. He lingered on certain words to avoid as it were a hiatus, but the pauses when they occurred were timed and still full of sound, like the musical pauses in the execution of a master. This cadenced utterance was most characteristic. When emphasis was needed he would introduce a hard metallic note, and this when passion intruded was like the clash of sword-blades. His myopic gaze as he spoke was turned within, looking into the darkness, where, as he himself said, 'there is always something'.[19]

The only overt reference to a memory from these tours is in 'His Phoenix' (*CP*, p. 170), a poem written some years later. Here, among a list of attractive and beautiful women, he remembers a certain Miss Marlowe, an actress whom he had seen as Juliet. But she, with all the others, is not equal to the proud, lonely Maud Gonne.

I knew a phoenix in my youth, so let them have their day.

France

PARIS   Compared with T.S. Eliot, who spoke French fluently, Yeats was little influenced by visits to Paris and meeting French writers. He went in 1894, 1895, 1896 and 1899, usually to see Maud Gonne or MacGregor Mathers. The meeting with Synge was by chance. In 1894 he was taken by Arthur Symons to see Verlaine, who died in January 1896, and was then considered *the* poet of the day (fortunately, he spoke English). But it seems that he never went to the *mardis* of Stephane Mallarmé in the rue de Rome, though he heard all about them from Symons, and later copied the idea at Woburn Buildings. On his final visit in 1921 he was the delegate to Sinn Féin at the Irish Race Congress.

NORMANDY   Yeats often visited Maud Gonne MacBride, her adopted daughter Iseult, and her son, Seán, at her house at Coleville, near Calvados in the summers of 1910, 1912, 1916, and 1917. It was on the beach there that he read her 'Easter 1916'.

CAP MARTIN AND ROQUEBRUNE, ALPES-MARITIME   Yeats and his wife spent January–March 1938 (when he was recuperating from his illness) at the Carlton Hotel on the sea-front at Menton, in the south of France. Then, after moving round in Ireland and England in the spring, summer and autumn of 1938, they again went to the French Riviera in late November 1938, to the small Hôtel Idéal Séjour above Cap Martin, two kilometres from Menton, amid pine trees and olive groves, very different from the cosmopolitanism of Menton. He was mentally active right up to his death, writing some of his *Last Poems*, correcting proofs of *The Death of Cuchulain*, and corresponding with friends. He died on Saturday 28 January 1939 and was buried in the cemetery of the Chapel of St Pancrace at Roquebrune, a small town clinging to a terraced and rocky hillside, overlooking the sea and Cap Martin. Not until 1948 was his body brought home to Drumcliffe.

Notes

1. Joseph Hone, *W.B. Yeats: 1865–1939* (London: Macmillan, 1942; 2nd edn 1965, repr. 1989).
2. V.S. Pritchett, *Midnight Oil*, vol. 2 (London: Chatto and Windus, 1971).
3. Virginia Moore, *The Unicorn: William Butler Yeats's Search for Reality* (New York: Macmillan, 1954), p. 282.
4. Lady Gregory, *Gods and Fighting Men* (repr. Gerrards Cross: Colin Smythe, 1970).
5. Stephen Spender, *The Destructive Element* (London: Cape, 1935), p. 117.
6. Louis MacNeice, *The Poetry of W.B. Yeats* (Oxford: OUP, 1941).
7. John Masefield, *Some Memories of W.B. Yeats* (Dublin: Cuala Press, 1940).
8. Hone, op. cit.
9. Douglas Goldring, *South Lodge: Reminiscences of Violet Hunt, Ford Madox Ford and the 'English Review' Circle* (London: Constable, 1943), p. 49.
10. Masefield, op. cit.
11. Ibid.
12. Kathleen Raine (ed.), *Letters on Poetry from W.B. Yeats to Dorothy Wellesley* (Oxford: OUP, 1940; reissued 1964).
13. Sir William Rothenstein, *Since Fifty. Men and Memories, 1922–28* (London: Faber and Faber, 1939), p. 349.
14. D.J. Gordon and Ian Fletcher, *Images of a Poet, Exhibition Catalogue* (Manchester: 1961), p. 820.
15. Jon Stallworthy, *Between the Lines* (Oxford: OUP, 1963).
16. Gordon and Fletcher, op. cit., p. 83.
17. Shri Purohit Swami, *An Indian Monk: His Life and Adventures* (London: Macmillan, 1932); see *E&I*, pp. 426–37 and 449–85.
18. T.R. Henn, *The Lonely Tower: Studies in the Poetry of W.B. Yeats* (London: Methuen, 1950; 2nd edn 1965).
19. Hone, op. cit., pp. 201–2.

Places referred to either directly or by inference in the poems

PLACE	POEM
The Glen at Alt. Co. Sligo	The Man and the Echo
Ballinaford, Co. Sligo	The Ballad of Father O'Hart
Ballisodare, Co. Sligo	Down by the Salley Gardens
Ballygawley, Co. Sligo	Red Hanrahan's Curse
Beltra Strand, Co. Sligo	The Valley of the Black Pig
Ben Bulben, Co. Sligo	Towards Break of Day
	Under Ben Bulben
	The Mountain Tomb
	The Tower, I
	Alternative Song for the Severed Head
Carrowmore, Co. Sligo	The Wanderings of Oisin
Castle Dargan, Co. Sligo	Red Hanrahan's Curse
Cumeen (Cummen) Strand, Co. Sligo	Red Hanrahan's Song about Ireland
Cloone, Co. Kilkenny	The Tower, II
Cashel, Co. Tipperary	The Grey Rock
	The Double Vision of Michael Robartes
Collooney, Co. Sligo	The Ballad of Father O'Hart
Cloyne, Co. Cork	The Seven Sages
Coole Park, Co. Galway	In the Seven Woods
	Upon a House shaken by the Land Agitation
	The Wild Swans at Coole
	Shepherd and Goatherd
	To a Squirrel at Kyle-na-No
	A Prayer for my Daughter
	The New Faces
	Coole Park, 1929
	Coole Park and Ballylee
	The Man and the Echo
	Beautiful Lofty Things
Croagh Patrick, Co. Mayo	The Dancer at Cruachan and Cro-Patrick

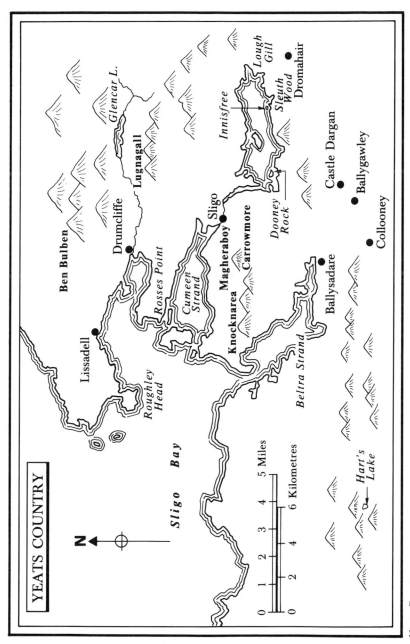

Yeats Country.

PLACE	POEM
Croghan (Cruachan), Co. Roscommon	The Hour before Dawn
	Tom at Cruachan
	The Old Age of Queen Maeve
Dooney Rock, Lough Gill, Co. Sligo	The Fiddler of Dooney
Dromahair, Co. Sligo	The Man who dreamed of Faeryland
Drumcliffe, Co. Sligo	Are you Content?
	Under Ben Bulben
Dublin, The Abbey Theatre	Beautiful Lofty Things
Dublin, the General Post Office	Three Songs to the One Burden, III
	The Statues
Dublin, Glasnevin Cemetery	To a Shade
	Parnell's Funeral
Dublin, Kilmainham Gaol	On a Political Prisoner
Dublin, St Patrick's Cathedral	The Seven Sages
	Swift's Epitaph
Dublin, various streets	The Three Monuments
	In the Seven Woods
	Easter, 1916
	The O'Rahilly
Ferrara, Emilia-Romagna, Italy	The People
Glencar, Co. Sligo	The Stolen Child
Glendalough, Co. Wicklow	Stream and Sun at Glendalough
	Under the Round Tower
Gort, Co. Galway	The Three Beggars
Hart's Lake, Co. Sligo	The Host of the Air
Howth, Co. Dublin	Beautiful Lofty Things
Innisfree, Co. Sligo	The Lake Isle of Innisfree
Kiltartan, Gort, Co. Galway	An Irish Airman foresees his Death
Kilvarnet, Co. Sligo	The Fiddler of Dooney
Knocknarea, Co. Sligo	Alternative Song for the Severed Head
	The Hosting of the Sidhe
	The Valley of the Black Pig
	The Wanderings of Oisin
	The Ballad of Father O'Hart
	Red Hanrahan's Song about Ireland
	The Black Tower
Kinsale, Co. Cork	The Ballad of Moll Magee
Knocknashee, Co. Sligo	The Ballad of Father O'Hart

PLACE	POEM
Lissadell, Co. Sligo	The Man who dreamed of Faeryland
	In Memory of Eva Gore-Booth and Con Markiewicz
	Easter, 1916
Lough Derg, Co. Clare	The Pilgrim
London	Vacillation IV
Lugnagall, Co. Sligo	The Man who dreamed of Faeryland
Moira, Co. Down	Are you Content?
Oxford, Christ Church	All Souls' Night
Oxford, Garsington Manor	Meditations in Time of Civil War I, Ancestral Houses
Penns-in-the-Rocks, Withyham, Sussex	To Dorothy Wellesley
Magheraboy (Mocharabuiee), Co. Sligo	The Fiddler of Dooney
Roughley Head, Co. Sligo	Tom O'Roughley
Ravenna	Long-legged Fly
Rome	Under Ben Bulben, IV
Rosses Point, Co. Sligo	At Algeciras – a Meditation upon Death
Sleuth Woods (Slish Woods)	The Stolen Child
	Three Songs to the One Burden
	The Black Tower
Slievenarnan (Slievenamon), Co. Tipperary	The Grey Rock
Sligo	Under Saturn
	Are you content?
	In Memory of Alfred Pollexfen
	The Meditation of the Old Fisherman
Tara, Co. Meath	The Two Kings
	Tara's Halls
Thoor Ballylee, Co. Galway	The Tower
	In Memory of Robert Gregory
	A Prayer for my Daughter
	A Dialogue of Self and Soul
	Blood and the Moon
	To be carved on a Stone at Thoor Ballylee
	A Prayer on going into my House
	Meditations in Time of Civil War II, V, VI, VII

PLACE	POEM
Tiraragh, Co. Sligo	The Ballad of Father O'Hart
Urbino, The Marches, Italy	The People
	To a Wealthy Man . . .
Venice	To a Wealthy Man . . .

Yeats's spelling is often erratic. 'Magheraboy' above is an example of this.

Yeats's symbols: their origins, connections and attributes

SYMBOL	ORIGIN	CONNECTIONS	ATTRIBUTES
I			
Tower	Babylon	Aspiration to Heaven	Isolation
	Alexandria	Gyres (winding stair)	Security
	Ballylee	Norman Conquest	Night
	Milton	Crumbling roof	Scholar
	Shelley	Battlements	Warfare
	Samuel Palmer		
Troy	Homer	Leda	Cyclic periods
	Virgil	Destruction	Burning of a city
		Achilles	'femme fatale'
		Helen	
		Deirdre	
		Maud Gonne	
Annunciation	Myth	Leda	Origins of love and war
	Iconography	Logos	Cyclic reversals of civilization
	New Testament	Swan	
		Dove	Arrow
II			
Swan	Myth	Soul	'Free from all elements'
	Iconography	Purity	Woman–bird–spirit
	Irish folklore	Fidelity	
	Coole	Death-song	Subjective man
		Leda	
Falcon and Hawk	Egyptian and Irish folklore	Soul Guardian	Spirit
			Immortality
			Freedom
			Strength
			Nobility (heroic)
			Subjective man
			Ferocity

Reference Section

SYMBOL	ORIGIN	CONNECTIONS	ATTRIBUTES
Heron (*Herne, Crane*)	Iconography Myth Folklore Visual experience	Solitary fisher Metamorphosis Hunchback	Solitary man
Curlew	Experience	Loneliness Moorland Sea	'Crystalline cry' Souls in Company
Crow and Raven	Myth Folklore	Omens Blackness and death	Morrigu

III

Hare	Myth Folklore	Soul Metamorphosis	Hunter/Hunted Pursuit of female Pity Magic (of collarbone)
Cat	Myth Folklore Egyptology	Woman Moon	Grace Influence of moon Grimalkin Witchcraft Eyes
Dolphin	Myth Iconography	'Love-beast' Man's rescuer Arion Fidelity	Rescuer from sea Life Sex Joy Vitality
Serpent	Old Testament Myth Hindu Iconography		
Cherub	Iconography	Innocence	Man's return to innocence

IV

Phidias	Greek sculpture	Perfection of Greek art	Creator of perfect human form
Michelangelo	History Iconography	Last synthesis of Renaissance Ending of gyre	Creator of perfect human form
Locke	History	'Mechanized' mind with Newton	Mind bound to mechanic world

SYMBOL	ORIGIN	CONNECTIONS	ATTRIBUTES
V			
Fire	Arrow	Hound Dance	Sea voyage
Sword	Spear	Horn	Climbing of the hill
Forge	Cave Well Fountain	Deer Boar Bell	

Note: a list of this kind must be used with caution. Not every reference to a symbol will automatically call up all the connections and attributes. But the list does have its uses, as Yeats's symbols are both public e.g. *Troy* calls up Helen, and esoteric: the connection of Samuel Palmer and Milton has generated for Yeats the association of *Tower* with 'Scholar', which is not immediately obvious to the general reader. Yeats's private 'system' has also contributed the 'gyres', and his magical studies have produced some of the bird and animal symbols.

Having said all this, the table can be used to generate insight. One can see why the *dolphins* come in to 'Byzantium' and 'News for the Delphic Oracle' as symbols of positive life-affirming values. Similarly, the *swans* which appear in so many famous poems are never just white birds, but carry an immense weight of symbolic meaning. Yet the table shows that even the symbols with many associations are still limited to well-defined conceptual areas. *Herons*, whatever they suggest which might seem unusual, are never gregarious or jolly. A Yeats poem will often leap across the connections that the table tries to illustrate e.g. the association of the *falcon* with positive ideas is crucial to understanding the opening of 'The Second Coming'.

Common Irish (Gaelic) place names

Derivations

There are many variations in spelling: names are often given in the anglicized form by Yeats and by the Ordnance Survey.

Bal, balla, bally, baile	town, settlement, e.g. *Ballisodare*
beg(g) beag	small
ben, bin	peak, mountain, e.g. *Ben Bulben*
carrow	a district or quarter, e.g. *Carrowmore*
cashel, castle	fort or castle, e.g. *Cashel*
clon, cloon	meadow, e.g. *Clonmel*
cool(e)	back, e.g. *Coole*
croagy	a rick or rick-like hill, e.g. *Croagh Patrick*
croaghan, cruachan	diminutive of above
curragh, currach	a marsh, e.g. *Curraghmore*
drom, drum	a ridge, e.g. *Drumcliffe*
glan, glen, glin	a valley, e.g. *Glendalough*
inch, inis(h), ennis	island, e.g. *Inishmaan*
kil, cill	cell, church, e.g. *Kilcolman*
knock	hill, e.g. *Knocknarea*
lough, loch	lake, sea-inlet, e.g. *Lough Gill*
mor, more, mir	big, great
rath	ringfort, e.g. *Rathmines*
slieve, slew, sliabh	mountain, e.g. *Slieve-Da-Ein*
tibber, tipper	a well, e.g. *Tipperary*
tir	country, territory, e.g. *Tiraragh*
toor, tore, thoor	a milking enclosure, e.g. *Thoor ballylee*

Pronunciation

'C' is always hard. 'Ch' is guttural as in Scottish 'loch'. The spelling varies even in the best Irish authorities.

Aedh (anglicized Hugh)	Ay (as is 'day')
Almhuin	Alloon
Aoife	Ee-fa
Aughrim	Ochrim

Baile	Boi-la
Beltaine	Bal-tinna
Caoilte	Cweelta
Conchubar	Conn-ahar
Cruachan	Croc-han
Cuchulain	Cu-hóolin or Cú-hullin
Cumhal	Coo-al
Dáil Éireann	Dau-il-Ayrun
Danaan	Donnan or Dannan
Diarmid (anglicized Dermot)	Dee-armid
Emir	Aevir or Eemir
Eochan	Eohee
Eoghan	Owen
Fianna	Fee-anna
Guiare	Gorey
Knocknarea	Knock-na-ray
Maeve	May-va
Muirthemne	Muir-ev-na
Naoise	Nee-sha
Niamh	Nee-av
Oisín	Usheen
Ribh	Ree-v
Robartes	Ro-bart-ees
Samhain	Sou-in
Sinn Féin	Shinn Fayn
Sidhe	Shee
Usna	Ushna

Further reading

The poems

Throughout this book references have been given to *The Collected Poems of W.B. Yeats* (2nd edn, London; Macmillan, 1950); *CP* in the text. In spite of a number of problems connected with the text and the order of Yeats's three latest volumes, this is the last edition which was – to a large extent – overseen by Yeats himself, and may be taken as supplying 'the final text'. He was, as we have noticed, particularly concerned with revising the text of his poems and with the order in which the poems were placed within each volume. At the other extreme, as it were, *The Variorum Edition of the Poems of W.B. Yeats*, eds Peter Allt and Russell K. Alspach (New York, 1957 and London: Macmillan, 1966) supplies variant readings, and should be consulted in order to understand the changes which Yeats made in the text of his poems from time to time. Recently there have been several new editions, complete and selected, of the poems: the first volume of the new collected edition of Yeats's works is *W.B. Yeats: The Poems*, ed. Richard J. Finneran (London: Macmillan, 1984; new edn 1991), which includes a revised text of the *Collected Poems*, together with approximately 128 additional poems at the end; since these poems are mainly excerpted from the plays they are not by and large 'unknown'. Selections by A.N. Jeffares, *Poems of W.B. Yeats: A New Selection* (2nd edn; London: Macmillan, 1988) and Timothy Webb, *W.B. Yeats: Selected Poetry* (Harmondsworth: Penguin, 1991) are annotated and incorporate helpful additional material. A.N. Jeffares has also produced a useful companion volume to *Collected Poems* and the Finneran edition, because it incorporates the page numbers of both: this is *A New Commentary on the Poems of W.B. Yeats* (London: Macmillan, 1984). It should be emphasized that the ideal edition of Yeats is still a matter of controversy, and one should always think carefully about the text and the placing of poems under discussion.

Plays

These are available in a standard text – *The Collected Plays of W.B. Yeats* (London: Macmillan, 1952) and later editions – and, as in the case of the poems, a variorum edition – *The Variorum Edition of the Plays of W.B. Yeats*, ed. Russell K. Alspach with Catherine C. Alspach (London: Macmillan, 1965). A new edition of the plays by David R. Clark is in preparation.

Prose Works

Macmillan publish the standard editions of the following prose
works, most of which were originally issued in some form by Yeats
in his lifetime; many of them are now available in paperback:
Autobiographies (1988); *Essays and Introductions* (1961); *Memoirs*, ed.
Denis Donoghue (1988); *Mythologies* (1978); *The Secret Rose* (1988)
and *A Vision* (1988). There is a variorum edition of *The Secret Rose;
Stories by W.B. Yeats* (London: Macmillan, 1991). Minor prose
materials of a miscellaneous nature were made available in *Uncollected
Prose by W.B. Yeats*, 2 vols. ed. John Frayne and Colton Johnson
(London: Macmillan, 1970, 1975) and *Prefaces and Introductions*, ed.
William H. O'Donnell (London: Macmillan, 1989); further collec-
tions are to be issued. It should be noted that most of the standard
prose works are soon to be re-edited and published in the new
collected edition by Macmillan. There will also be texts available of
Yeats's autobiographical novels.

   A Vision (*VIS* throughout this book), which came out in two
versions in Yeats's lifetime, will also be reprinted in both texts in the
new collected edition. It was based upon Mrs Yeats's automatic
writings i.e. dictated to her by spirits, and various notebooks, and
these have now been 'unscrambled', and are available as *Yeats's
'Vision' Papers*, the first two volumes edited by Steve L. Adams,
Barbara J. Frieling and Sandra L. Sprayberry, and the third by
Robert Antony Martinich and Margaret Mills Harper (London:
Macmillan, 1991).

Life

Immediately after Yeats's death, a charming semi-official life, *W.B.
Yeats 1865–1939*, was written by his friend Joseph Hone, and first
published by Macmillan in 1942. It is full of information, though
the quotations – I suspect from memory – are sometimes inaccurate,
and the index incomplete. The book was enlarged in 1962 and a
reprint is now available from Macmillan. A later work, A.N. Jeffares,
W.B. Yeats: Man and Poet, 1949, reissued with corrections.
(London: Routledge & Kegan Paul, 1962), was very scholarly and
full, but perhaps overemphasized the influence of Maud Gonne on
the poet. Later Jeffares wrote *W.B. Yeats, A New Biography* (London:
Hutchinson, 1988). For all sorts of reasons a satisfactory 'factual' life
is not yet forthcoming though an 'official biographer' has been
appointed; but see below for Ellmann and other interpretative
critical biographies. It must be remembered that Yeats's autobiographical works are patchy, and very much a history of his imagination. A good deal of reliable and unreliable reminiscence is to be

found in memoirs of his contemporaries. A useful list of these may be found at the end of Catherine Fahy, *W.B. Yeats and his Circle* (Dublin: The National Library of Ireland, 1989); this is a record of an exhibition of the same title at the library and contains many photographs of Yeats and his associates.

Letters

To a certain extent letters provide a verifiable version of events; they do, however, still need extensive annotation to avoid misunderstanding. The poet's letters were originally edited by Allan Wade, *The Letters of W.B. Yeats* (London: Hart–Davis, 1954).

There is now (in progress) a full edition: *The Collected Letters of W.B. Yeats*, Vol. 1: 1865–95 John Kelly and Eric Domville, (Oxford: the Clarendon Press, 1986). At the time of writing the sequence has reached Vol. 3, 1901–04, (ed. John Kelly).

Also available is Yeats's correspondence with Maud Gonne, *The Gonne–Yeats Letters: 1893–1938*, eds Anna Macbride White and A. Norman Jeffares (London: Hutchinson 1992; Paperback Pimlico, 1992). The letters of Yeats's circle are also useful: e.g. John Butler Yeats, *Letters to his Son, W.B. Yeats, and others, 1869–1922* ed. Joseph Hone (London: Faber and Faber, 1944), and *Letters on Poetry from W.B. Yeats to Dorothy Wellesley*, reissued with an introduction by Kathleen Raine (Oxford: OUP, 1964).

Bibliography

Allan Wade's *A Bibliography of the Writings of W.B. Yeats* (1951), was revised by Russell K. Alspach (London: Hart–Davis, 1968). A list of critical writings down to 1978 is provided in K.P.S. Jochum, *W.B. Yeats: A Classified Bibliography of Criticism* (Ill.: University of Champaign–Urbana, 1978).

Interpretation and Criticism

For contemporary reviews of Yeats's work as it appeared, see *W.B. Yeats: The Critical Heritage* ed. A. Norman Jeffares (London, Henley and Boston: Routledge and Kegan Paul, 1977). This takes us down to 1940. Since that time work on Yeats has generally been focused on interpretation: (a) trying to make sense of the poet's life and works generally; and (b) detailed studies of particular works. These productions are abundant, and tend to assume that the object of their attention is worth studying in the first place. There is, in my opinion, a dearth of genuine criticism, and those who have produced hostile critical accounts, e.g. Yvor Winters, *The Poetry of W.B. Yeats* (1960), are laughed out of court by the devotees. Winters contrived to choose some of Yeats's most memorable phrases such as 'A terrible beauty is born' and to dismiss them as 'pure Yeatsian fustian'.

The earliest and still in many ways the best general interpretative biography was written by Richard Ellmann, *Yeats: The Man and the Masks* (1948, revised 1979; Harmondsworth: Penguin, 1987). A further study, *The Identity of Yeats* (London: Faber and Faber, 1954; 2nd edn, London: Macmillan, 1964) is a companion volume, helpful in understanding the poet's ideas. Another very important study of Yeats's ideas was provided by T.R. Henn in *The Lonely Tower: Studies in the Poetry of W.B. Yeats* (London: Methuen, 1950; 2nd edn 1965). This is especially valuable for its attempt to explain *A Vision* – with diagrams – and for its account of the influences on the poet of the world of art.

Detailed criticism is often at fault if insufficient attention is paid to the poet's drafts and first intentions; here Jon Stallworthy's textual studies are fascinating to follow: *Between the Lines; Yeats's Poetry in the Making* (Oxford: Clarendon Press, 2nd impression 1965); and *Vision and Revision in Yeats's Last Poems* (Oxford: Clarendon Press, 1969). He sometimes disagrees with Curtis Bradford, *Yeats at Work* (Ill.: Southern Illinois University Press, 1965), after examination of the same manuscripts. However, such disagreements reveal much about the MSS: how difficult the writing of verse was for Yeats; his illegible handwriting, erratic spelling and eccentric punctuation; how mistakes were still printed in the final text because of Yeats's method of composition – dictating to a secretary, who often misheard or misread Yeats's drafts, and finally because of errors in proof-reading. Books on Yeats now proliferate to the extent that several are published every year and articles in periodicals similarly abound. Useful siftings of these are provided by collections of essays which often bring together materials which are otherwise inaccessible to the general reader. One of the best was that edited by John Unter-ecker, *Yeats: a Collection of Critical Essays* (London: Prentice-Hall, Spectrum Books 1963), which contains fourteen contributions, sum-ming up the early phases of Yeats studies, and including, for exam-ple, a valuable essay by T.S. Eliot; nearly a quarter of the book is taken up by an analysis of the Byzantium poems by Curtis Bradford.

Such collections of critical essays have often been brought together subsequently, but it must be said that they seem to show their age more obviously than monographs; the most recent example is *Yeats and Post-Modernism*, ed. Leonard Orr (Syracuse: Syracuse University Press, 1991).

A useful way of keeping up to date is to consult the annuals published by Macmillan; see, for instance, *Yeats Annual 9: Yeats and Women* ed. Deirdre Toomey (London: Macmillan, 1992). *Yeats Annual 8*, 1991, included some early essays by Yeats and his dialogue, *The Poet and the Actress*.

General Index

Abbey Theatre
  debates, 21, 122, 130, 131
  designer, 128
  Eliot at, 20
  players, 113, 189
  playwrights, 39, 138–9, 156
  political meeting at, 144
  riots, 154, 158
  subsidy, 114
  Y.'s dramatic activities, 87–8, 172
AE, see Russell, George
Aedh, 29
Aherne, 170
Andersen, Hans, 104
Anglo-Irish
  aristocracy, 92–4, 119, 125–7,
    136, 140, 166, 175
  Protestant ascendancy, 31–5, 43,
    57, 161, 175
  Y. as, 25, 176
Anima Mundi, 47, 49, 50, 53, 55, 67,
  73–4
Annunciation, 90–1
Antichrist, 98
anti-mask, 72–3, 112, 155
anti-self, 129, 155, 169
Apocalypse of St John, 95–8
Aran Islands, 154–5, 157
Arnold, Matthew, 19, 85
Athene, Pallas, 120, 125, 171
Auden W.H., 137
Aughrim, 31

ballad, 82, 107, 147
Ballylee, 41, 99–101, 168–71
Balzac, 16
bards, 28
Bax, Clifford, 115
Beardsley, Aubrey, 133, 180
Bedford Park, Chiswick, 16, 115,
  118, 158, 175, 177–9
Ben Bulben, 17, 173–4, 175, 176
Berkeley, George, 32, 35, 45, 49,

55–7, 59–60, 142, 161
'Black and Tans', 41, 182
Blake, William, 58–61
  edition by Ellis and Y., 114–5,
    143
  Four Zoas, 73
  imagination, belief in, 54–5
  influence on Y., 18, 172, 179
  pictures, 60, 180, 189
Blavatsky, Madame Helen
    Petrovna, 46, 48, 49, 50, 177
Blueshirts (Fascists), 139–40
Boer War, 40, 135
Book of Kells, The, 29, 161
Boyle, Richard, 30
Boyne, Battle of the, 31
Bowra, Maurice, 182
Brian Boru, 29–30
Bridges, Robert, 182
British Museum, 179
Buddhism, 46
burial, Y's, 163, 177, 191
Burke, Edmund, 32, 35, 57–8, 63,
    125, 142, 161, 170
Butler family, 31, 157
Byzantine art, 185–6
Byzantium, 103–5

Calvert, Edward, 60, 189
Canada, 190
'cantilating' i.e. cantillating, 115
Cap Martin, 191–2
Carson, Edward, 40, 41
Castiglione, 183–4, 188
Cathleen ni Houlihan, 34, 118, 120
Catholic emancipation, 32–6
Celtic
  Mysteries, see Order
  revival, see Gaelic
Celts, 25–8
censorship, Y. on, 43
Charles I, 30
Charles II, 31

Chatterjee, Mohindi, 46
Chesterton, G.K., 179
Christchurch bell, 181
Christianity
    arrival in Ireland, 25–8
    in Nietzsche, 61–3
    in T.S. Eliot, 70–2, 90
    in Y.'s thought, 70, 88, 90, 95–8,
        171, 177
Church of Ireland, 31, 33, 37
Churchill, Winston, 142
Civil War, *see* Irish
Clarke, Austin, 22
coinage, Y. and Irish, 43
Coleridge, S.T., 81
Colum, Pádriac, 21, 39–40
Conchobar, 27
Connaght, 27, 30
Connolly, James, 40, 112–3, 119,
        136, 145–6
Connolly, the player, 113
Coole, (i.e. Coole Park), 22–4, 34,
        38–9, 41, 123, 125–8, 130,
        131, 137, 149, 154, 165–8
    paintings of by Y., 180
    period, 120–1, 147
Corbet, Robert, 113, 161
Cosgrave, William, 113, 114, 141,
        142
Croce, Benedetto, 53
Cromwell, Oliver, 30
Cuala
    Industries, 164
    Press, 87
Cuchulain, 26, 27, 39, 53, 62, 85,
        109, 140, 147, 172–3
    statue, 141, 163
curlew as symbol, 135
Curragh mutiny, 114
cyclical view of history, 54–5, 62,
        67–9, 90–1, 97, 98, 104

Dáil Éireann, 41, 42, 92, 113, 136,
        142
da Montefeltro, Federico, 184
    Guidobaldo, 134, 184
Danaan, 25–6
dance as symbol, 71
Dante, 105

Daughters of Ireland, 119
Davis, Thomas, 36, 143, 162
Deidre, 26, 27, 65, 120
de Markievicz, *see* Markievicz
Derry, 30, 31
Descartes, 53–4, 57
Desmond's rebellion, 30
de Valera, Eamonn, 41, 42, 113–4,
        136, 139, 142, 144, 146
Diarmuid, 26, 27, 173
divorce, Y.s views on, 43
Dolmetsch, Arnold 87–8, 115–6
Dooney Rock, 174
Drogheda, 30
druids, 28, 171
Drumcliffe, 17, 163, 176–7, 191
Dublin, 18, 29, 35, 40, 42, 119, 152,
        158, 161–5
    architecture, 34
    Art Gallery, 133–4
    General Post office, 107, 112, 135,
        141, 144–5, 163–4
    Hermetic Society, 46
    and see St Stephen's Green etc.
Dun Emer Press, 87

Easter Rising, 40, 92–3, 107, 112–3,
        119, 135, 136, 144–7, 163
Edward VII, coronation of, 167
Éire, 43, 130
Eliot, T.S., 20–1, 70–3, 74, 90, 96,
        150, 187
Ellis, Edwin, 59, 114–5
Emain, 65
Emer, 26–7, 85
Emery, Mrs Florence, née Farr,
        115–6, 131, 138, 177–9, 180
Emmet, Robert, 35, 36, 38, 135
Empedocles, 62
England, Y.'s residences in, 177–83
Eramus Smith High School, Dublin,
        18–19

Faculties, Four, in Y's thought, 72–3
fairies, 80–1
falcon, as symbol, 97
fanaticism, 93–4
Farr, Florence, *see* Emery
Fascists, 43, 74, 95, 98, 139–40

Feis, 28
Fenians, 37, 142
Fenellosa, Prof. Ernest, 149
Fergus, 109
Fianna, 28, 29, 37,140,173
Fianna Fail, 139
Finn, 26, 28, 37, 140, 173
fire, as symbol, 71, 104–5, 186
First World War, 40, 128–9
Fitzgerald, Lord Edward, 33, 36, 135
'Flight of the Earls', 30
'flight of the wild geese', 31, 135
foolishness, in Y.'s thought, 107
France, 190–1
Franco, 139
Free State Constitution Bill, 42
French Revolution, 32–3, 57
Friends of Irish Freedom, 119

Gaelic
    epic and legend, 25–8, 40, 109,
        120, 140–1, 147, 163, 172–3
    Ireland, 25–30, 34–5, 36, 43
    Lady Gregory's work, 125–6
    League, 130, 144
    placenames, 200
    pronunciation, 200–1
    revival, 39–40, 77, 130, 136, 140,
        144, 162
    Society of Trinity College, 162
    Y.'s acquaintance with, 17, 29,
        39–40, 126, 130–1
Garsington Manor, 181
George II of Greece, 114
George IV, 35
Georgeville, 161
Gibbon, Monk, 20
Gill, Lough, 174–5
Gladstone, W.E., 37–8
Glasnevin Cemetery, 38
Glendalough, 118
Godolphin School, Hammersmith,
    16–19, 21
Gogarty, Dr Oliver St John, 21,
    141, 162
'golden bough', 105
Goldsmith, Oliver, 35, 58, 142, 161
Gonne, Iseult, (Mrs Francis Stuart),
    117–8, 190

Gonne, Maud, 36, 38, 40, 47, 109,
    112, 113, 117, 118–25, 135,
    145, 151, 153, 167, 172, 177,
    189, 190
Gore-Booth family, 136, 175–6
    Constance, *see* Markievicz
    Eva, 92, 175
Gort, 168–9
Gough, General Sir Hubert, 114
Grainne, 26, 27, 173
Grattan, Henry, 32–4, 35, 58, 161
Great Memory, 47, 74
Great Wheel, 67–9
Great Year, 69
Gregory family, 165–8
    Anne, 22, 24
    Augusta, Lady, 22, 26, 28, 38,
        39, 41, 63, 125–8, 131, 133–
        5, 137, 138–9, 145, 147–8,
        149, 151, 153, 156, 157,
        166–7, 172, 180, 182, 183,
        189
    Robert, Major, 41, 112, 128–30,
        131, 157, 183
    William, Sir, 125, 166
Grierson, Sir Hebert, 20
Griffith, Arthur, 40, 42
Guaire, King, 165
gyres, 67–9, 71, 73, 95, 97, 104, 186

Hanrahan, Red, 173
Helen of Troy, 65, 120
Henry II, 30
Heraclitus, 52, 62, 67, 69, 71, 73
Hermetic
    Order of the Golden Dawn, 46,
        48, 98, 115, 138
    Society, *see* Dublin
hero, in Y.'s thought, 62, 112, 135,
    147, 154
heron, as symbol, 129
High King, 27, 29
Hinduism, 46
Hitler, Adolf, 139
Home Rule, 37–8, 40–1
Homer, 62, 87
Hone, Joseph, quoted, 35, 86, 135,
    138, 140, 161, 179, 189–90
Horton, W.T., 138

Hyde, Douglas, 39, 126, 130–1, 141, 149, 171
Hyde-Lees, Miss Georgie, *see* Yeats, Mrs
Hynes, Mary, 168

Indian religions, 46, 70, 152
    poems by Y., 80
Innisfree, 174–5
Ireland
    history of, 25–44, *and see below under* Irish
    places connected with Y., 161–77
Irish
    architecture, 34–5
    civil war, 42, 43, 55, 99–101, 113, 114, 164, 166, 169
    Famine, 36
    Franchise Act, 36
    Free State, 41–2, 113, 139, 141–2
    Labour Party, 112
    language, *see* Gaelic
    legend, *see* Gaelic
    Literary Renaissance, 36, 39–40, 43, 132, 151, 152, 175, 189
    Literary Societies, 58, 132, 143, 149
    National Brotherhood, 21
    People, The, 142
    pronunciation, 163–4, *and see* Gaelic
    Race Congress, 190
    Rebellion
        of 1798, 33, 134–5
        of 1916, *see* Easter Rising
    Republican
        Army (IRA or 'Irregulars'), 41, 42, 136, 139, 141, 164, 169
        Brotherhood (IRB), 37, 40, 135, 136, 142, 143, 144
    saints, 28–9
    Statesman, The, 152
    Volunteers, 40, 144
Irishness, 58, 80, 99
'Irregulars', *see* Irish Republican Army
Italy, Y.'s visits to, 183–6

James I, 30, 37

James II, 31
Japan, Yeats Society of, 152
Japanese
    plays, *see* Noh
    sword, *see* Sato
John, Augustus, 21, 24, 131, 141
Johnson, Lionel, 49, 131–3, 153, 154
Joyce, James, 20, 28, 74, 150, 152
Jubilee Riots (1897), 119, 145
Jung, 50, 52

Kabbalah, 46, 48, 148
Keats, John, 77, 82, 103–4
Kerry, 107
Key, Lough, 171–2
Kilcolman, 30
Kiltartan, 126, 128–9, 165, 168, 171
Knocknarea, 17, 172–3, 175

lamp, as symbol, 170–1
Land Acts, 36–9
Lane, Sir Hugh, 24, 127, 133–5, 158, 185
La Téne culture, 26, 28
Latin, Y.'s command of, 17–19, 162
Leda, 65, 120
Leinster, 27
Liberal party, Gladstone's, 37
Limerick, 31, 34
Lissadell, 92–3, 136, 175–6
Lloyd George, David, 41, 146
Locke, John, 56, 57, 59, 61
London,
    colonization of Ireland, 30
    Y.'s residences in, 177–81
    Y.'s youth in, 14–17, 158, 174
lunar phases, *see* moon
Lutyens, Sir Edwin, 169
Lyttleton, Mrs Alfred, 22

MacArt, Cormac, 27–8
MacBride, Major John, 40, 118, 135, 145–6
    Mrs, *see* Gonne, Maud
MacDonagh, Thomas, 135, 136, 145–6
MacMurrough, Dermot, 30
Maeve, 27, 172–3

magical beliefs, Y.'s, *see* occult
    studies
Magnus Annus, 69
Mahaffy, Dr, 162
Majorca, 150–1, 187–8
Mallarmé, 71, 148, 191
Markievicz, Constance, Countess
    de, 92, 124, 136–7, 175
Masefield, John, 137–8, 157, 175,
    180, 182
mask, Y.'s theory of, *see* anti-mask
Mathers, MacGregor, 47, 98, 115,
    138, 177, 190
    Mrs, 49
Merrion Square, Dublin, 34, 152,
    164, 169
Menton, 191–2
Metropolitan School of Art, Dublin,
    19, 151, 158, 163
Milan, 183
Millevoye, Lucien, 119
Milton, John, quoted, 50, 130,
    170–1
Mitchel, John, 36
Monreale, 103, 186
moon, phases of the, 62, 67–70, 72
Moore, George, 21, 22
Moore, Sturge, 100 (illus.), 105
Morrell, Lady Ottoline, 181
Morris, William, the poet, 85, 87,
    179
Morris, William, Lord Nuffield, 114
mosaic, 104, 185–6
Munster, 27, 30
Music, Early, 87
Mussolini, Benito, 139
myth, 50, 54, 55, 59, 65–7, 74, 109,
    112, 147, 163, 171–3, 177

Naisi, 26, 27
National Gallery, London, 134
National Volunteer Force, *see* Irish
    Volunteers
natural history
    Y.'s early love of, 17–18
    later ignorance of, 22
Neoplatonism, 46, 49–53, 56, 59, 67
New York, 149, 158, 189
Niamh, 27

Nietzsche, Friedrich, 45, 61–3
nightingale, 103–5
nineties, the 1890s, 133, 154
Nirvana, 46
Nobel Prize, 188
Noh plays, Japanese, 149
Norman rule in Ireland, 30
Normandy, 117, 190
Norsemen, 29
Northern Ireland, origin of, 42

'objectivity' in Y.'s thought, 70, 129,
    169
O'Casey, Sean, 39, 40, 124, 126–7,
    138–9
O'Connell, Daniel, 35–8
O'Connor, Frank, 27
occult studies, 45–9, 67, 90–1, 103,
    105, 138, 143, 148, 170–2
O'Duffy, Eoin, 43, 114, 139–40
O'Grady, Standish, 39, 126, 140–1,
    158
O'Higgins, Kevin, 42–3, 57, 114,
    141–2
Oisin, 26–9, 140
O'Leary, John, 48, 135, 142–3, 158
opposites, in Y.'s thought, 60, 69,
    72–3
O'Rahilly, The, 107, 144
Order
    of Celtic Mysteries, 138, 171–2
    of the Golden Dawn, *see*
        Hermetic
Orwell, George, 74
Oxford, 24, 137, 170, 181–2

painting, Y.'s, 19, 180
Palermo, 187
Palladius, 28
Palma, 150, 187–8
Palmer, Samuel, 51 (illus.), 60, 99,
    170–1, 189
Parliament
    British, 32–3, 36, 38, 40
    Grattan's, 32–5, 164
    Irish, 31–5
    Irish Free State, 42
Parnell, Charles Stewart, 37–8, 114,
    134, 135, 142, 143, 190

Patriot Party, 32
Pearse, Pádraic, 40, 143–7, 162, 163
Pembroke, Earl of, 30
Penns-in-the-Rocks, 156, 182
perne, 67, 104
phases of the moon, *see* moon
physical frailty, Y.'s, 14, 16–17, 22
Pitt, William, 33–4, 57
Plato, 42, 49–53, 55, 67, 73, 112, 170–1
playboy of the western world, The, 154, 189
    riots at, 139, 154, 158
Plotinus, 49, 50, 52, 53, 56
politics, Y.'s attitude to, 43, 57, 74, 92–4, 95, 119, 123, 129, 136, 139–40, 147, 175–6
Pollexfen, Y.'s mother's family, 14–16, 147–8, 157–8, 176, 177
    Alfred, 147–8
    George, 133, 147–8, 157, 173, 174
    John, 148
    Susan, *see* Yeats, Mrs, (mother)
    William, 14, 147–8, 156, 176
Porphyry, 49, 50, 53
portraits of Y., 21, 131, 180
Post Office, General, *see* Dublin
Pound, Ezra, 20, 77, 148–9, 153, 179–80, 182
Powell, York, 179, 181
Pre-Raphaelitism, 19, 21, 85, 90, 91, 120, 155, 158, 180, 182
Pritchett, V.S., 164
Protestant
    ascendancy, *see* Anglo-Irish
    plantations, 30
    Y.'s ancestors, 31, 113
psaltery, 87, 115–6
Purohit, Shri, Swami, 150, 187–8
Pythagoras, 52–3, 138, 147

Quinn, John, 61, 141, 149–50, 157, 158, 189

Raftery, 168
Raleigh, Sir Walter, 30
Rathfarnham, 137, 164–5
Ravenna, 103, 185–6

refrain, use of, 82, 101, 106–7
reincarnation, 46, 49, 73
Renaissance, Italian, 184–5
Rhadamanthus, 52
Rhymers Club, 131–2, 154
Richard II, 30
Riversdale, 139, 164–5, 189
Robartes, Michael, 95, 97, 170
Romans, 27
Rome, 185–6
Roquebrune, 190–1
Rosaleen, Dark, 34–5
rose as a symbol, 120
Rosicrucians, 46–7
Rosses, 80–1, 156, 175
Rothenstein, Sir William, 183
Roxborough House, 125, 127
Royal Hibernain Art School, 19
Ruddock, Margot, 150–1
Russell, George, known as 'AE', 23(illus), 39, 48, 120, 141, 149, 151–2, 158, 172, 187
Russia, 95, 97

St Brigit, 28–9
St Colman, 29, 165
St Columba, 18, 28, 29, 176
St Enda's School, 136, 144
St Patrick, 17, 27, 28, 29, 162
St Patrick's Cathedral, Dublin, 162–3
St Stephen's Green, 136–7
Sandymount Castle, 113, 161
Saorstát Éireann, 41
Sarsfield, Patrick, 31
Sato, Junzo, 152–3, 189
Scott, Sir Walter, 16
Seanad Éireann (Irish Senate), 34, 42–3, 141, 164
Senator, Y. as, 43, 141, 164
Shakespear
    Dorothy, 149
    Olivia, 149, 150, 153
Shakespeare, 18, 81
Shaw
    George Bernard, 115, 166
    Norman, 177
Shawe-Taylor, Captain John, 39
Shelly, P.B., 77, 96, 130, 170–1

Sheppard, Oliver, 163
Sicily, 103, 185–6
sidhe, 26, 173
Sinn Féin, 40-1, 113, 190
Sinnett, A.P., 46
Six Counties, 41–2, 113
Sligo, 14, 16, 17, 20, 80–1, 138,
        147–8, 156–7, 174–7, 190–1
    Co., 172–5
Smith, F.E., 114
sound, of Y.'s verse, 22, 157, 175
Spanish Civil War, 139
spelling, Y.'s, 131
Spencer, Hebert, 19
Spenser, Edmund, 30
Sphinx, 96, 98
spiritualism, *see* occult
Spiritus Mundi, 97–8, *and see Anima*
        Mundi
stare, 101
Stead, William Force, 24
Stevenson, R.L., 174
Stafford, Earl of, 30
Strong, L.A.G., 181
Strongbow, 30
Stuart
    Francis, 20, 118
    Mrs Francis, *see* Gonne, Iseult
style, changes in Y.'s, 77, 89, 91,
        107, 129
'subjectivity', in Y.'s thought, 70,
        129, 169–70
Sussex,
    Steyning, 22
    Stone Cottage, 20, 149, 182
Sweden, 189–90
Swift, Jonathan, 31–2, 34, 35, 37,
        38, 55, 57, 61, 142, 161,
        163
symbolism, Y.'s, 48, 53, 59, 65–7,
        71, 93–4, 97, 99, 101, 112,
        152, 154, 169–71, 172,
        197–9
Symbolists, 71, 81, 148, 154, 179
Symons, Arthur, 154, 190
Synge, John M., 23(illus), 39, 133,
        139, 148, 149, 154–6, 157,
        158, 161, 166, 189, 190
syntax, 91, 101, 109

Taín Bó Cualgne, 27
Tara, 25, 27
Taylor, Thomas, 50, 52
Thame, 182
Theosophical Society, 46, 48, 177
Thoor Ballylee, 41, 99–101, 168–71,
        181
Thoreau, Henry, 174
Tibet, 46
Tir-na-nÓg (country of the young),
        27, 53, 104
Todhunter, Dr., 179
Tone, Wolfe, 33, 35, 36, 37, 38, 135,
        161
    centenary, 40, 113, 119, 166
tower, as symbol, 169–71
Trinity College, Dublin, 19, 29, 31,
        33, 37, 56, 58, 130, 140, 142,
        154, 157, 161–2
Troy, 65
Tullylish, 157
túatha, 27
Túatha de Danaan, 25
Turner, 19
Tynan, Katharine, 21, 181

Ulster, 27, 30, 37, 40, 142, 151, 157
Union, Act of, 33, 35
United Irishmen, 40
United Irishmen, Society of, 33, 166
United States of America, Y.'s tours,
        36, 149, 181, 182, 189–90
Upanishads, 46
Urbino, 123, 134, 183–5
Usna, 65

Venice, 183
Verlaine, 191
'Vernon, Diana', *see* Shakespear,
        Olivia
Vico, Giambattista, 45, 53–5, 62, 67
Victoria, Queen, 119
Vikings, 29
violence, Y.'s views on, 119
Virgil, 105
Voysey, 180–1

Wellesley, Dorothy, 21–2, 24, 153,
        156, 174, 182–3, 187

Wentworth, Thomas, 30
Wexford, 30
Wexford, 30
Whiggery, 55
Wilde, Oscar, 145, 161
William of Orange, 31
Woburn Buildings, 137, 148,
    170, 175, 177, 179–81,
    190
Wood, William, 32
Wordsworth, William, 81–2,
    107

Yeats
    ancestors, 176
    Elizabeth (sister 'Lolly'), 87
    Georgie, Mrs (wife 'George'), née
    Hyde-Lees, 53, 65–7, 117–8,
        152, 163, 164, 171, 180–1,
        182, 186, 189, 189, 190
    John Butler (brother 'Jack'), 133,
        149, 156–7, 158, 166, 176,
        177, 180
    John Butler (father 'J.B.'), 14, 16,
        59, 61, 63, 114, 143, 148,
        149, 154, 157–9, 161, 166,
        177, 189
    Michael (son), 19
    Susan, Mrs (mother), née
        Pollexfen, 14, 157
    Susan Mary (sister 'Lily'), 87,
        158, 177
Yoga, 46
Young Ireland party, 36

Index of references to Yeats's works

'Acre of Grass, An', 58–9
'Adam's Curse', 120
'Adoration of the Magi, The', 90
'After Long Silence', 153
'Against Unworthy Praise', 122
'All Souls' Night', 103, 115, 138, 181
'Among School Children', 53, 71, 124
'Appointment, An', 134
'Are You Content?', 113, 176
'Arrow, The',120
'At the Abbey Theatre', 130
Autobiographies, 14, 16–17, 18, 19, 29, 38, 46–7, 130, 131, 133, 136, 138, 141, 143, 145, 148, 156, 171–2, 174, 179, 184, 190–1

BBC broadcasts, 59, 103, 151, 167
'Beautiful Lofty Things', 125, 141, 143, 151, 154, 158, 166
'Black Tower, The', 173
Blake, edition of the works of, 114–5
'Blood and the Moon', 43, 57, 58, 142
Book of Irish Verse, A, 162
'Bounty of Sweden, The', 156, 190–1
'Bronze Head, A', 125
'Byzantium', 60, 71, 105, 185–6
Cathleen ni Houlihan, 126, 189
Cat and the Moon, The, 101
'Circus Animals' Desertion, The', 77, 107–9
'Cold Heaven, The', 122–3
'Coole Park', 167
'Coole Park and Ballylee, 1931', 34, 77, 127–8, 166–7
Countess Kathleen, The, 109, 143
'Countess Kathleen in Paradise, The', 120
'Crazed Girl, A', 150–1
'Crazy Jane', 155

'Cuchulain's Fight with the Sea', 83–6, 109

'Death', 43, 142
Death of Cuchulain, The, 85, 191
Deirdre, 21
'Delphic Oracle upon Plotinus, The', 52
'Dialogue of Self and Soul, A', 129, 151–2
'Dust hath closed Helen's Eye', 168

'Easter 1916', 92, 107, 117, 135–7, 145–6, 190
'Ego Dominus Tuus', 129, 133, 169
'Epilogue to a Vision', *see* 'All Soul's Night'
Essays and Introductions, 39, 47, 56, 60, 87, 115, 131
'Estrangement', 184
Explorations, 34, 65, 167

'Fallen Majesty', 122, 148
'Fiddler of Dooney, The', 174
'Folly of Being Comforted, The', 120, 122
'Friend's Illness, A', 126
'Friends', 122, 126, 153

Green Helmet, The, 122, 136
'Grey Rock', 132–3

'He Bids his Beloved be at Peace', 153
'He hears the Cry of the Sedge', 120
'He thinks of those who have Spoken Evil of his Beloved', 120
'Her Praise', 123
'His Phoenix', 123, 191
'Hour before Dawn, The', 155

'Ideas of Good and Evil', 47
'In Memory of Alfred Pollexfen', 148

'In Memory of Eva Gore-Booth and Con Markiewicz', 92, 175
'In Memory of Major Robert Gregory', 129–30, 133, 148, 155
In the Seven Woods, 87, 120–2
'In the Seven Woods', 120–2, 167
'Irish Airman Foresees His Death, An', 128–9
'Irish Theatre, The', 189

'King and No King', 122

'Lake Isle of Innisfree, The', 82, 174–5
'Lamentation of the Old Pensioner, The', 78
Land of Heart's Desire, The, 180
Last Poems, 57, 108–9, 112, 118, 125, 141, 146, 155, 191
lectures in USA, 144, 189
'Leda and the Swan', 69, 90–1, 152
'Letter to Leo Africanus', 91
Letters, 81, 82, 131, 140, 145, 148, 150, 153, 170, 181, 187
Letters on Poetry from W.B. Yeats to Dorothy Wellesley, 156, 183
'Living Beauty, The', 123
'Lover mourns for the Loss of Love, The', 153

'Magi, The', 89–91, 97
'Man and the Echo, The', 145, 151
'Man Young and Old, A', 124
'Mask, The', 156
'Meditations in Time of Civil War', 42, 53, 55, 99–101, 102–3, 181
'Men Improve with the Years', 117
Michael Robartes and the Dancer, 92, 95, 123–4
'Modern Poetry', 131
'Mohini Chatterjee', 46
'Mountain Tomb, The', 173
'Municipal Gallery Revisited, The', 112, 142, 155

'Never Give All the Heart', 120
'New Faces, The', 126
New Poems, 107
'News for the Delphic Oracle', 53

'Nineteen Hundred and Nineteen', 41
'No Second Troy', 122, 124

'O Do not Love Too Long', 120
'On a Political Prisioner', 91–4, 136
On Baile's Strand, 85, 109
On the Boiler, 43, 55, 176
'On those that "The Playboy of the Western World", 1907', 154
'O'Rahilly, The', 106–7, 146–7
'Owen Aherne and his Dancers', 118
Oxford Book of Modern Verse, The, 24, 77, 126, 133, 156
Oxford Union speech, 41, 182

'Parnell's Funeral', 38, 114, 142
'Paudeen', 135
'Peace', 122
'People, The', 123, 183–4
'Phases of the Moon, The', 62, 69–70, 170
'Pity of Love, The', 120
'Players Ask for a Blessing on the Psalteries and on Themselves, The', 86–8
Poet and the Actress, The, 205
'Poet Pleads with the Elemental Powers, The', 48, 120
'Politics', 109, 117
Pot of Broth, The, 126
'Prayer for my Daughter, A', 97, 123
'Prayer on Going into my House, A', 169
Preface to Lady Gregory's *Cuchulain of Muirthemne*, 26–7
'Presences', 117
'Private Thoughts', 34
Purgatory, 72, 156

'Quarrel in Old Age', 124–5

'Reconciliation', 122
'Red Hanrahan's Song about Ireland', 120
'Remorse for Intemperate Speech', 25

Responsibilities, 89, 118, 122
  prefatory poem, 31, 122–3
Resurrection, The, 62, 65, 88, 152,
  164
Reveries over Childhood and Youth, 14,
  148, 174
Rose, The, 120, 132
'Rose of the World, The', 120
'Rose Tree, The', 146

'Sailing to Byzantium', 60, 71, 88,
  102–5, 185–6
'Second Coming, The', 67–8, 94–8,
  104, 140
Secret Rose, The, 151
'Secret Rose, The', 120
'September 1913', 134–5, 143
'Seven Sages, The', 55, 57
'Shepherd and Goatherd', 130
'Sixteen Dead Men', 136, 146
Sophocles' King Oedipus, 188
'Sorrow of Love, The', 120
'Speaking to the Psaltery', 115
'Stare's Nest by my Window, The',
  42, 53, 99–101
'Statesman's Holiday, The', 114
'Statues, The', 53, 147
'Stolen Child, The', 79–82
'Supernatural Songs', 49, 70
'Sweet Dancer', 151
'Swift's Epitaph', 163
'Symbols', 152

'That the Night Come', 122–3
'Those Images', 60
'Thought from Propertius, A', 123
'Three Hermits, The', 155
'Three Marching Songs', 140
'Three Songs to the One Burden',
  147
'Three Songs to the Same Tune',
  140
'To a Child Dancing in the Wind',
  117
'To a Friend whose work came to
  Nothing', 135
'To a Shade', 38, 135
'To a Wealthy Man who promised
  a Second Subscription to the

Dublin Municipal Gallery if it
  were proved the People wanted
  Pictures', 134–5, 185
'To be Carved on a Stone at Thoor
  Ballylee', 169
'To Dorothy Wellesley', 183
'To Ireland in the Coming Times',
  143
'To Some I have Talked with by
  the Fire', 48
'Towards Break of Day', 173
Tower, The, 99, 102, 124
'Tower, The', 33, 53, 57, 73, 101,
  112, 169, 173
'Tragic Generation, The', 133
'Travail of Passion, The', 153
Trembling of the Veil, The, 29, 38,
  47–8, 138, 145, 171–2, 174
'Two Songs from a Play', 54, 69,
  88
'Two Songs of a Fool', 118
'Two Trees, The', 48, 120
'Two Years Later', 117

'Unappeasable Host, The', 26
'Under Ben Bulben', 173–4, 177
'Under Saturn', 176
Upanishads, The Ten Principal
  (translation), 187–8
'Upon a House Shaken by the Land
  Agitation', 38

Vision, A, 45, 48, 55, 62, 63, 65–74,
  90, 95, 97, 103

Wanderings of Oisin, The, 29, 80, 85,
  109, 143, 154, 173
Wheels and Butterflies, 34
'What then?', 147, 165
'When Helen Lived', 122
'When you are Old', 120
'White Birds, The', 120
Why should not Old Men be Mad?',
  176
'William Blake and the
  Imagination', 60
Wild Swans at Coole, The, 118, 123
'Wild Swans at Coole, The', 65, 123,
  166

Wind Among the Reeds, The, 26, 120
Winding Stair, The, 124
'Woman Homer Sung, A', 122

'Words', 122
Words Upon the Window-Pane, The, 35